W9-CFC-840

The Fight of the Century

THE
FIGHT
OF THE
CENTURY

ALI vs. FRAZIER
March 8, 1971

Michael Arkush

John Wiley & Sons, Inc.

This book is printed on acid-free paper. ∞

Copyright © 2008 by Michael Arkush. All rights reserved

Published by John Wiley & Sons, Inc., Hoboken, New Jersey
Published simultaneously in Canada

Wiley Bicentennial Logo: Richard J. Pacifico

All photos except bottom of page 141 AP Images. The photo on bottom of page 141 is courtesy of Leroy Johnson.

No part of this publication may be reproduced, stored in a retrieval system, or transmitted in any form or by any means, electronic, mechanical, photocopying, recording, scanning, or otherwise, except as permitted under Section 107 or 108 of the 1976 United States Copyright Act, without either the prior written permission of the Publisher, or authorization through payment of the appropriate per-copy fee to the Copyright Clearance Center, 222 Rosewood Drive, Danvers, MA 01923, (978) 750-8400, fax (978) 646-8600, or on the web at www.copyright.com. Requests to the Publisher for permission should be addressed to the Permissions Department, John Wiley & Sons, Inc., 111 River Street, Hoboken, NJ 07030, (201) 748-6011, fax (201) 748-6008, or online at http://www.wiley.com/go/permissions.

Limit of Liability/Disclaimer of Warranty: While the publisher and the author have used their best efforts in preparing this book, they make no representations or warranties with respect to the accuracy or completeness of the contents of this book and specifically disclaim any implied warranties of merchantability or fitness for a particular purpose. No warranty may be created or extended by sales representatives or written sales materials. The advice and strategies contained herein may not be suitable for your situation. You should consult with a professional where appropriate. Neither the publisher nor the author shall be liable for any loss of profit or any other commercial damages, including but not limited to special, incidental, consequential, or other damages.

For general information about our other products and services, please contact our Customer Care Department within the United States at (800) 762-2974, outside the United States at (317) 572-3993 or fax (317) 572-4002.

Wiley also publishes its books in a variety of electronic formats. Some content that appears in print may not be available in electronic books. For more information about Wiley products, visit our web site at www.wiley.com.

Library of Congress Cataloging-in-Publication Data:

Arkush, Michael.
    Fight of the century : Ali vs. Frazier March 8, 1971 / Michael Arkush.
      p. cm.
    Includes bibliographical references and index.
    ISBN 978-0-470-05642-4 (cloth : alk. paper)
    1. Boxing matches—New York (State)—New York. 2. Ali, Muhammad, 1942– 3. Frazier, Joe, 1944– 4. African American boxers—Biography. 5. Boxers (Sports)—United States—Biography. I. Title.
    GV1125.A75 2008
    796.8309747'1—dc22

                                  2007034274

Printed in the United States of America

10 9 8 7 6 5 4 3 2 1

To Pauletta,
the greatest champion I have ever known

Contents

Photo section begins on page 137.

Preface

I was sitting alone in the lobby of the Eden Roc hotel in Miami Beach one evening in mid-November 1970. I was twelve. Six weeks had gone by since I lost my father to Lou Gehrig's disease. He was only fifty-one. More than ever, the world of professional sports consumed my time and energy. Nobody died in that world. Not on the field, at least.

Then, suddenly, I saw Muhammad Ali. He was walking in the lobby and was alone, too. We chatted, just the two of us. About what and for how long, I don't remember. I asked for his autograph, and soon it was over.

From that moment, I loved reading about Ali in the paper, and there certainly was a lot to read. Nobody in the world I relied on to protect me generated more news more frequently, and certainly with more flair, than Muhammad Ali. Not Joe Namath. Not Willie Mays. Not Wilt Chamberlain. Nobody.

When February 1971 came around, everybody seemed to be talking about Ali's upcoming fight against the heavyweight champion of the world, Joe Frazier. I did not understand everything I read, but I understood enough. I became more excited about a single sporting event than any before—or, I might add, since. I did not see the fight. For many years, I wished I had been in Madison Square Garden that evening. I wished I could have seen those two proud gladiators during one of their most courageous hours.

As the years went by, I moved on to other interests: girls, college, work, life. I became a journalist and was fortunate enough to meet other childhood heroes and attend many glorious events.

I was in Dodger Stadium when a limping Kirk Gibson hit his historic ninth-inning home run against Dennis Eckersley to win the first game of the 1988 World Series. I saw my alma mater, the University of Michigan, capture the 1989 NCAA basketball title in Seattle over Seton Hall. I walked inside the ropes in Arizona to watch Jack Nicklaus rally to win a senior major in 1996, his last official tournament victory. These are wonderful experiences I will always cherish, but I would trade all of them to have been in the Garden on March 8, 1971.

I've never understood why the fight has meant so much to me, then and now. Maybe because my father was taken from me before I ever learned who he truly was, I was drawn to these two men in their late twenties, full of life, indestructible, which is how I will always remember them.

1

Beating the System

Some Georgia politicians—Andrew Young, Julian Bond, Maynard Jackson—who launched their careers in the 1960s and 1970s became famous. One, an ex-peanut farmer from the town of Plains, rose to the highest office in the land. Another became Speaker of the House. Yet there was one man in the state who, it could be said, was the most gifted of all in the art of power. He was not particularly well known outside of Georgia back then, and never would be, but inside, many folks heard of the Honorable Leroy Reginald Johnson, the Democratic state senator from the 38th District, the first African American to serve in the State Legislature in almost ninety-two years.

"He had this marvelous facility for getting along with other people," Bond said. "My brother had some kind of traffic ticket problem, and I remember going with my parents to see Johnson. He said, 'I'll take care of it.' My father said, 'Well, what do I owe you?' He was a lawyer, you expect to pay him. 'That's okay,' Johnson responded. 'You can do something for me sometime.' Without the criminal element, he was the Godfather. He was the guy that you came to see to get things done, things that you could not do for yourself."

Leroy Johnson was the first person Harry Pett thought of when, during the summer of 1970, his son-in-law, Robert Kassel, who was recently involved in the promotion of his first boxing card, called him in Atlanta to find out if he knew of anyone in the city with real clout. Kassel, an ambitious thirty-year-old New York corporate attorney, did not expect too much. He knew that his father-in-law, who operated a small spice business, did not exactly mingle with society's movers and shakers, but Kassel did not know where else to turn. Over the previous three years, not a single city in the entire nation demonstrated the courage to permit Muhammad Ali to resume his boxing career. The only reason Kassel thought of Atlanta was that Atlanta was where he had attended college, at Emory University, for undergrad and law school, and where he met his first wife. Atlanta would serve his purpose as well as any other city. Pett, who had once met Johnson at a function, placed the call.

"Senator, do you think that you might be able to get a license for Muhammad Ali to fight in Atlanta?" Pett asked Johnson. "If you can somehow find a way to put this together, we can make sure that Ali gets a contract."

Johnson was no expert on the fight game, but he was definitely an expert on picking fights in the arena which he mastered, fights he won more often than he lost, and here was one with enticing possibilities.

If he was successful, he would make history, helping to put Ali back where he belonged, between the ropes, and he would make money—lots of it. For a black man in 1970, in the Deep South no less, Johnson, in his early forties, did quite well for himself. He owned a house in northwest Atlanta and a cottage about fifteen miles outside of town. But Johnson, who also worked in a downtown law practice, didn't get to where he was by running from opportunities to rise even higher. He told Pett he would check with his contacts and call him back in a few days. "My mission was to beat the system," Johnson recalled, "to say to the world that you cannot do this to a man just because of his color."

On April 28, 1967, at eight o'clock in the morning, Muhammad Ali walked into the United States Armed Forces Examination and Entrance Station at 701 San Jacinto Street in Houston. For much of the morning, Ali and the other recruits went through routine physical examinations and filled out paperwork. At about 1 p.m., they were taken to a room for their formal induction. After the ceremony, they would go by bus to Fort Polk, Louisiana, to begin their basic training.

One name after another was called, each man stepping forward to symbolize his entrance into the armed forces. Then came Ali's turn.

"Cassius Marcellus Clay!" an officer said.

Ali did not step forward.

The officer called him by his preferred name, Ali, but it made no difference. Navy Lieutenant Clarence Hartman then brought Ali to a room down the hall to explain that his act of defiance was a felony that could be punished by five years in prison and a $10,000 fine. But, upon returning to the first room, Ali again failed to move when his name was announced. Hartman asked Ali to write down the reason he would not accept service.

"I refuse to be inducted into the armed forces of the United States because I claim to be exempt as a minister of the religion of Islam," he wrote.

His refusal came as no surprise, and it epitomized the dramatic transformation in Ali, and how he was perceived, since he first became a public figure when he captured the gold medal at the 1960 Olympic Games in Rome. Back then, he was known as Cassius Clay from Louisville, Kentucky, a hero adored for his charm, wit, and innocence. In 1964, he slayed the heavyweight champion, the mighty Sonny Liston, and "shook up the world," as he put it. Within weeks, however, he changed his name to Muhammad Ali, a member of the Nation of Islam. Nothing, however, alienated Ali from his detractors as much as the famous comment he made in February 1966 after his draft status was reclassified to 1-A: "Man, I ain't got no quarrel with them Vietcong." To Ali, it made no sense to fight in a war to liberate the people of South Vietnam when members of his race were being mistreated back home.

Within hours of refusing service, Ali was stripped of his crown by the New York State Athletic Commission and the World Boxing Association. Ali's decision was "regarded by the commission to be detrimental to the best interests of boxing," stated Edwin B. Dooley, the chairman. On June 20, 1967, Ali was convicted by a federal jury in Houston of violating the Selective Service Act. He was sentenced to five years in prison and fined $10,000, the maximum penalty. The jury took only about twenty minutes before reaching a guilty verdict. Ali's lawyers filed an appeal.

By the summer of 1970, when Harry Pett called Senator Leroy Johnson, Ali remained free on bail, hoping the Supreme Court would review his case. If the court chose not to hear it, Ali would have to serve his sentence. He had not appeared in an official bout since March 22, 1967.

For blacks in Georgia, a proud member of the old Confederacy, the system was stacked against them from the start. Leroy Johnson, who grew up in an Atlanta ghetto, was no exception.

One afternoon, during the mid-1930s, instead of waiting patiently at the front door as he did every day to greet his cherished Aunt Minnie, a housekeeper being dropped off by her white female employer from the other side of town, the *rich* side, he ran to the car. He hugged his aunt and then, instinctively—he was seven or eight, too young, too loving, to comprehend bigotry—started to embrace the other woman, who was usually very friendly with him. The woman quickly pulled herself away, as if this harmless child would infect her with a horrible disease. Aunt Minnie seized Leroy's hand and ushered him immediately into the house.

"Why didn't she hug me?" the boy wondered.

"You will understand as you grow older," Aunt Minnie assured him, "that there is a difference between *us* and *them*."

Aunt Minnie told Leroy something else that day he would never forget. "I want you to know that when God made you," she explained, "he was at his highest and best and that you are as good as anybody."

The message was constantly reinforced at Morehouse College, the distinguished private black liberal arts school in Atlanta that Johnson attended in the late 1940s with, in the class a year ahead, another student who dreamed of a color-blind America in his life-time, Martin Luther King Jr. Morehouse made an impact on John-son on his very first day when, during a rousing speech welcoming the student body, President Benjamin Elijah Mays, regarded later by Dr. King as his "spiritual mentor and intellectual father"—he would give the eulogy at King's funeral—warned, "You cannot and must not ever take segregation. When you go to a segregated the-ater, you are paying for segregation." Johnson became convinced that the president's stern words were meant specifically for him. A few days earlier, he had gone to see a picture at the Fox The-atre downtown, taking a seat, as usual, in the upstairs balcony, the section set aside for blacks. "I thought Mays had seen me go into the theater," Johnson recalled. "I never again went to a segregated theater."

After graduating from Morehouse in 1949, Johnson taught history and geography in the city's black schools for several years until he realized that his true calling was not in academia but in the legal profession, where he felt he could make the greatest dif-ference on the major issues of the day. He earned his law degree from North Carolina College at Durham in 1957 and became the first African American investigator in the district attorney's office in Atlanta.

In 1962, he ran for a seat in the State Senate. The obstacles were enormous. A black man had not served in the Georgia legisla-ture since Reconstruction. The system simply did not allow it. The system dictated that voters from all over Fulton County cast their ballots for each of the county's seven seats instead of only for a sin-gle district. Residents from predominantly white areas were not about to choose one of *them* to protect their interests. On the cam-paign trail, especially in more rural towns, Johnson was heckled or, perhaps worse, ignored. In the fall election, he prevailed among the voters in his district but did not capture a majority countywide. But Leroy Johnson was a Morehouse man, and Morehouse men were taught never to give up. When a judge ruled that each seat was to be selected only by the voters within their respective district, Johnson was declared the victor.

Gaining recognition from his peers proved to be just as challenging. During Johnson's first thirty days in office, none of the other legislators uttered a word to him. "I would walk from the courthouse to the Senate chamber, meeting senators going in the opposite direction," he remembered. "I would say, 'Good morning, Senator.' They would just look away. They thought that my being there was like a plague, that the ceiling would fall in and the seats would crumble. I was all alone in a lion's den."

The silent treatment finally came to an abrupt end when Johnson arrived late one morning for an education committee meeting. Several senators rushed to his side. Johnson was, for the moment, no longer a black man trespassing on sacred white ground. He was a vote that counted as much as the others, a vote they needed to break a deadlock. Johnson put aside any resentment he might have still harbored—this was no time to let his hurt feelings get in the way of attaining the influence he coveted—and made the first of countless bargains, aligning himself with the senators who agreed to back several of his bills. "I learned you get not what you deserve in politics," he said, "you get what you can negotiate." At times, Johnson was criticized by members of his own race for not shaking things up enough in the white-dominated body, but he strongly believed the most prudent way to achieve long-term progress for blacks in the South was to not only beat the system but, as often as possible, to work within it.

On the other hand, he recognized that not every right could be obtained through skillful negotiation. Some rights needed to be seized. Johnson was adamant from the day he was sworn in that he deserved to receive the same privileges as every other member of this exclusive club. One afternoon, with assistance from one of his few friends in the chamber, Senator Joe Salome, Johnson decided he would attempt to desegregate the cafeteria in the Georgia State Capitol.

"Senator Johnson and I are going to have lunch," Salome told senators headed toward the cafeteria. "Please come and have lunch with us."

Nobody accepted the invitation, which, of course, did not come as a tremendous shock. After all, this was early 1963, before the March on Washington and Dr. King's "I have a dream" speech on the steps of the Lincoln Memorial, before the landmark 1964 Civil Rights Bill, before the South finally surrendered for the second, and last, time. The rejections did not deter the Morehouse man for one second. He picked up a tray, filled it with a few items, and calmly joined his friend in the checkout line.

"We can't serve you," said the agitated woman behind the register.

Johnson did not budge. "Young lady," he replied without raising his voice, "I am a state senator and I intend to eat here in the state cafeteria."

The woman went to see her supervisor. A few minutes later, she returned, defeated. "Give me your money," she told him.

Johnson and Salome found a table, but as soon as they sat down, senators on both sides stood up and walked away. The two did not let this demonstration spoil their moment of triumph. The cafeteria in the State Capitol of the commonwealth of Georgia was officially desegregated.

"I had done what Morehouse College had trained me to do," Johnson said.

The fight to obtain a boxing license for Muhammad Ali, if Johnson was to take it on, would be among the toughest of his political career. Since Ali's last official appearance in the ring—against the aging Zora Folley at the old Madison Square Garden on Eighth Avenue between Forty-ninth and Fiftieth streets in New York City, in which he defended his crown for the ninth time with a seventh-round knockout—people who knew a heck of a lot more about the sweet science than an outsider from, for heaven's sake, *Georgia*, had failed in dozens of attempts to put the deposed champion back to work. Georgia was, after all, where the Ku Klux Klan still held rallies at Stone Mountain, noted for its monumental carving of Civil War generals Robert E. Lee and Stonewall Jackson and Confederacy president Jefferson Davis on horseback, and where an ardent segregationist, Lester G. Maddox, resided in the governor's mansion.

Elected officials and boxing commissioners throughout the United States refused to support Ali's bid for a boxing license. "The boxing commissioners were afraid that they would lose these patronage jobs, which is all they were," said the *New York Times*'s Robert Lipsyte, who wrote about Ali extensively in the 1960s and 1970s. "It was very easy to turn him down. It was a wonderful way for all these hacks to show their allegiance to the governors or mayors who appointed them."

Nor was Ali permitted to leave the country while he remained free on bail. Proposals for title bouts in Japan and Canada were turned down. In Canada, Ali was to be escorted by federal marshals after posting a $100,000 cash bond and to stay on foreign soil for less than twenty-four hours, but the Fifth United States Circuit Court of Appeals in New Orleans denied his request without comment. The Gila River Indians in Sacaton, Arizona, whose reservation was outside the jurisdiction of the state's Athletic Commission, refused to sanction a rematch between Ali and Folley. The Gila River tribal council determined that giving Ali a license would "desecrate the land some of our brave boys have walked on," although other factors may have played a role in its decision. "The story I got," former *Newark Star-Ledger* columnist Jerry Izenberg said, "was that there was a call from the Interior Department asking whoever was on the tribal council, 'Do you really want to keep getting that poverty money?' and then there was a change of heart."

Despite the growing antiwar movement on college campuses, and the profound effect on public opinion of the ghastly images appearing in dying color on the evening news and in the weekly magazines, many Americans stood behind the Johnson, and subsequently the Nixon, administration's campaign in Vietnam, or at the very least considered Ali unpatriotic for his refusal to serve. Nonetheless, those lured by the potential record-setting payday of an Ali comeback fight continued to search for a receptive politician and, on several occasions, it appeared they just might succeed.

In December 1969, Florida governor Claude Kirk loaned his support to a bout in Tampa between Ali and a certain fighter out of Philadelphia. This fighter did not possess a long reach, did not throw many traditional combinations, and could, at times, be quite vulnerable. Yet he did not back off for an instant, and in the view of those who closely followed boxing, he was more formidable than anyone Ali ever faced, and that included Sonny Liston. The fighter was Smokin' Joe Frazier. "I think Mr. Frazier can easily beat Mr. Clay," Kirk said. "You know, there was some talk that Mr. Clay lost his title because of politics, instead of due to fisticuffs. And I'd be glad if we could promote a fight in Tampa to settle this." Within days, however, after fierce opposition emerged—an editorial in the *Tampa Tribune* proclaimed, "We Object Conscientiously"—the governor changed his mind.

"While I would like to see Frazier put his fists right on Mohammed Blah," Kirk said, "I have heard from enough people in Florida to know that they do not want the fight to take place in Florida. It comes as a surprise to me that a man who lacks the courage to fight for his country could have the guts to get into the ring. . . . I see no reason why an alleged draft dodger should be in a position to lay claim to any title."

Months later, Ali's attorney, Bob Arum, launched an effort to stage the fight in the future capital of professional boxing, Las Vegas, Nevada. Arum, who along with Don King would become the premier promoter during the last quarter of the twentieth century, persuaded Ali and Frazier to sign contracts. Meanwhile, the well-known handicapper Jimmy "the Greek" Snyder secured the approval of Governor Paul Laxalt. Nobody stood in the way—well, almost nobody. Arum was about to go into a meeting in the basement of a hotel on the Strip with members of the Nevada Athletic Commission, Governor Laxalt, and Snyder when the phone rang. It was Bob Mayhew asking for Snyder. Mayhew was an important player in Vegas. "Jimmy went white," Arum recalled. "You work with us for the resort's interests," Mayhew reminded Snyder. Snyder did indeed. Mayhew explained that their boss did not want Ali to fight in his state. The call ended and so did the negotiations. Their boss was Howard Hughes. The reason for his opposition was the usual one: Ali's stance on the draft.

"The governor was embarrassed," Arum said, "but I got him off the hook. I told him, 'Look, I'm going to pull the application,' which is what I did."

Some proposals were downright bizarre. One was for Ali to fight in a bull ring in Tijuana, another at a rodeo arena in Tulsa.

Perhaps the most unconventional of all surfaced from the mind of Murray Woroner, a Miami promoter who achieved a degree of success with *The First Christmas, Easter the Beginning*, and *July 4, 1776*, radio recreations of historic events delivered as modern newscasts. Woroner had already put together Ali's only "fights" during the exile, the results decided by machine instead of man. Over a hundred variables (the ability to absorb a punch, punching power, tendency to get cut, courage, and so on) compiled by boxing experts were fed into a National Cash Register computer in Dayton, Ohio. Among sixteen greats in Woroner's *All-Time Heavyweight Tournament and Championship Fight*, broadcast over nearly four hundred radio stations, Ali lost to James Jeffries, the Great White Hope from the early twentieth century. Ali filed a $1 million suit against Woroner for defamation of character for losing to Jeffries, but it was dropped when he was paid $10,000 for a computer match in 1969 against Rocky Marciano. Marciano, forty-five, who retired undefeated in 1956, took the challenge seriously, shedding about fifty pounds and putting on a new toupee.

"He was so happy to be back," said Ferdie Pacheco, Ali's longtime doctor, who took part in the production. "He wanted to fight for real." Too real, for Ali's comfort. "He did hit Ali several times hard," Pacheco said. "Ali told him, 'Hey, if we play *that* game, then I'm going to start punching you and they're going to start sewing you up.'" Marciano was quite impressed with Ali. "My God, the kid is so fast," he kept saying.

The finished product drew a fair amount of coverage, a commentary on a sport lacking in excitement since the banishment of its charismatic leading man. Love Ali or hate Ali, it would be nearly impossible to find anyone in America who was neutral toward the man in the late 1960s. People wanted to see him between the ropes, no matter how contrived or commercial the enterprise might be. "I could announce tomorrow that Muhammad Ali will walk across the Hudson River and charge twenty dollars admission," Teddy Brenner, the Madison Square Garden matchmaker, once said, "and there would be twenty thousand down there to see him do it. And half of them would be rooting for him to do it and the other half would be rooting for him to sink."

The computer fight was shown on closed-circuit television on January 20, 1970, a Marciano left hook knocking Ali out in the thirteenth round. It was reported at the time that after fans complained in England about the outcome, a new version was shown a week later with Ali triumphant. Marciano, the story said, was seen with his arms raised in protest after the fight was halted because of cuts. However, David Woroner, Murray's son, who was involved in a documentary about the fight in recent years, said the England story was a hoax. In any case, Marciano died in a plane crash in Iowa on August 31, 1969, only three weeks after the filming was completed. He never knew the outcome, since seven different endings were shot to protect against any leaks.

According to Pacheco, for Ali's official comeback Woroner proposed that Frazier (recognized as the titleholder in New York and several other states), Jimmy Ellis (the survivor of the eight-man elimination tournament organized by the World Boxing Association in 1967 to fill the vacancy), and Ali slug it out in, of all places, a movie studio in South Miami, with two fights needed to produce the champion: Ellis versus Frazier, then the winner versus Ali. Under one plan, only the combatants, their corners, a film crew, a physician, and the judges would be allowed to attend, and then, immediately afterward, the entire group would be sequestered for several weeks to keep the results secret until the film could be developed and distributed to closed-circuit outlets. Not surprisingly, Pacheco said, the project proved far too enormous for Woroner, a novice in the high-stakes universe of professional boxing, to pull off. "We had a child playing with dynamite," he explained. "All we needed was a Don King or a Bob Arum to come in and take the reins of the thing and put a few million dollars behind it, and we would have been off and gone, but we did not have a Don King or a Bob Arum, and we did not have a million dollars. All we had was a good idea and nobody to do it."

In July 1970, Ali flew to Charleston, South Carolina, to fight for real. So what if it was only an exhibition and instead of Frazier, Ali was to square off against a much less imposing Joe (Bugner), and the equally unspectacular Jeff Merritt? He would be back in his comfort zone, the spotlight, tossing punches and barbs, doing the famous Ali shuffle, *being* Ali, presumably a huge step toward a fight against Frazier or another high-caliber opponent. What mattered was that the barrier would finally be torn down, and that boxing commissioners from other states might then reconsider and offer him an opportunity to earn a living in his chosen profession while he awaited his fate in the judicial system. In 1970, with the nation more opposed than ever to U.S. involvement in Southeast Asia, these political pawns were not dealing with the same pressures they encountered in 1967, 1968, and 1969. ABC prepared to tape the exhibition for its popular Saturday afternoon show *Wide World of Sports*, while writers from some of the top newspapers made the trip. The long-delayed return of Muhammad Ali to the ring against anyone, anywhere, was a major story.

The fights were scheduled for County Hall, the proceeds going to help subsidize young, underprivileged boxers. Everything was proceeding smoothly until, only two days before the event, the county council voted unanimously to call the whole thing off. To this day, the event's promoter, Reggie Barrett Jr., blames the cancellation on South Carolina congressman L. Mendel Rivers, the conservative Democratic chairman of the House Committee on Armed Services, who, Barrett claims, complained to former council chairman J. Mitchell Graham that he was being ridiculed by his fellow legislators in Washington for allowing a convicted draft dodger to fight in, of all places, *his* district. Barrett quickly suggested an alternative site, the Charleston Speedway, a dirt racetrack about ten miles outside of town, but when he took Ali to check it out, the ex-champ's response closed the matter for good.

"When I parked the car," Barrett recalled, "he said, 'Let's go. I ain't getting out here in any ring and letting a bunch of rednecks shoot me like they did Martin Luther King and Medgar Evers. I'm out of here.'" (Evers, a prominent Civil Rights activist, was gunned down after returning from a meeting with NAACP lawyers on June 12, 1963.)

A dispirited Ali, his hopes dashed once again, flew back to his home in Philadelphia. "For days, I refused even to answer the phone," he wrote in his 1975 autobiography. "I had resolved that Charleston and Jackson [an earlier effort to obtain a license in Jackson, Mississippi, fell through] would be my last rejections, and if all that was left now was to serve the five-year jail term and forget boxing, I was prepared."

Leroy Johnson worked the phones. Johnson was not about to spend hard-earned political capital on trying to beat the system if the system was not beatable. He needed a road map to circumnavigate the anti-Ali forces that would surely mobilize in opposition as they did in Tampa and every other city when a fight appeared on the horizon. Within a few days, he found one. Georgia did not have a state boxing commission, which meant that the authority to sanction prizefights was solely in the hands of local governing bodies— in the case of Atlanta, the city's Board of Aldermen. Johnson could not believe his good fortune. A number of the board members, black and white, owed their positions to his influence. "It was like putting a rabbit in the berry patch," Johnson said. On the night before every election, the Negro Voters League in Atlanta, in which he was one of the leading figures, passed out a ticket to black voters that listed the candidate for each contest who had received the league's endorsement. "You took it to the polls with you and you voted for whoever the ticket said," Julian Bond said. Johnson then asked a friend in the Fulton County district attorney's office to conduct a thorough investigation of Robert Kassel and his New York associates. If there was one thing Leroy Johnson knew about professional boxing, it was what everyone else knew, that practically since the days of bare knuckles, the sport has attracted more than its share of shady characters.

Johnson, once he was informed that the group was not connected to organized crime, phoned Kassel's father-in-law, Harry Pett. "I can get Ali a license to fight in Atlanta," Johnson said.

To understand why Johnson was so confident requires more than an awareness of his considerable political skills. An examination of how far Atlanta had advanced over the previous decades, especially on the important issue of race relations, is also imperative. Leroy Johnson would have gotten nowhere in the Atlanta of 1950 or 1960. The Atlanta of 1970 was the centerpiece of the *New South*, a term used in the 1880s by *Atlanta Constitution* editor Henry Grady to describe a region that, with the breakup of the pre–Civil War plantation economy, was evolving into a more industrial society.

"The old South rested everything on slavery and agriculture, unconscious that these could neither give nor maintain healthy growth," Grady said. "The new South presents a perfect democracy, the oligarchs leading in the popular movement—a social system compact and closely knitted, less splendid on the surface, but stronger at the core . . . and a diversified industry that meets the complex need of this complex age." Hailing the arrival of a New South became a recurring theme in the land of Dixie. "There have been about four 'New Souths' announced over time," Bond said. "'*This* is the New South,' and fifty years later, '*this* is the New South.'"

This was, undoubtedly, a *new* Atlanta, described by ex-mayor William Hartsfield in the late 1950s as "the city too busy to hate." Black police officers, required for years to put on their uniforms and receive their daily assignments at the Butler Street YMCA, were now based at headquarters and allowed to perform the same functions as their white counterparts. Prior to those changes, "if you were a black policeman and you saw a white guy coming out of a bank with money in one hand, a gun in the other," Bond pointed out, "you had to hold the guy but you could not arrest him. You had to call for a white policeman."

A prominent role in the city's evolution was played by Ralph Emerson McGill, the former editor and publisher of the *Atlanta Constitution*. "It was Ralph McGill and others like him who bridged the gap between the black and white communities and made it possible for Atlanta to be different from Mississippi and other areas of the South," Johnson contended. "His articles always created an atmosphere of tolerance, of moving forward, and, without that kind of atmosphere, I'm not so sure we would've been able to do anything." Also helping to bridge the gap was the arrival of the Atlanta Braves baseball franchise from Milwaukee, which, featuring future all-time home-run king Hank Aaron, began play in the spring of 1966. "Whenever you can get blacks and whites in the same forum," Johnson said, "it tends to release and remove some fears that might have existed between the two."

Advances in the city's business community were just as momentous. The Atlanta Life Insurance Company, established by Alonzo F. Herndon, a former slave, had grown into a very prominent financial institution. The *Atlanta Daily World*, founded in 1928, was one of the nation's most influential black papers. In the 1940s, WERD became the first African American-owned and operated radio station in the United States. With black institutions such as Morehouse College, Spelman College, Clark College, Atlanta University, and Morris Brown College, the academic environment was thriving as well. "Black people flocked to Atlanta," Bond said. "It had this reputation as a center of black middle-class life. You could get a job at Delta or Coca-Cola, where, in New York, you might not be able to work for these companies. Things appeared to be going on. It was a place you wanted to be."

The accumulation of political power was perhaps the most significant development. During the election of 1969, the number of African Americans on the Board of Aldermen rose from one to five while Sam Massell, who received more than 90 percent of the black vote, was elected the first Jewish mayor in the city's history. The victories gave Johnson more leverage than ever. When the moment became appropriate, he would surely collect on those IOUs. With the opportunity to help launch Muhammad Ali's comeback, and pick up a nice paycheck, the moment had arrived. Johnson went to city hall to meet with Massell. Johnson was not about to take any chances with such a delicate matter. "The mayor could always, because he was the mayor, flex his muscles," Johnson explained. "Could we override that? Possibly, but you try to anticipate problems and resolve them. If I had the Board of Aldermen and the mayor, then I would have a clear shot."

Massell, in office for less than a year, was not overly thrilled with the idea. Believing he knew the pulse of the city better than anyone—a special light was installed in his car allowing him, between engagements at night, to read every local publication, including the Greek, the Jewish, and the union newspapers—the mayor recognized that despite evidence of improved relations between whites and blacks there were still people in Atlanta who were not too busy to hate. After hesitating briefly, he gave his consent. "I owe you one," Massell said, according to Johnson. The mayor served on the draft board during World War II and was familiar with the laws dealing with conscientious objectors. "I knew it was a legal position, so that was part of what dictated my opinion and judgment," he said. In exchange for his support, Massell extracted a commitment from Kassel's group to hand over a check for $50,000 on the night of the fight to the Metropolitan Atlanta Commission on Alcoholism and Drugs for information leading to arrests and convictions. The drug problem in the city "was just surfacing," Massell recalled. "We had a large influx of hippies, flower children, maybe second to San Francisco. They flooded the streets."

The next assignment for Johnson was much tougher. The governor of Georgia did not owe Leroy Johnson a damn thing. Furthermore, the suggestion that Lester G. Maddox, who ascended to power largely on his opposition to integration and refused to attend Dr. King's funeral in 1968, calling him an "an enemy of the country," might actually assist a black convicted draft dodger seemed ludicrous. In fact, he had opposed a bid a year earlier for an Ali match in Macon.

Maddox became famous, or infamous, in July 1964 when he and his supporters, wielding pick handles, prevented five blacks from entering the Pickrick, a fried chicken restaurant he owned. Maddox also waived a pistol in the air. A photo of the incident, which took place the day after President Lyndon Johnson signed the Civil Rights bill, appeared in papers throughout the country. Three years later, Maddox became governor even though he lost the popular vote to conservative Republican Howard "Bo" Callaway. Because of a write-in campaign for former governor Ellis Arnall, Callaway failed to secure a majority, sending the decision to the Democrat-controlled Georgia State Assembly, which, naturally, chose a fellow Democrat, Maddox.

The meeting got off to a rough start, with Maddox insisting to Johnson that an Ali bout in downtown Atlanta would incite violence. "Governor, there is nothing in Ali's history which suggests that he's an instigator," Johnson countered. The senator made a strong argument, but Maddox was not swayed. Johnson moved on to the subject of welfare. He believed that the governor was one of many Southerners during that era who assumed that every black person's fondest desire was to remain forever on the public dole. "Ali wants to work for a living," he told Maddox, "and not be on welfare. To do that, he needs to fight." Maddox held his ground again.

Finally, Johnson pulled out his last card. A few months earlier, the governor's son, Lester Maddox Jr., twenty-six, had been arrested for burglary. Remembering he heard a judge explain that he was giving the governor's son "another chance" by keeping him out of jail, Johnson said to Maddox, "Governor, everybody deserves *another chance*." The use of the identical phrase did not escape Maddox. "On with the fight," he told Johnson. The phrase apparently stuck in the governor's mind. "I think Clay deserves another chance," he said at a press conference. "Clay's proud of his race. I think a man should be proud of his race. Besides, if I was against him, what could I do about it? . . . At least he was expressing his real convictions. And if he's made some mistakes, everyone else has made some, too, you know."

Soon afterward, however, Maddox reversed course, claiming he gave his initial blessing without knowing that Ali had been formally convicted of draft evasion. Johnson was stunned. He became convinced that the White Citizens' Council, adhering to the same segregationist views as the Ku Klux Klan, must have gotten to Maddox. Yet the senator was savvy enough to recognize that the last thing he could afford at this critical juncture was to be involved in a public fight with the governor of Georgia, a fight he would most likely not win, and which might very well cost him his only opportunity to stage the Ali bout in Atlanta. Johnson referred to Maddox as "a man of great compassion," certain "he meant the kind things he said about giving Mr. Clay the opportunity to redeem himself."

Maddox might have come to a sincere change of heart or been simply posturing in an appeal to his supporters. Under Georgia law, though ineligible to run in November for a second consecutive term, he was a candidate for lieutenant governor. (Maddox was victorious, serving in the post from 1971 to 1975. Elected to replace him as governor was Jimmy Carter.)

If a fight could be arranged, if Leroy Johnson were to prevail against Lester Maddox, or anybody else who might attempt to thwart his efforts, who would then be Ali's ideal opponent in the ring? Who would draw the most attention—or, more precisely, the most dollars? Making history was an admirable objective, but prizefights are made, first and foremost, to make money, not history. The obvious answer was Joe Frazier, who, with his victory over Jimmy Ellis at the Garden in February, was the only official heavyweight champion, the heir to the throne Ali was forced to abdicate. Yet landing Frazier was not the first order of business for Johnson and Kassel. Frazier was not going anywhere. He and Yancey "Yank" Durham, his trainer and manager, could not possibly turn down the opportunity to rid themselves of the one remaining obstacle in their path and secure the most lucrative payday of their careers.

The first order of business was landing Muhammad Ali. Nobody took very seriously Ali's declarations that he was done with boxing.

"They can come up tomorrow," Ali wrote in *Esquire* during the spring of 1970, "and say: 'We want you to fight Joe Frazier in Madison Square Garden for millions of dollars with no taxes. Here's your license to fight. We're all ready.' I'll just tell them: 'I'm sorry, but I'm through now. . . . I can't sleep under but one roof, can't eat but one meal, can't wear but one suit, and can't ride in but one car, and I got plenty of that. So why do I want to fight? I don't need no prestige at beating up nobody. I'm tired. And I want to be the first black champion that got out that didn't get whipped.'" Ali even volunteered to hand over his belt to the Frazier-Ellis winner in the middle of the ring, but the offer did not prove he was finished. The only reason Ali was not fighting was that no boxing commission or politician let him fight. Boxing was what made him famous.

"Had somewhere during that period he discovered that he had as much talent with the trumpet as he had in the ring and could get as much attention as the world's greatest brass player, I think going back into the ring would not have mattered," the *Times*'s Robert Lipsyte suggested. "But I think that a lot of this goes back to that desperate striving for affirmation, and the only way he had ever gotten it, and would continue to get it, was as a boxer." In fact, in the same *Esquire* article, Ali described how he would approach Frazier differently in the ring from the way his former sparring partner, Ellis, did. He did not exactly sound retired.

"Ellis wore himself out, got weak," Ali wrote, "couldn't take no punishment in close . . . *I'd be pickin' and pokin'* . . . *throwing water on Joe's smokin'*. . . . *It might shock and amaze ya, but I'd destroy Frazier.*"

In April 1968, Lipsyte was strolling down Van Ness Street in San Francisco in search of breakfast when he was spotted by Ali, who was on his way to address an antiwar gathering at the Civic Center Plaza. His car pulled up to the curb. "He was looking for people to talk to him," Lipsyte said, "particularly people who remembered him when he was the champ. He was glad to see reporters. He wasn't getting the attention that he wanted." The most attention Ali received in the late 1960s came during the lectures he delivered on college campuses. The students applauded his courage in taking on the Establishment, and let him know they still considered him the true heavyweight champion.

"They loved him," Pacheco recalled. "We walked in there, and you would think that he was ready to run for president."

Ali needed more than attention. He needed money. The limited streams of revenue during his hiatus—lectures for about $2,500 a crack, a short-lived appearance in a Broadway musical called *Buck White*, a $225,000 deal with Random House for his autobiography—could never come close to the riches available to him in the fight game. (*Buck White* closed after only four days. According to producer Zev Buffman, Ali gave an inspired effort when he performed in front of a preview audience but could not maintain the same level the following night when the critics showed up. "There was no fire," Buffman said.) "For a brief moment in life," according to Pacheco, "he tasted the wonderful fruits of having a lot of money, and then, all of a sudden, he tasted poverty again. Ali was stone broke." So broke, Pacheco said, that friends gave him money. "You're talking about $100 here, $200 there," he added. "You love the guy, and he means something to you, you just don't want to see him scuffle."

Even people who did not know Ali personally assumed he was in financial trouble. A New York Hilton Hotel employee once informed him that he owed $53.09 in charges billed to his room and, from then on, needed to pay for room service in cash.

"This don't bother me none," Ali said. "Word probably got around, he's not the champ no more, he's busted, you better get your money up front. That's the way it is. When you the champ, you can sign and sign and sign." Ali handed the clerk a fifty and a five. "The manager of the hotel was so apologetic, asking for autographs," Lipsyte said. "The whole thing was really bizarre." Ali coped as well as possible, given the circumstances. "You could put him in the worst dump of a hotel and it would not bother him at all, as long as there was a bed, a wash basin, and a bathroom to use," Pacheco said. "He didn't give a shit. He didn't seem to get insulted."

To this day, one question related to Ali's economic difficulties remains: did Joe Frazier give him money?

In the 2000 HBO documentary *Ali-Frazier I: One Nation . . . Divisible*, Frazier claims he put "some love in his hand," meaning cash. Butch Lewis, a friend, said Frazier gave Ali $2,000 for an overdue hotel bill. Joe Hand, an administrator for Cloverlay, the Philadelphia corporation established in 1965 to oversee Frazier's finances, recalled that during a board meeting, "somebody in the office said, 'We just lent Ali some money.' Yank and Joe said they wanted to do it. I don't know if it was Cloverlay's money or not." Ali biographer Thomas Hauser said, however, that when he ran the Lewis story by Ali in 1990, Ali was emphatic that it was not accurate. Hauser left it out of the manuscript. "There were lots of other anecdotes in the book that one might consider equally embarrassing that Ali had no problem with," Hauser said. "From that, it seemed to me he was probably correct in denying that it happened." Pacheco also expressed his doubts. "I don't think Ali would have asked for it or accepted it," he said. "Frazier is a tough guy from Philadelphia. He had no reason to give anything to Ali."

In April 1969, Ali opened up about his troubles, and it cost him dearly. During an interview with Howard Cosell, Ali acknowledged that he hoped to return to boxing to clear up some of his debts.

The Black Muslims suspended him for one year and took away something far more valuable to him than his crown: his name.

"Mr. Muhammad plainly acted the fool. Any man or woman who comes to Allah and then puts his hopes and trust in the enemy of Allah for survival is underestimating the power of Allah to help them," Elijah Muhammad, the group's head, said in a statement that ran in *Muhammad Speaks*, the Nation of Islam publication. "This statement is to tell the world that we, the Muslims, are not with Mr. Muhammad Ali, in his desire to work in the sports world for the sake of a 'leetle' money." Ali retracted his comments. "He was right and I was wrong," he said several months later. "I don't need boxing to make a living. What my leader did was worse than my five-year sentence, worse than 15 years at hard labor." At the same time, however, he added, "I don't want to fight Frazier—he wants to fight me—but I would fight him if the terms are agreed."

By the summer of 1970, Ali was still often referred to by the media as Cassius Clay even though six years had gone by since he went public with his new identity, declaring Clay a slave name. As Ali did not formally change his name, the *New York Times* typically added the phrase "also known as Cassius Clay" after calling him Ali in the original reference. In the late 1960s, Robert Lipsyte argued to his superiors against any references to *Clay*, but it did no good. A. M. Rosenthal, the paper's conservative managing editor, Lipsyte said, "waited a long time before he would allow Ms. in the paper." Ali understood. Once, when a friend started reading to Ali a story written by Lipsyte, the writer apologized for referring to him as Clay. Ali put his hand on Lipsyte's shoulder.

"I know it's not you," Ali assured him. "You're just a little brother of the white power structure."

To members of the fourth estate who grew up in the 1940s and 1950s and believed that black professional athletes were supposed to be respectful, subservient, and eternally grateful for the privilege of amassing more fame and fortune than they could have ever imagined, Ali was still Cassius Clay. Unlike their icon, Joe Louis, who proudly served his nation in World War II, the seminal event of their lifetime, Clay was precisely what an athlete was *not* supposed to be: bombastic, defiant, pontificating on social and political issues outside his limited scope. Conversely, to many younger writers, Ali was a pivotal figure in American culture precisely *because* he saw beyond the narrow parameters of his sport. They, too, greatly admired Joe Louis, but World War II had not shaped their value system.

Despite his popularity among college students, Ali did not buy into the whole left agenda and was not afraid to let them know it.

"He could be kind of off-putting when he made fun of dope or when he mocked interracial relationships," Lipsyte said. For the speech in San Francisco, "he had a beautiful day, a big audience, everyone thrilled that he was there. The first thing he did was kind of twitch his nose at the cloud of pot that was coming up from the audience and he made some comment about that. The heads [potheads] got up and left, and then he got into one of his redbirds stay with redbirds and bluebirds stay with bluebirds and the checkerboard [interracial] romances got up and left. Later, he told the booking agent, 'I guess I'm just too strong for the audience.'"

Whatever his social or political leanings, few attracted a crowd as easily as Muhammad Ali. One day, he and Ferdie Pacheco were in a limo heading down Broadway with the British promoter Jarvis Astaire, who was, according to Pacheco, considering the idea of hooking Ali up for a third time with English heavyweight Henry Cooper. Ali won both fights, in 1963 and 1966. In the fourth round of their initial encounter, Cooper became only the second opponent to put Ali on the deck. Ali was in real danger of suffering his first defeat. Enter Angelo Dundee to the rescue. He bought some much-needed extra time by enlarging a split that had already opened up in Ali's gloves. Ali recovered and stopped Cooper in the fifth round.

"How do I know if you still have any drawing power?" Astaire asked.

"How much money do you have in your pocket?" Ali responded.

"Two thousand dollars," Astaire said.

"I'll bet you two thousand dollars," Ali proposed. "Let me out at this corner. I'll walk up to that corner over there. I won't say anything. I won't holler or raise my arms or acknowledge who I am. I'll walk straight to that corner and I'll stand still. By the time I get over there, I'll stop traffic. The police will have to come."

Astaire accepted the bet.

Ali stepped out of the limo. He walked only a few yards before people began to chant his name.

"By the time we got to that corner," Pacheco said, "you could not move on Broadway and Forty-second. From sidewalk to sidewalk, you couldn't see the street. It was all just people."

According to Pacheco, Ali did not believe his banishment from the ring would last too long. "They can't help but get to me," Ali told him. "I'm the best there is. I'm where the money is. If not this year, next year." Maybe he was the best there was and maybe, with all the people in the business who stood to profit from his return, *they* would have to get to him eventually. Then again, maybe not. With every rejection, every time a boxing commissioner or elected official blocked his path, Ali, in his most insecure moments, must have wondered if his career was, indeed, over. "There were a lot of ups and downs that raised and lowered his spirits," Lipsyte acknowledged.

There was another concern: Ali was running out of time. In boxing, time is every fighter's one truly indestructible opponent. The day comes, whether it's Jack Johnson or Jack Dempsey or Joe Louis, when the punches are no longer as powerful, the reflexes as precise, the will as persistent. In his normal style, Ali relied heavily on speed and intelligence to overcome flaws—he held his hands low and leaned away from punches instead of slipping them. The longer Ali, twenty-eight, stayed away from competition, the longer the odds of him staging a successful comeback. "I knew that unless my exile ended soon, the tools of my trade would wither," Ali acknowledged.

Pacheco was also worried. Prior to the layoff, because of Ali's ability to escape any sustained punishment, "there was nothing for me to do," Pacheco said. That would certainly not be the case after the layoff. "He was getting too flabby, and the edge wasn't there anymore," he added. "I wasn't worried about a comeback happening. I was worried it would happen too late for him. But even if it had been too late, he would have done it anyway."

During the exile, Ali jogged on occasion and trained at his familiar hangout, the Fifth Street Gym in Miami Beach. He sparred with Jimmy Ellis. Yet no amount of working out could possibly compare with getting into a real fight against an opponent out to knock him senseless.

Ali was skeptical about the comeback happening in Atlanta. Anybody would be skeptical that, of the fifty states in the Union, Georgia, with its shameful record on civil rights and governed by Lester Maddox, would be the one to embrace a black man who chose not to obey the law of the land. During their first conversation, Leroy Johnson stressed to Ali that Atlanta was everything the rest of Georgia was not—progressive, tolerant, a beacon for a New South. "I want history to show that it was a black man that assisted you in beating the system," Johnson told Ali. "Brother, I like that," Ali replied.

In August 1970, the Board of Aldermen approved a permit for Ali to fight, presumably against Frazier, on October 26 at Municipal Auditorium, a dusty 5,000-seat arena perhaps best known for Friday night wrestling shows put on by the promoter Paul Jones (the state-of-the-art Omni would not be completed until 1972). Robert Kassel arranged for a press conference at the Marriott Hotel in downtown Atlanta to make the formal announcement. Ali came in from Philadelphia, but after so many failures, he was not about to celebrate his return to the ring just yet. After schmoozing with Sam Massell and other city leaders, Ali retreated to his room. According to Kassel, the press was not informed he was in the building. "I told Ali I would call his room and have the phone on speaker," he said, "so he could hear the goings-on, so that when he realized we were presenting a license, he would come down."

The key players in securing the permit—which included Jesse Hill, the chief actuary of Atlanta Life—came to the press conference, except for Massell. It was one thing for the mayor to give his official support; it was quite another, given the amount of antagonism that remained toward Ali, for Massell to be seen on the dais with the other dignitaries. "I had done what I needed to do," he explained. "I knew it was not a popular thing." Midway through the session, Kassel took the phone off the speaker. "Champ," he whispered to Ali, "why don't you come down. Everybody is here. The flashbulbs are going and the cameras are on." A few minutes later, Ali made his grand entrance. Nobody made grand entrances like Ali. The reaction, Kassel said, was "pandemonium. They were shocked he was there."

Within a few days, Johnson spoke with Yank Durham, who made the important decisions in the Frazier camp. Johnson soon realized that Durham might be even tougher to bring on board than the hesitant mayor and the segregationist governor back home. The close calls in recent months made Durham perhaps even more wary than Ali. "We've been down the primrose path before, and it always collapsed," he told the senator. Yet Johnson emerged from the conversion with a ray of hope. Durham, he claims, assured him that if he was able to put Ali in the ring against another fighter first, he would have a date with his man.

Johnson went to work right away on arranging an Ali exhibition bout. He ruled out Municipal Auditorium, because it was too accessible to the white community, which might incite the kind of violent response Maddox warned him about in their earlier meeting. Maddox would then be able to make a pretty strong case that staging another Ali fight in October would be too risky. Johnson contacted his good friend Hugh Gloster, the president of Morehouse College, who agreed to allow the school's gym to be used for the event. Morehouse was situated in an African American neighborhood. Johnson believed it would insulate the bout from the "intrusion of the White Citizens' Council and the Ku Klux Klan." The Klan, in fact, was planning to hold a rally at Stone Mountain three days after the Ali exhibition. The group, in an advertisement that appeared in the *Atlanta Journal,* promised "prominent speakers" and "cross lighting" and reminded people to bring their robes.

Ali went into training and dropped about 15 pounds, though on the eve of the exhibition he tipped the scales at a portly 221, still about 10 pounds above his standard fighting weight. Asked about his return to fighting, he said, "I have a lot to see in eight rounds."

What he—and everyone else—saw, in three separate bouts against the unheralded heavyweights Johnny Hudgins, Rufus Brassell, and George Hill, in a hot, crowded college gymnasium, was not very impressive. Against Brassell, his first opponent, he threw light jabs. Against Hudgins, he let himself get hit. Finally, after the first of four rounds against Hill, some of the 2,700 fans registered their disapproval with a response rarely associated with an Ali show: they booed. Ali's assistant trainer and lead booster, Drew "Bundini" Brown, who coined the slogan "Float like a butterfly, sting like a bee," decided to do something about it. "I kept talking to him in the corner, reminding him of what he went through to get here, and he perked right up," said Brown, in Ali's corner for the first time since he was kicked out five years earlier for pawning his championship belt to a barber in Harlem for $500. "Bad financial straits characterized Bundini's life," Pacheco said. "He couldn't hold on to a nickel. As soon as he got money, he spent it."

Brown drank too much, but nobody fired Ali up as well as he could. If Ali did not feel like training, Brown found a way to make him train. Ali was so fond of him that, according to Pacheco, even Dundee could not do anything about it. "Angelo recognized he had to accept Bundini because the kid wanted him," Pacheco said. "If he didn't accept Bundini, the likelihood was that *he* would get fired. He tried to just act as if Bundini wasn't there. When he stole the belt, Angelo didn't say anything. Ali thought he was funny. It was like a court jester."

Responding to Brown's pep talk at Morehouse, Ali began to show flashes of the preexile Ali—the famous footwork, the flurry of combinations, the crowd-pleasing entertainer. The boos ceased and the cheering got loud, and soon Ali was done for the evening, though it was clear that he was a long way from being at his best and that nothing less than his best would be necessary to reclaim the crown. Although Ali downplayed Frazier's abilities, he was aware of how formidable an adversary Frazier would be. "In 1967, I was working for WKCR, a student radio station at Columbia," Ali biographer Thomas Hauser said. "I taped an interview with Ali. That was the first time I met him. It was right before he fought Zora Folley. I asked him who he thought would be the toughest of the young heavyweights out there for him and he said, 'Joe Frazier.'"

Ali's showing at Morehouse was not the point. He would have nearly two months to work himself into prime fighting condition. The point was that Johnson did exactly what Durham proposed, and the city didn't burn. There was little Lester Maddox could say now. "Way down in our hearts, we didn't know if the bell would ring," Brown said. "We didn't know if we could even enter the ring here until we walked out there and did it. . . . I think everyone was expecting someone to stop the fights just as they were about to begin." For many, the evening signified more than the return of one of the world's greatest athletes. "At the time, among Morehouse students, there was enormous interest in Afro-American consciousness and pride," said Alvin Darden, the school's dean of freshmen, who attended Morehouse at the time. "That's why we loved Ali. He was fighting for his liberation—to be recognized as a Muslim, to be recognized for his stance on the war—and this was a metaphor for what we were going through. So it wasn't a boxer in our gym. It was part of a movement."

Johnson was more optimistic than ever. He was on the verge of pulling off something the established boxing promoters failed to do in the nearly three and a half years since Ali was stripped of his title. He was about to land—with respect to Joe Louis and Max

Schmeling, and their historic June 1938 duel in Yankee Stadium—
the fight of the century. But Durham was not swayed by the exhibition. He told Johnson that Frazier would not fight Ali in Atlanta.
Plans were already in motion for Frazier to take on the light heavyweight champion, Bob Foster. Johnson was angry. "The man gave
his word, and I went to a lot of trouble getting a place for him to
fight," he said.

Kassel and Johnson needed another opponent for Ali, and time
was definitely not on their side. In the late summer of 1970, there
remained a distinct possibility that the Supreme Court would
decide at any moment against hearing Ali's appeal, which meant he
would have to report to the federal penitentiary. "It became abun-
dantly clear that we were sort of pissing against the wind," Kassel
said. "Our attitude was to strike while the iron was hot. We couldn't
sit around negotiating, trying to convince Yank Durham to do
something."

Thanks to Harold Conrad, they found their backup. Conrad,
a tall, skinny, ex-sportswriter, was entrusted with an assortment
of tasks, many invaluable. He was the model for Budd Schulberg's
1947 novel, *The Harder They Fall*, in whose film version a down-
and-out Humphrey Bogart promotes a series of fixed fights involving a trumped-up boxer from Argentina.

"Conrad was a throwback right out of Damon Runyon," Schulberg recalled. "He was running around the boxing world and the
mob world. He had no illusions about anything." In February 1964,
it was Conrad who suggested that Ali, during his last week of training in Miami Beach for the first Liston bout, visit with four young
men from Liverpool. Ali and the Beatles posed for a group of price-
less photos. During the exile, Conrad crisscrossed the country in
hopes of landing a license for Ali. He was especially useful to Kassel, who, prior to Atlanta, had worked on the promotion of only
one bout, Ellis versus Frazier. Also on the payroll was Mike Malitz, a
closed-circuit expert, whose father, Lester, was a pioneer in the technology that changed boxing forever. "I wasn't one of the gang," Kassel
said. "To be one of the gang, you had to be around for ten years."

The backup was Jerry Quarry. Although he was not particularly consistent (losses to Eddie Machen and George Chuvalo stood out) or clever (he attempted to out-box Ellis and out-slug Frazier), Quarry was ranked number one by *Ring* magazine, the sport's unofficial bible, and was extremely popular. He was a superb counterpuncher, with victories over former champion Floyd Patterson and the highly regarded Thad Spencer. There was an added benefit to bringing Quarry into the equation: Quarry was white. While Ali was adored by many white fans, and the sport and society had come a long way since the search for a white fighter to dethrone the despised heavyweight champion Jack Johnson in the early twentieth century, introducing the element of racial conflict could not help but generate broader interest. There were also many fans who abhorred Ali, including those who would like nothing better than to see a black draft dodger knocked on his ass by a white man defending the United States of America.

On September 10, 1970, Muhammad Ali and Jerry Quarry met at the Hotel Berkshire at Madison Avenue and Fifty-second Street in midtown Manhattan to sign the contracts for their scheduled 15-rounder at Municipal Auditorium. Ali was guaranteed $200,000 against 42½ percent of the net income, and Quarry $150,000 against 22½ percent—the largest purses either fighter had ever secured for one night's work. Established immediately as a 3–1 favorite, Ali wasted no time in selling the fight. Shortly before the press conference began, he approached his opponent.

"I want you to say that you're going to beat me up," he told Quarry, according to Quarry's wife, Kathleen. "You just lay into me and I'll lay into you. People come to my fights for two reasons, either they love me or they hate me. Either way, I make money."

When Quarry took the podium, he was no Ali, but he played the part as well as he could. "I've always wanted to fight him," Quarry said. "He's quick but he's not a big puncher, and I can punch with either hand. I can take a lot out of him. I don't know if he'll be as good as he was. That remains to be seen. But he better be."

Afterward, Ali bumped into Quarry and his wife in front of the hotel. They shook hands and laughed.

"You did good," Ali told him. "You did good."

For Leroy Reginald Johnson, Muhammad Ali versus Jerry Quarry was not exactly the duel he anticipated when he took on the cause. Ali versus Quarry was not the fight of the century. Nonetheless, at long last, Muhammad Ali was scheduled to appear in an official heavyweight bout for the first time since March 22, 1967.

Leroy Johnson was beating the system. Again.

2

"Back in My Old Life Again"

Leroy Johnson did not feel secure. It did not matter that the permit for Ali was approved, the contract signed, the money earmarked, and the auditorium booked. Johnson knew better. He knew he would not feel secure until around 10:40 p.m. on the evening of October 26, until he heard the bell, until the only person on the planet with the power to stop Muhammad Ali was coming from the opposite corner. Six weeks were left before fight night, and anything could happen in six weeks. Too many people hated Ali and what he represented. Lo and behold, in late September, Governor Maddox asked State Attorney General Arthur K. Bolton there was any legal action the state could take to halt the event. Whether this was the governor's true intent or he was again appealing to his constituency is unclear. Either way, the attempt was not successful. Bolton, in a letter to Maddox, indicated there was no state law "which disqualifies a person from participating in a sporting event because of a pending criminal conviction or a final criminal conviction." Johnson was relieved but felt certain other challenges would emerge in the month ahead.

Ali began to train in earnest at the Fifth Street Gym. He needed the work. The problem was not only the rust. The problem was the body. The body he inhabited was not the same one that had made him seem invincible in the mid-1960s against Sonny Liston, Floyd Patterson, Ernie Terrell, Cleveland Williams, Zora Folley—against any mortal daring to challenge his crown. Long gone was the heavyweight with the look of a middleweight. In his place was a man approaching thirty, never to seem invincible again. "You looked at him before," Ferdie Pacheco said, "and you did not see any fat. I kept telling Angelo, 'Hey, this is a different guy. This guy is bigger now and his legs are weaker.' His answer was, 'Oh, he'll get right back in shape.'"

Ferdie Pacheco was there in the beginning, in the fall of 1960, when a brash youngster from Louisville, Kentucky, fresh from capturing the gold in Rome, walked into his life. His life would never be quite the same again. In those days, Pacheco was operating clinics in the black ghetto of Overton and the Cuban district. He treated pimps, hookers, and drug dealers. On Thursday afternoons and weekends, he hung out at the Fifth Street Gym.

"I needed some relief from the agony of that misery of the ghetto all the time," Pacheco said. "Boxing was that relief."

At first he went to soak in the atmosphere, but it was not long before his skills were put to use. "In the corner with me was Angelo all the time and he was nothing then, just a guy in the corner," Pacheco said. "We kept talking. Finally, one of the fighters got hurt. He was a black guy and they had nowhere to take him; he had a huge cut. So I said I would take care of him at my office and sew him up. Angelo says, 'You know, we don't have anybody to take care of black fighters.' I started to do that, and the Cubans, as well. I was young. I had a wonderful time."

One afternoon, Pacheco was told by Mable Norwood, his nurse, that there was "some huge guy" in the waiting room. The huge guy was Cassius Clay, sent over by Angelo's brother, Chris, who ran the gym, to receive a shot. Clay, eighteen, was not fond of needles. He went around the room, his pants down to his knees. The nurse, holding a syringe, finally pinned him down. "That chile is either gonna be locked up in the crazy house or he is gonna be the heavyweight champion of the world," she said. Both, Pacheco told her.

In early 1961, former champ Ingemar Johansson, training at the Fifth Street Gym for a third duel with Patterson (they split the earlier encounters), needed a sparring partner one day. What happened next became part of the Ali lore, a glimpse of the remarkable journey ahead for this rarest of athletes and for those lucky enough to go along for the ride.

"They were going to send Willie Pastrano over," Pacheco said, "but Pastrano [a future light heavyweight titleholder] did not want to get hit by Johansson. So we sent the kid." After only two rounds, "Johansson said, 'Get him the fuck away from here, and never, ever put him back in here again. I can't touch him. Nobody is going to touch the guy! I'm just looking like a fool here.' We all knew we had something."

Maybe so, but that had not always been the case. When the Louisville Sponsoring Group, the eleven white businessmen who financed Ali's entry into professional boxing, offered Angelo Dundee a choice between $125 per week and 10 percent of the earnings to become his trainer, Chris Dundee, according to Pacheco, advised his brother to go for the sure thing.

Pacheco said Chris told Angelo, "Take the fucking money and run. This kid is not going to be around here long." Pacheco could not believe it.

"Chris, you know boxing," he said. "This guy is really good. Did you see the Olympics? Did you see how big he is? He's going to grow. Wait till he finishes growing. And did you see how fast he is? You're going to take $125 a week?" Chris Dundee held his ground. His brother took the guaranteed money, though after Ali won the rematch against Sonny Liston on May 25, 1965, Angelo Dundee was able to rework the deal, receiving a percentage of his fighter's future purses. "You never look back," Dundee said in 2006. "Then you're a loser."

Angelo Dundee came aboard officially in December 1960, guiding Ali a week later, in his second professional fight, to a fourth-round knockout over Herb Siler. Dundee's real name was Angelo Mirena Jr., and he was from South Philadelphia, the sixth of seven children born to Italian immigrants. His older brother,

Joe, adopted the name of Dundee because, Angelo said, "he didn't want the old man to know that he was fighting." Angelo fought as well, when he was in the air corps in Louisiana during World War II. After the war he moved to New York City, where Chris, a manager, occupied an office in the Capital Hotel on Eighth Avenue. Angelo spent just about every day at Stillman's Gym on Fifty-fourth Street, close to the old Garden, absorbing every ounce of knowledge he could about the sweet and brutal science from top trainers such as Ray Arcel and Charley Goldman, who worked with Marciano. Once he learned his craft, he was in the corner with one elite fighter after another: Carmen Basilio, Ralph Dupas, Luis Rodriguez, Sugar Ramos, and Pastrano.

Dundee met Ali in 1957, when he brought Pastrano to Louisville to fight John Holman. Ali, the local Golden Gloves champion, boldly tracked down Dundee at his hotel room. "He gave me a long list of championships he was planning to win," Dundee recalled, "including the Olympics, and then the heavyweight championship of the world, and then he said he wanted to come up to the room to meet us." Dundee agreed. Two years later, he let him spar a round with Pastrano. Dundee knew exactly how to handle Ali.

"Later on in his career, he said, 'Angelo never trained me.' People took offense. I didn't take any offense," Dundee said. "I didn't make him feel like I trained him, that I was the governing body behind this big, beautiful fighter. I just got the end result. I didn't give a darn about getting accolades or anything else. What the kid did spoke for me."

Pacheco, however, believes Dundee was not afforded the respect he deserved. "In the middle of the career, when the Muslims were really in charge, Ali treated him shabbily," Pacheco insisted. "I'd see Angelo at the Fifth Street Gym, and say, 'How can you take this shit from the guy?' And he would say, 'Well, it's Ali.' I'd say, 'Fuck him.'" Especially galling to Pacheco was that, in his opinion—and he was hardly alone—Ali would not have won the title without Dundee. During the first Liston bout, a solution that some thought had been used on a cut Liston sustained got into Ali's eyes near the end of the fourth round, blurring his vision. Ali was ready to give up, but Dundee cleaned out his eyes and sent him back out. When Liston failed to get off his stool for the seventh round, Ali became the new heavyweight champion of the world. (There are different theories about the solution, including the suggestion that it had been put intentionally on Liston's gloves.)

"Had he not gotten that stuff out of his eye, he would have quit," Pacheco said. "I mean, he wasn't asking us. He was *telling* us to cut off his gloves. It would have taken him forever to find his way back up to the top. Angelo saved his ass." Pacheco admired how fiercely Dundee believed in the men he trained. "He never thought his fighter could lose," Pacheco said. "It's not good to say [in the corner during a fight], 'By the way, they're going to kill your ass.'"

In dealing with Ali, a uniquely intelligent fighter, there was a limit to the effectiveness of Dundee's cheerleading. If Ali, for instance, believed that Dundee was being overly optimistic, Pacheco went on, he "would say to him, 'Shut up, Angelo, this guy is killing me.' Angelo might say, 'That was an even round,' and Ali would say, 'That was not an even round,' and he was right almost all the time. He fought as hard as he could, and then would come back and listen to us. If we were wrong, he would tell us, 'Shut up.' If we were right, he would get ready to go again. He was very honest, realistic, and that's what made him great."

The punch thrown by Al "Blue" Lewis, one of Ali's sparring partners, in Miami Beach, nailed him in the ribs. Ali fell to the floor. Some of the fans, who included singer Petula Clark (best known for the song "Downtown"), cracked up. They figured he was clowning around. Only this time, he was really hurt. The pain, he described in his autobiography, was "like a terrible toothache shooting through bones, up the spine, up the back of my head." In the dressing room, Pacheco recommended that Ali go for X-rays. Ali decided to hold off, but when the pain did not subside, he saw a radiologist Pacheco knew could be trusted to remain quiet. The last thing Ali could afford was for the news of the punch and its possible damage to make the papers. He hung out in the waiting room while the results were being processed. If, as he feared, the ribs were broken, the Quarry fight would be postponed. He sat there "trying to overcome the feeling," he later wrote, "that I am doomed never to fight again, and that each time I come near a fight something will stop it." The X-rays revealed only a bruise. The fight would go on.

In mid-October, leaving his wife, Belinda, and their children in Philadelphia, Ali flew to Georgia for the last two weeks of training. Typically, the Ali entourage set up its base at a luxurious downtown hotel that could cater to its needs, which were many and constant. Not this time. Leroy Johnson felt that staying downtown, close to where the white folks lived, would send the wrong message to the blacks who supported Ali during his long battle with Uncle Sam. They would think that Ali was siding with *them*. Johnson owned a 60-acre cottage on Austin Road about 15 miles from downtown. Five minutes from the nearest paved road and surrounded by trees and a pond, the cottage was quite isolated. One visit and Ali was sold. Johnson enlisted his sister, Lillian, to serve as Ali's cook. She made steaks, his favorite meal. There was another advantage to Ali's being sheltered in the sticks. Although he was unlikely to stir up trouble—he understood perhaps more than anyone how closely he would be scrutinized in the days ahead—the further away he was from potential problems, the better for everyone concerned.

"Once we get in the ring," Johnson told Ali, "we got it made. The White Citizens' Council and the Ku Klux Klan are looking for an opportunity to invoke some kind of activity to stop the fight, and right now we have everything going for us." Ali seemed surprisingly comfortable during his two weeks in the Deep South. "Shoot, I been out there running on them red clay roads at five, six o'clock in the morning and people come by, they spit tobacco and say, 'How you doin' boy? How's it goin, champ?' I say it's just fine, sir," Ali said. "Man, it's beautiful in Georgia. These newspapers down here, they don't try to embarrass you. Up North, they say, 'What's your religion? What meeting you go to last week?'"

Nonetheless, the police received death threats against Ali. Assigned to protect him was J.D. Hudson, the first African American detective lieutenant on the Atlanta Police Department's vice squad, a member of the force since 1949. Every morning, Hudson mapped out the precise route for Ali to do his roadwork. Nobody else was aware of the route in advance, not even Ali. After answering his daily wake-up call from his wife at 4 a.m., Ali jogged in the darkness, Hudson trailing in a car. A welterweight who appeared in six amateur fights before serving in World War II, Hudson did not care one iota about ingratiating himself with the famous Ali or any of his associates. The fact of the matter was that he became quite annoyed with the whole crew, which apparently figured that they could boss him around. Nobody bossed J.D. Hudson around.

"They were a pain in the ass," he recalled. "I had to constantly remind them, 'I don't work for you. My only job is to keep this man alive. If you don't like what I do, you can go to hell!' I had to cuss out [Rahaman, Ali's younger brother] a couple of times. You would have thought that he was the champ, the way he was telling me what to do and what not to do." Ali intervened several times on behalf of Hudson, whom he referred to as "the police." "You all leave the police alone," Ali told the others. Hudson offered no apologies about the way he approached his job. "Everything good you've heard about a cop," Hudson said, "that was me. Everything bad you've heard about a cop, that was me." Ali, Hudson claims, was never in any danger during his stay in Atlanta, although two incidents, neither of which was made public, exemplified the times.

One incident took place on Larchmont Drive in the cozy neighborhood of Collier Heights. Leroy Johnson and his wife, Cleopatra, were about to go to sleep. Their son, Michael, twenty, was in his room down the hall, when everyone heard a noise. "My neighbors went into their bathroom and closed their door," Cleopatra said. "That's how loud the noise was. They didn't know what was going on." The noise came from gunshots fired at the couple's bedroom window upstairs and the den downstairs. "We always thought somebody would be trying to harm Ali," Leroy Johnson said, "but when they shot in our home, we realized that Ali was not just the target. I had never thought about the personal danger." From then on, Cleopatra, a supervisor in the city's public school system, was given police protection. One afternoon she returned home to discover that the family's houseguests had permitted workers, whom they believed to be repairmen, to tinker with the telephones. Cleopatra became convinced the phones were bugged. Also raising suspicions was an unfamiliar car parked down the street for several days.

The other incident took place at the cottage on Austin Road. Ali was inside when, according to Reggie Barrett, the promoter from the aborted Charleston exhibition, passengers in a gray Plymouth fired a volley of shots that landed in the pond, shouting, "Let's get them niggers, let's get them niggers!" before speeding away. Ali was adamant, he indicated in his autobiography, that he did not want Barrett to say a word about the shooting, fearing that the news would "draw more nuts and Maddox will say my presence is a nuisance. You'll wake all the sleeping dogs that want to get at our throats. They got nothing to rally around now." Not even threats against his wife and children in Philadelphia deterred Ali from going ahead with the Quarry fight.

"It's in God's hands," Ali said after he was notified, according to Gene Kilroy, a member of the entourage. "If someone is going to get you, they're going to get you. We called some friends, and they watched over the house." Pacheco was not overly worried after the shooting at the cottage. "They were bullshit shots," he said. At the same time, he admitted, "I wouldn't go walking in the woods alone. I wasn't *that* crazy."

There were others out to get Ali. They did not want to scare him; they wanted to seduce him. One evening, Hudson said, "four or five of the most beautiful women in the world" tried to sneak onto the grounds of Johnson's cottage by rowing across the lake. Hudson forced the women, who were black and of college age, to turn around, and he believes that during the two weeks he watched over Ali he kept members of the opposite sex away. Whether Hudson truly succeeded remains uncertain. "We were never without women . . . *never*," Pacheco maintained. "What is so surprising about that? You have got the world's greatest sex symbol, and he's as kind as can be. Jack Johnson did the same thing. Joe Louis did the same thing."

Ali, though, according to Pacheco, only fooled around with black women. Once, Pacheco said, when a popular white actress from the 1950s and 1960s slipped the key to her hotel room into Ali's hand, Ali let it drop to the ground and walked away. "I'm sorry, I don't see white women," he told her.

The conventional wisdom forever in boxing has been that too much sex can jeopardize a fighter's condition. That did not apply to Ali, his former doctor said. "He was one of these guys who could fuck and fight," Pacheco said. "It's not the physical act that hurts you anyway. It's the woman who brings jealousy, envy, manipulation. That is where someone gets hurt."

In New York, Robert Kassel, assisted by Mike Malitz and Harold Conrad, worked on the arrangements for the big night. The first choice to do the blow-by-blow for the closed-circuit telecast was, naturally, Howard Cosell, Ali's partner in the comedy act (Cosell was the straight man, of course) that would forever link the two, the top entertainers in their fields. Cosell, a lawyer by training, strongly defended Ali during the exile, arguing that he was denied due process. However, Cosell, Kassel claims, asked for a "ridiculous amount of money" and would not compromise. "You'll pay that, kid, or you won't have anybody," Cosell said, according to Kassel. "He sort of suggested that Ali would push for him," added Kassel, who promptly secured Tom Harmon, the 1940 Heisman Trophy winner, as lead announcer, and the comedian Bill Cosby as the commentator. In his 1973 autobiography, Cosell wrote about the Ali-Quarry bout but did not address the issue of why he didn't do the telecast. During the bout, Harmon referred to Ali as Clay, which Cosell, obviously, would never have done.

Interest in Ali's comeback spanned the globe, with Malitz making arrangements for the fight to be shown in France, Australia, Mexico, Japan, England, Germany, Canada, South America, and, for the first time, the Soviet Union. In Scranton, Pennsylvania, however, the screening was canceled after State Commander E. Thomas

Cammarota of the American Legion objected to the fight being aired in auditoriums "owned by organizations that normally display, in both act and deed, a high sense of patriotism and civic responsibility."

These were exciting times for Kassel, an unknown corporate attorney. In October, he claims, Herbert Muhammad, Ali's manager and the son of Elijah Muhammad, told him that in return for promoting the Ali-Quarry bout, he and his New York group would be given the first crack at the next one. Kassell knew what that meant. The next one would probably be the big one, *the* fight, Ali versus Frazier, the payday to end all paydays. These were also, however, anxious times for Kassel. "I was constantly being asked for money for his entourage," he said. "Somebody would come to my office and say, 'I'm the secretary of the world of Islam,' or whatever the title was and say, 'I need $20,000.' I'd call up Ali's camp and say, 'Do I give this guy the money?' They'd say, 'Yeah, give him the money.' That made me uncomfortable. We had a budget for the fight and this was not some small amount of money." Kassel estimates he handed out close to $100,000 in the final weeks before the fight.

Kassel received one call that was particularly disturbing. "How does a nice Emory boy arrange this fight and let this nigger come down here?" the caller said. "Your family better be careful." The threat was considered serious enough by the authorities that Kassell sent his wife and two young kids to his father-in-law's home in suburban Atlanta. For the night of the fight, the FBI advised Kassel to wear a bulletproof vest. He didn't. "I tried to put it on," he explained, "but I couldn't get my tuxedo on right. It wouldn't fit. I was not seriously worried. I was a jerk. I should have been."

Ali and Kassel were not the only ones who were threatened; so was Jerry Quarry, according to his family. During the fight his family was seated within several rows of the exit, "to get us out the door just in case anything happened," Quarry's mother, Arwanda, claims. The Quarrys did not rely on the authorities to keep them safe. Returning to the hotel after the fight was over, Kathleen Quarry was startled when her brother-in-law, Jimmy, removed a gun from his trench coat. Kathleen said she did not know of the threats. Otherwise, she would not have brought their three-year-old son, Jerry Lyn, to the auditorium.

No doubt the prospect of a white versus black prizefight in a country with deep social and racial divisions helped promote the Ali-Quarry duel in some quarters, but the prefight buildup coming out of Atlanta did not revolve around this issue. "The excitement was about Ali's return," the *Times*'s Lipsyte said. "It was not about trying to flog, as Madison Square Garden did so many times, the equivalent of neighborhood brawls between different ethnic minorities." Yet Ali clearly did his part to exploit the racial element, making comparisons between himself and Jack Johnson and their struggles against the white power structure. Johnson, the world champion from 1908 to 1915, was vilified for his romances with white women, including two prostitutes. In 1913, he was convicted of violating the Mann Act, which outlawed the transportation of women across state lines "for the purpose of prostitution, debauchery, or for any other immoral purpose." He left the United States but surrendered when he returned in 1920, and spent a year in prison.

"It's about *me*," Ali reportedly said after seeing *The Great White Hope*, the Broadway play chronicling Johnson's life. "Moves were made to strip him of the title, like what happened to me. He had a jail term comin' up, as I have. And at ringside fellows would yell, as they did at my fights: 'Knock that nigger out.'" Coincidentally, the movie version, starring James Earl Jones and Jane Alexander, opened only a few weeks before the Ali-Quarry fight. Jones, in fact, was one of several dozen celebrities who allowed their names to be included in a November 1969 article in *Esquire* calling for Ali's right to defend his title. Other high-profile figures in the piece included Truman Capote, Elizabeth Taylor, Ali McGraw, Sammy Davis Jr., Jackie Robinson, and Elia Kazan.

At the same time, Quarry was not always innocent of injecting race into the fight game. In late January 1970, he said, "Boxing needs a white champion to replace Cassius Clay," but, to his credit, in the final weeks before the Ali fight, he did not make it an issue. Those who knew him well insisted that Quarry thought of himself as a fighter, not a white fighter. In 1965, during a trip back from Kansas City, when his black sparring partners were denied service at a restaurant, Kathleen Quarry remembered that Jerry told the waitress, "If they aren't welcome, we're not welcome," and took off.

How Ali would fare against his opponent was not the overriding issue either. Very few boxing experts believed that Quarry, a 17-to-5 underdog, could possibly pull off an upset against one of the sport's all-time greats, even if Ali was appearing in his first official bout in forty-three months. The overriding issue was how the twenty-eight-year-old Ali, facing a younger foe for the first time (Jerry was twenty-five) would fare against the old Ali and against the high standard he set between 1964 and 1967, between Liston and Folley, the artistry he and his followers expected every time he answered the bell. History was not in Ali's corner. One superb champion after another—John L. Sulllivan, James Corbett, Jim Jeffries, Joe Louis—could not win the title back after a long layoff, perhaps tarnishing the image each fought so gloriously to attain. Would Ali suffer a similar fate?

"He was, don't forget, a human being," said the former light heavyweight champion Jose Torres. "Ali had to be conscious that time takes stuff out of you. The mind is telling you what to do but you cannot do it like you did it before." Except that Ali could not be compared to the other ex-champions. They were in their thirties when they came back, their best far behind them. "I should reach my peak at about 30," Ali predicted. "And with my speed afoot, I might be 35 before I start to slow down."

Ali's daily workouts, held at the decrepit Sports Arena, a barn used primarily for square dancing and wrestling, offered few hints of what might transpire on October 26. Ali was, as Dundee put it, "the worst gymnasium fighter in the world. The other guys worked to fight in the gym. He just worked. He would toy and play. I couldn't break him out of that. 'I know what I'm doing,' he would say. 'I know what I'm doing.' He would get in shape. He never tried to win a decision in the gym." Dundee realized, from the Ellis-Quarry fight in 1968, that the most prudent strategy for his man was to maintain a safe distance from the ropes, to keep Jerry, the excellent counterpuncher, in the center of the ring, to entice him to be the one to lead. Dundee gave him all the pointers he could, but even he was uncertain about what would take place once Ali squared off for the first time in three and a half years against some-body aiming to beat his brains out. "I don't know how he'll react if he gets hit with a chopper," Dundee said. "He hasn't gotten wet since Folley." During the weigh-in, Ali tipped the scales at 213½, only two pounds more than he weighed for the Folley fight.

The plan for Quarry, put together by his trainer, Teddy Ben-tham, was to crowd Ali, to pound him in the body, to limit the dancing as much as possible. Quarry trained hard, sparring with his brother Mike, a promising light heavyweight, and Eddie Jones, another light heavy, for about 130 rounds. Both were quick, serv-ing as the ideal preparation for Ali. Quarry also did about 140 miles of road work. Because of the layoff, the longer the 15-round fight went on, presumably the better Quarry's chances.

Irish Jerry Quarry first stepped into the ring around the age of five. All the Quarry boys got started early. That was the way their father, Jack, wanted it to be, and he was the boss. Jack, who grew up in Oklahoma, did not live a charmed life—that much was obvi-ous. In the mid-1930s, when he was only fourteen, he ran away from home, hopping from train to train, town to town, until he ended up where many ended up, in America's land of opportu-nity, California. The future would always be uncertain for folks like Jack Quarry. Years later, each of his knuckles had a letter in indelible blue ink, which, when the hands were extended, read HARD LUCK. In 1942, he was introduced to Arwanda Tolbert, who became his wife. Of their eight children, Jerry was the second oldest, born May 15, 1945. Jack raised Jerry to be tough, which was the way he himself had survived, but at the age of thirteen, Jerry contracted nephritis, an acute inflammation of the kidneys. Doctors told the Quarrys their boy needed to stay in bed for a whole year and would probably be a semi-invalid for the rest of his life. Under his mother's care, however, and with medication, Jerry recovered.

Tutored by the veteran trainer Johnny Flores, who owned a gym in Pacoima, north of Los Angeles, Jerry developed into a ferocious puncher. He and his older brother, Jimmy, sparred against each other all the time. Fighting, it turned out, was not for Jimmy, who quit at twenty. Fighting was for Jerry. As an amateur, he won well over a hundred fights.

When Jerry was in high school, he met Kathleen Casey at the Tastee Freeze in Bellflower. Jerry was working the hamburger counter, Kathleen the ice cream counter. Jerry made a bet with the other guys that he would take her out and "get somewhere" on the first date. She made it a policy not to date anyone she worked with, but when word of Jerry's bet got back to her, Kathleen figured she would teach this boy a lesson he would never forget. He was not going to get anywhere, not with her, anyway. By the end of the night, she was kidding herself and she knew it. Kathleen was crazy about Jerry. They spent the night necking, and, while stuck for a few minutes on a Ferris wheel at the local amusement park, he professed his love for the first time. "You can't love me," she told him. "You don't know me." It was not long before he popped the question. Her answer was an unequivocal no. Kathleen told Jerry he would have to wait a full year and if he was still interested, maybe then her answer would be different.

Month after month went by. Then one day Kathleen was in the kitchen with her mother, peeling potatoes, when Jerry stopped by, put Kathleen in his car, and, without revealing his intentions, drove to the nearest stationery store. He pointed to the calendar. Exactly one year had passed since he proposed on the Ferris wheel. Jerry and Kathleen were married in June 1964.

Jerry's breakthrough came at the National Golden Gloves in Kansas City, one of the sport's most prestigious events for amateur fighters. Despite suffering from the flu, Jerry accomplished something none of them ever did and no heavyweight has done since. He knocked out five consecutive opponents, two in the same night, the bouts lasting a *total* of eighteen minutes and two seconds. "The first night, we went back to our little room, with the two twin beds we pushed together," Kathleen said. "I could see how energized he was, how it overtook him. He was walking on air. When he went into the ring the second night, I don't think his feet were even touching the floor. Because it was even more than he thought he could do."

Two months later, on May 7, 1965, Jerry, about to turn twenty, made his professional debut in Los Angeles, prevailing in a four-round decision over Gene Hamilton. Fighting the majority of the time at Olympic Auditorium in downtown L.A. and comanaged by his father and Flores, Jerry began to move up the ranks of heavyweights. "I was put on this earth to do something," said Jerry, who quit his job at Greyhound, "and I know it wasn't to change 300-pound bus tires." By the summer of 1966 his record was an outstanding 17-0-3, the draws coming against Tony Doyle and Tony Alongi. Even Marciano was interested in purchasing a piece of him––until, it seems, July 14, when Jerry faced Eddie Machen. Machen, thirty-three, who went the distance against past champions Liston and Patterson, was supposed to be washed up. He wasn't. Machen earned a unanimous 10-round decision. Jerry was the one who looked washed up. He could not lift his arms in the final rounds. "Are boxing fans finally getting the idea about Jerry Quarry?" a *Los Angeles Times* columnist wrote. "Eddie Machen merely exposed officially what several have felt all along. Young Jerry has a handsome left hook, but he can't fight much and never could."

For a few weeks Jerry thought about quitting, but plenty of prizefighters think about quitting when they lose, and then once their wounds, both mental and physical, begin to heal, they think about their next fight and their next check, and any thought of quitting goes away—until the next loss. Besides, as Jack Quarry preached to his kids, "There's no quit in a Quarry." Nonetheless, doubts about this Quarry's level of commitment lingered. "Training camp was a holiday for him," Kathleen suggested. "He had all this attention from people who offered him dinners just so they could be around the fight game." Among those seeking his attention were members of the opposite sex. According to Kathleen, a young woman walked up to Jerry once and said, in her presence, "If you ever get sick of sleeping with *her*, you can put your shoes under my bed any day."

Claude Sutherland, a friend and sparring partner in the early days, was with Jerry on the night that Joe Frazier, staying at the same hotel in Los Angeles, stopped by his room; both were getting ready for upcoming fights. "Someday, if we keep it going like we are, we can make a lot of money together," Frazier told Jerry, according to Sutherland, who detected a sharp contrast between the two men. "You could see the passion in Joe that you couldn't see in Jerry," he said.

In the fall of 1966, Jerry rebounded with victories over Bill Neilsen and Leslie Borden. Next up, on December 15, was Joey Orbillo, another California native. After spending nearly a year at army training camps, there was more on Orbillo's mind than Jerry Quarry. Orbillo was days away from a much tougher fight, for his life, in Southeast Asia. Aided by a knockdown in the fourth round, Jerry won the decision, although the beating Orbillo received might have been the best thing that ever happened to him. Due to a perforated eardrum he suffered in the bout, he was shipped back to the States after only a few weeks in Vietnam. Orbillo had taken part in search-and-seizure missions for the 199th Light Infantry. His job was looking out for booby traps. The solider who replaced him did not make it. "Don't think that doesn't cross my mind at least twice a week, even now," Orbillo said in 2006.

On October 28, 1967, Jerry faced Floyd Patterson for the second time. Four months earlier, they battled to a draw in Los Angeles. Jerry knocked Patterson down twice in the second round but failed to put him away. In their rematch, also in L.A., much more was at stake for the combatants. The bout was one of the quarterfinal matches in the World Boxing Association's eight-man elimination tournament to determine a successor to the deposed Ali. "This was an important sport, and nobody wanted to see it just lay fallow while everyone worried about what was going to happen to Ali," said Fred Hofheinz, the executive vice-president of Sports Action, which promoted the event. "Everybody had to make a living."

Plus with Ali dominating the division since ousting Liston in 1964, the tournament was an opportunity for the WBA, a loose body representing several dozen states, to drum up more competitiveness.

With the top-rated Joe Frazier declining to participate, just about any of the contenders—Quarry, Patterson, the former WBA title-holder Ernie Terrell, Jimmy Ellis, Leotis Martin, Oscar Bonavena, Thad Spencer, and Karl Mildenberger—had a legitimate shot to become the new world heavyweight champion. The money was good, too. Each quarterfinalist collected $50,000, the semifinalists $75,000, and the finalists $125,000. Whoever prevailed would pick up a cool quarter million.

Against Patterson, Jerry escaped with a split 12-round decision. Next, on February 3, 1968, he stopped the favored Spencer in the twelfth round. At twenty-two, Jerry was only one victory away from the title. His opponent in the final would be Ellis, Ali's former sparring partner, trained by Angelo Dundee. From May 1965 through December 1967, Ellis won ten fights in a row. In the tournament, he disposed of Martin in the ninth round and secured a 12-round decision over Bonavena. The match with Jerry was set for April 27, 1968, in Oakland, California. Jerry was not at his best, according to his mother, when he arrived in Oakland because of a fight he got into weeks earlier with his brother Jimmy on the floor of the Neutral Corner, a bar Jerry co-owned in the Los Angeles suburb of Norwalk. Jerry severely injured his back. Years earlier, at the same bar, he found himself in an altercation in the parking lot with a customer trying to steal two pool cues. The customer hit Jerry over the head with one of the cues. Jerry promptly knocked him out cold.

Despite his back problems, Jerry went to training camp, although he was not the same Jerry Quarry. X-rays taken afterward revealed that Jerry went through the whole fight with a broken back. "He couldn't commit," said Orbillo, who was now one of his sparring partners. "The punches weren't as hard. He was more defensive because of not wanting to get hit." Orbillo said he was offered free ringside tickets to the bout but decided to stay away because he was afraid of what might happen to his friend.

Ignoring the game plan laid out by Teddy Bentham, Jerry tried to outbox Ellis, one of the slickest boxers in the business. "Jerry always fought the fight he wanted to fight," Kathleen said. "He listened to his corner men. He listened to his trainer. He listened to his manager. But when he got in the ring, it was that man against him." The decision went to Ellis, who stuck to the game plan laid out by Dundee. Ellis stayed in the center of the ring and did not allow Jerry to do what he did best: counterpunch.

"Angelo said, 'We're gonna stink out the joint and win a title,' and that's what we did," said Ferdie Pacheco, who was in the Ellis corner.

Jerry won his next five fights, including a unanimous decision over Buster Mathis at the Garden. Then, on June 23, 1969, he encountered his toughest opponent yet, Joe Frazier. Frazier was right about what he told Jerry at the hotel in Los Angeles. The two made a lot of money and were in position to make a lot more. Jerry was only twenty-four, Frazier twenty-five. Yet it was Frazier who separated himself from the pack, becoming the champion in several states. Of course, one fight could change everything.

"Finally the time has come," Jerry admitted, "when I find just what I'm all about."

Despite Jerry's inconsistency, he did not lack confidence. One night, a few weeks before the fight, also set for the Garden, he went to the Lancer Lounge, a saloon in Downey, outside Los Angeles. Everyone told Jerry he was going to win. What else were they going to tell the local hero? Yet what Johnny Ortiz, who ran the joint, remembers four decades later is not what the patrons said but what Jerry said, and the emphatic way in which he said it. "I can knock this guy out," Jerry insisted, according to Ortiz. "He can't take my left hook." Ortiz claims that Jerry was so certain of victory that he placed a $5,000 bet on himself. "I think I'm going to stop him," Jerry told Ortiz.

Early on, Jerry looked as though he might just cash in. He took the first round from Frazier, a normally slow starter. Yet again, Jerry Quarry fought the wrong fight against the wrong guy and it cost him any chance of an upset. Up to that point, nobody had outslugged Joe Frazier.

In the second round, Frazier cut off the ring and pinned Jerry against the ropes. In the third round, a left hook opened an inch-long slice under Jerry's right eye. The fight was not stopped until after the seventh round, but it was over much sooner. Jerry protested, but his eye was shut, and so was his case to become the new champion. Why did Jerry go on the offensive against the most punishing puncher in the sport? Perhaps because he believed he had something to prove to those who questioned his commitment. "I've had too many complaints in the past about not fighting," Jerry said. "Well, the first man who says I didn't fight tonight, better be ready. I still have plenty left."

That much was true. At times over the next fifteen months, Jerry was impressive, with seven wins, highlighted by a sixth-round knockout of the unbeaten Mac Foster. Other times, he was ordinary. The lowest moment came in his loss to the Canadian George Chuvalo on December 12, 1969. Chuvalo was a brawler, but Jerry was in control of the fight until he hit the deck in the seventh round. He was not seriously hurt and seemed ready to rise at any moment, but, inexplicably, he lost track of the count and was still on one knee when it reached 10. "It was terrible," said Johnny Flores Jr., the son of Jerry's former trainer. "Chuvalo was a fat guy behind a desk, no muscle, no nothing. Everybody beat the hell out of Chuvalo."

In the late summer of 1970, the phone rang.

"When he hung up," Kathleen Quarry said, "he turned around and smiled. Muhammad Ali was Jerry's favorite fighter. He followed him from the beginning."

Lester Maddox was not through yet. Proclaiming Monday, October 26, 1970, a "day of mourning" in the state of Georgia, the governor called for patriotic residents to express their outrage over an individual who would not fight for his country but was being allowed to fight for himself. "I would hope that Clay gets beat in the first round," Maddox said, "and that he's flattened out for a count of 30." When someone informed Ali that Maddox basically considered it a "black day" for the state, he responded, "Oh, yeah, there'll be a lot of my folks here." Mayor Massell issued a proclamation of his own, declaring a "Sports Spectacular Weekend" encompassing the fight, as well as contests involving the Atlanta Falcons of the NFL, the Atlanta Hawks of the NBA, and the Georgia Tech football team.

One spectacular event in Atlanta was already under way. The scene was downtown, at the new Regency Hyatt House, which, designed by John Portman, featured an atrium lobby, glass-enclosed elevators, and, on this most historic weekend, a procession of black stars from sports, entertainment, and politics who came to town to celebrate the return of one of their own, and to celebrate themselves, a proud race no longer willing to be marginalized in American society. The spoils of success, of the American Dream, were open to them as well, to be enjoyed in any way they deemed fit. The message was, as Julian Bond put it in 2006, "Here we are, this is us. This is our man. We're glad to be here."

Blacks from less reputable professions—pimps, whores, hustlers—also joined in the coming-out party. They came, they saw, they spent.

"There were all these black guys in fancy clothes with fancy girls with wads of money," Budd Schulberg said. "The white bartenders were in shock." On several occasions during the weekend before the fight, Ali stopped by the Hyatt, the shepherd greeting his flock. "Everybody would go to him like he was a magnet," said Stan Sanders, a former Rhodes Scholar, who hung out at the hotel. "It would take him the better part of an hour to work his way across the lobby. Ali was the only person who could have drawn together such a wide cross-section of so many prominent people in the community. A Martin Luther King—dead by two years—could have drawn a great crowd, but no hustlers would have shown, and not too many of your All-American athletes would have shown."

Another party took place on the eve of the fight. This party was for the press, which descended on the city in huge numbers for a prizefight, bringing its pens, pads, and, as always, prejudices. The party was held at the Playboy Club in Atlanta. The club was normally closed on Sundays, but thanks to Harold Conrad, who seemed to know everybody, Kassel was put in contact with the premier playboy himself, Hugh Hefner. Hef opened the club when

House of Sports, Inc., the company promoting the fight, agreed to set up a special feed of the closed-circuit telecast at the Playboy Mansion in Chicago. The party was a great success. "Guys were drinking too much, groping at the girls, and standing on the tables," Kassel said, "middle-aged men who had nobody watching them, telling them what they could or could not do."

Not every move by Kassel worked out. Without running the idea by Conrad or Mike Malitz, Kassel arranged for cheerleaders, pom-poms included, and a marching band from a local high school to perform during the weigh-in ceremony on the morning of the fight. The band hit only a few notes before Conrad hit the ceiling. "What the fuck is this?" he barked. "Who let these people in here?" Kassel did not say a word. "I disavowed any knowledge," he admitted. "I didn't protect them."

More pressing issues surfaced in the final days, such as finding a ring. A 19½-foot ring was not large enough to accommodate Angelo Dundee, who asked for one measuring 20 feet.

"I enjoyed big rings," Dundee explained, "because the kid was able to move. Small rings, his calves were hitting the ropes." Because there was not a single ring in the entire city that met Dundee's specifications, one was transported from the Charleston Naval Base. Coincidentally, the ring belonged to Reggie Barrett, the promoter of the canceled exhibition, who had stored it at the base after a recent bout. The irony was inescapable—a ring from the same city that had rejected Ali only three months earlier, and from a branch of the armed forces, aiding a man convicted of draft evasion.

October 26 arrived at last, a day for punches, not proclamations. Other cities blew their opportunities, bowing to the political pressures. But three and a half years after Muhammad Ali refused to step over the line in Houston, so much was different now about the war in Vietnam, and the war at home, about an angry and confused America searching for a way beyond the dissent and destruction to chart a more promising future. Bobby Kennedy and Martin Luther King Jr. were dead, as were four students at a college campus in Ohio. In 1970, Ali was viewed in a much different light than he was in 1967. Even those who did not share his convictions about the Vietnam War, or at least the manner in which he chose to express them, showed a new willingness to forgive and allow him to resume his career.

In the morning, Ali headed to Municipal Auditorium for the weigh-in ceremony. He was on his best behavior. He did not try to antagonize Jerry Quarry or create a scene. Back at the cottage, he received calls from the baseball greats Hank Aaron and Willie Mays, the football star Gale Sayers, the actor Sidney Poitier, and the civil rights activist Whitney Young. He watched a new film on Jack Johnson, which played continuously on a bed sheet converted into a screen. During the afternoon, the Reverend Jesse Jackson arrived. To Jackson, who later rode with Ali to the arena, the fight symbolized a much broader struggle than one between two individuals. An Ali defeat, Jackson contended, "would suggest that the forces of blind patriotism are right, that dissent is wrong, that protest means you don't love the country. . . . He's a hero, and he carries the same mantle that Joe Louis did against Max Schmeling or Jesse Owens when he ran in Hitler's Berlin. . . . For the downtrodden, they need the high example—that their representatives, the symbol of their own difficulties, will win."

Around eight o'clock, Ali left the cottage. He stopped at the Hyatt first, helping to manage accommodations for two busloads of supporters who did not have tickets, the shepherd tending to his flock again. He waited about thirty minutes for the arrival of Coretta Scott King, but when she failed to turn up, he took off for the auditorium. Once inside his dressing room, he put up a fuss about wearing a foul protector, used for hits below the belt, fearing it would make him appear chubby. He finally agreed to put on a protector that belonged to his brother Rahaman, who fought in a preliminary bout, knocking out Hurricane Grant in the third round. (Rahaman Ali, known originally as Rudolph Valentino Clay, was a not a very good fighter. "He was more handsome than Ali," Pacheco said, "and he looked like he knew what to do in the ring because he mimicked Ali so good. He just did not have any reflexes. Just because he looked like Ali did not mean he knew how to fight like Ali, and it was apparent to everybody. Ali would beat the shit out of him every day in the gym. I said to Ali, 'You can't keep giving him those beatings. You're hurting him. What you're trying to *keep* him from doing, you're doing to him.' 'I'm not hurting him,' he'd say, 'he doesn't go out.' I told him, 'You don't have to go out to get brain damage.' ")

Ali taped his shoelaces to the top of his shoes. He looked at himself in the mirrors. When Sidney Poitier came into the room, they embraced. It was almost time.

"It's been so long," Ali said one day at the Fifth Street Gym. "I never thought I'd be back again, here again. Back in my old life again."

A stranger handed Robert Kassel some papers. Kassel was a lawyer. He knew what papers from a stranger meant. It was an injunction from a district court enjoining the fight from going forward. Kassel paused to review his options. He decided to do nothing. A piece of paper was not going to stop the fight, he figured. Let them, whoever they might be, come for him afterward. By then it would be too late. Kassel tore up the papers and tossed them into the garbage. Disposing of his anxieties would not be as convenient. "I thought maybe that federal marshals would come in and stop the fight," said Kassel, who now believes the papers were probably phony. Another last-minute hassle was locating seats for spectators holding tickets in rows A1, A2, and A3. According to Kassel, there were no such rows at Municipal Auditorium. Someone, he claims, printed and sold bogus tickets. "We started to get really concerned because you had people milling about and asking the ushers what the deal was," Kassel said. The ushers found a way to squeeze them in.

The 5,000-seat auditorium began to fill up. The list of celebrities included Diana Ross, Harry Belafonte, the Reverend Ralph Abernathy, Coretta Scott King, Julian Bond, and Sidney Poitier. Even more memorable than the people who came was what they wore. Men showed up in zoot suits, full-length ermine coats, mink hats, and double-breasted jackets; women in see-through body stockings, and beads down to the hem of their maxi-skirts. Ross sported a bouffant hairdo that stretched out ten inches on both sides. Some people took the short ride from the Hyatt in limos painted with psychedelic designs. Excitement was not the only thing in the air. "That was the first time I smelled marijuana in the men's room at a fight," said Dave Anderson, who covered the event for the *New York Times*. "There were more people, who, in Black America, are called 'players' than I had ever seen," Bond recalled. "As I was leaving, I ran into Mary Wilson of the Supremes. *The Supremes?* I didn't see the Supremes." The national anthem was performed by the singer Curtis Mayfield strumming a guitar.

It was 10:40 p.m. It was time. Jerry entered the ring first. He threw a few punches and headed to a neutral corner, rubbing his shoes over resin for better traction. Would this be Jerry Quarry's night? Then came Ali's turn. No moment in this sport, in any sport, can rival the excitement that begins to build during a fighter's march from the dressing room to the field of battle, in the way a gladiator marched into the Coliseum in Rome aiming to slay the beast. The march on this particular night was more dramatic than most, the gladiator rejected by the palace back in front of his adoring masses. Ali's entourage, with assistance from J.D. Hudson and other policemen, formed a cocoon around Ali. Even so, the march was treacherous.

"There was no aisle," Pacheco said. "If a guy wanted to slip a knife into your ribs, he could have done it in a minute. Let me tell you, it was not a good feeling. When we got back to our dressing room, it was, 'Man, we got by with that one,' because I really expected some of us would have been hurt, that Ali would be, at least, stabbed."

Ali entered the ring. He did the Ali shuffle. The fans roared. Ali and Jerry were introduced by the ring announcer, Johnny Addie. The ovation for Jerry was polite. The ovation for Ali was loud. The referee, Tony Perez, who would score the fight with judges Lew Eskin and Billy Graham, issued last-minute instructions while the fighters traded last-minute insults. Perez ordered the two to shut up. Referees realize that if they permit these exchanges to continue, maintaining order once the bout gets under way becomes more difficult. Ali and Jerry retreated to their corners.

The bell rang. Right away, Ali was the more aggressive. He capitalized on his five-and-one-half-inch reach advantage to pepper Jerry with one solid combination after another. Defensively, flashing his familiar quickness, Ali proved too elusive. Angelo Dundee was satisfied. During a talk in Ali's bedroom, Dundee had urged him to "make him know who's the doctor." Ali asked, "If I can knock him out in the first, should I?" "In the first minute," Dundee told him, "with the first punch. The faster, the better."

The message got through, and not only to Muhammad Ali's opponent. From his seat in the third row, Julian Bond, who did not consider himself an especially rabid boxing fan, started to echo Bundini Brown's familiar chant: "Stick him, Ali, stick him." Bond kept striking a woman in the row ahead of him on the back. "She didn't care," he said. "She didn't turn around." The whole week remains one that Bond will never forget. A few nights earlier, he had attended a party at Leroy Johnson's house. Bond and his then wife, who was wearing a lime green pantsuit, got into a conversation with Ali. "You coming to the fight?" Ali asked. Yes, she told him. "Don't wear that dress," Ali said. "I'm going to spill blood all over you."

Late in the round, Jerry landed a hard left hook to the body. The *Newark Star-Ledger*'s Jerry Izenberg was not shocked by Ali's sudden vulnerability. "He was absolutely magnificent in the first round," Izenberg pointed out, "but when he walked back to his corner, he looked like a beached whale. His mouth was open. He could hardly breathe." During the third round, however, an Ali right opened a cut over Jerry's left eye. The experienced Ali moved in to put him away. Jerry lasted until the bell, but when he reached his corner, Bentham took one look and told him he was done for the night. Jerry protested and struggled to break away, but Perez stopped the fight, officially recorded as a third-round TKO for the still-undefeated Ali. (After the fight, Kassel stood in the middle of the ring next to Dundee when he cut the laces off Ali's gloves. "He peeled back the part that's below the hand," Kassel said, "and inside, written in ballpoint pen, it said, 'TKO, third round.' Kassel hoped to acquire the gloves as a souvenir, but Ali gave them to Leroy Johnson.)

For Jerry Quarry, the opportunity for a major upset was gone. Nobody who was in Municipal Auditorium that night has ever disputed the severity of Jerry's cut, which required eleven stitches. "It was so bad, you could see the bone," Perez said. Even Jerry, after he calmed down, conceded that his trainer made the proper decision. "All that went through my mind was to get back in there because I'm a fighter," he said. "Then I felt the blood. It felt like it was gushing." If Jerry went out for the fourth round, it is conceivable he could have lost the sight in his left eye.

Nonetheless, why didn't Perez, as was the customary procedure, consult with a doctor before stopping the fight? Perez claims that none were near ringside. "I had to make a decision myself," Perez said. Interestingly enough, in an interview with Thomas Hauser during the late 1980s, Perez said, "There'd been a big controversy . . . about whether the doctors would be black or white." Only two doctors were used for the prefight examination five days earlier and both were black. "We wanted some assurance that no kind of foul play would go on," Leroy Johnson reasoned.

Jerry made his concerns known right away. "They want equal rights and that crap. I want it, too," he said. "I'm not climbing in there if there isn't a white and black doctor. I could have a slight nick and the doctor could say that's it." In the end, four doctors were assigned, two black, two white. Why none of them examined the cut remains a mystery, though Dr. Jerome Siegal was on his way into the ring when Perez stopped the fight. "In my 50 years in boxing, I've never seen a referee in an important fight such as this take the sole responsibility of stopping a fight without conferring with the ring doctor," said George Parnassus, a Los Angeles promoter. "It was a disgrace." The matter, however, did not attract much attention. "No one complained," said Ed Schuyler, the former boxing writer for the *Associated Press*, "because it wasn't Ali who got cut. If he had gotten cut, I'm sure there would have been a controversy."

No physician was needed to recognize that Ali, the winner of all three rounds on each judge's card, was the superior fighter on this night. Here was the unveiling of a new Ali, able to punch with greater authority than ever. Sadly, the new, more stationary, Ali also became a more vulnerable Ali, leading to its heartbreaking consequences. "What we found out after the layoff was very good news and very bad news, and that was he could take a punch," Pacheco said. "He could take a *mother* punch. That's bad. You take enough of those and they start to wear on you, and that's what happened to him. He took a lot of beatings, but people didn't see that because he kept winning at the end of the beatings."

In later years, Pacheco said, Ali was unwilling to believe his skills had deteriorated. "I used to tell Ali, 'Just because you get in front of a mirror and you look like you used to look, you're not the same fighter. You're not anything close to what you were. You can't even walk to the door the same way." In 1977, after Ali's hard-fought, 15-round decision over Earnie Shavers, Pacheco wrote him a letter to convey his deep concerns about the champion's severely damaged kidneys. Pacheco said Ali never responded. For Pacheco, it was finally time to leave. "I'm not going to watch you get killed," he told Ali. "'Don't call me. I'm not coming back.' And nobody ever tried to call me, *nobody*, not even Angelo. It was, 'Good riddance, there goes that pain in the ass.' I wasn't saying what they wanted me to say." Pacheco believes that, if anything, he waited too long. "Where I regretted not walking out," he said, "was after the third Frazier fight in Manila. He started mumbling. He started shuffling. He started doing all kinds of things."

From Ali's perspective, one negative from the fight in Atlanta was that three rounds after missing more than three and a half years was not nearly enough work. He needed a lot more to develop the stamina for the inevitable showdown with Joe Frazier. If there had been no cut and the bout had gone the distance, it is fair to speculate whether Ali would have been triumphant. Even he knew that the rust showed. "My jab was off target," Ali wrote in his autobiography. "My uppercuts were off. I saw openings I couldn't cash in on."

One aspect of Ali's game that worked as well as ever was his mouth. Afterward, he told reporters that because he finally had his license, Frazier was now merely another contender. In Pennsylvania, where Frazier was training for a November 18 title defense against Bob Foster, Yank Durham was equally dismissive. "As soon as we get rid of Foster," Durham vowed, "we'll stay in camp and destroy Clay." Durham, like Frazier, regularly referred to Ali as Clay. Frazier went to sleep before the fight started but received a full report from Durham. "For me," Frazier later wrote, "it meant that Clay was back on my radar screen . . . for years, Clay had been the wind that whipped the fire in me. . . . I'd wanted to bust his ass and show the world that Frazier, not Clay, was the greatest."

He would have to wait. For the time being, the stage belonged completely to Ali. A newspaper in Spain called him "a giant surrounded by dwarfs." Another, in Lebanon, stated that he remained "the wonder boxer of the 20th Century." The fight even solicited an official response from Tass, the Soviet news agency: "This win is actually a blow to racists and reactionary forces," Tass said, "that had unlawfully deprived him of the title of world champion." After the fight, Ali was presented with the annual Dr. Martin Luther King medal by the Reverend Abernathy, who called him a "living example of soul power, the March on Washington in two fists." Coretta Scott King added that Ali was "a champion of justice and peace."

There would be many more nights for Muhammad Ali. For the Georgia lawmaker and the New York lawyer who had made this one so memorable, there would never be another night quite like this. They pulled it off, two men from vastly different backgrounds, in a region of America nobody would have imagined, against great odds, and without provoking the trouble Lester Maddox predicted. The only incident occurred after the fight, when robbers got away with an estimated $1 million in cash and jewelry at an invitation-only party, the biggest robbery in Atlanta's history, in the northwest section. The partygoers, many of whom had attended the fight, were taken to the basement and forced to disrobe. Among the victims, according to Gene Kilroy, a member of Ali's entourage, was the ex-champion's father, Cassius Clay Sr. Tony Perez was also invited, but when he arrived, he said, "We saw about twenty police cars." The investigation, co-led by J.D. Hudson, first centered on Gordon "Chicken Man" Williams, a local hustler. Williams was later reportedly murdered in a contract killing. The story proved inaccurate. Williams had no part in the robbery and was very much alive. The real perpetrators, according to Hudson, were killed in Atlanta and New York.

After the Ali-Quarry fight was over, Leroy Johnson, who earned $175,000 for his work on putting it together, was standing near ringside when a black woman he did not know approached. "I never wanted to come south," she told him. "I was always concerned about my safety. But it was worth taking the risk to come see Ali fight again."

3

Joe

On May 4, 1967, less than a week after Muhammad Ali refused to step over the line in Houston, Joe Frazier stepped into the ring in Los Angeles. His opponent at the Olympic Auditorium was George "Scrap Iron" Johnson, a short ex-marine from Oklahoma. The fight took on an extra significance nobody would have predicted before Houston. Frazier was no longer simply a promising contender a year or two away from a shot at the title he first dreamed about while growing up in Beaufort, South Carolina, in one of the poorest areas in the nation, and where he heard about the great Joe Louis. With the heavyweight throne vacated, the shot at the title would likely come much sooner as long as Frazier continued to put away lesser fighters, such as Scrap Iron Johnson, who were carefully chosen by Yank Durham to serve that very purpose. Frazier and the deposed Ali were similar in that both were undefeated (Frazier, 15–0, with fourteen knockouts, and Ali 29–0) and gold medalists (Ali, a light heavyweight, at the 1960 Olympic Games in Rome; Frazier, a heavyweight, in Tokyo, four years later).

But Joe Frazier was not Muhammad Ali, and for that crime he would suffer. The comparison was grossly unfair; with the exception of Babe Ruth and Joe Louis, no athlete ever stood so large in his sport, and in his times, as Ali. Nonetheless, it was a comparison that Frazier would be forced to cope with, then and now—the two rivals in three epic battles over four years, enshrined symbols of a cultural war, inseparable forever.

The path from the amateurs to the pros was much rockier for Frazier than for Ali. After Ali returned from Rome, a group of white millionaires from his hometown of Louisville agreed to invest in him. He received a guarantee of $333 a month against his earnings and appeared in his first fight three days later, a sixth-round unanimous decision over Tunney Hunsaker, the police chief from Fayetteville, West Virginia.

After Frazier returned from Tokyo in the fall of 1964, his hand was in a cast—he fractured his left thumb during the semifinals—and his future was in limbo. No white millionaires came forward to invest in him, and no fights were on the horizon. Frazier was not even fit enough to resume his job at the kosher slaughterhouse in Philadelphia, where he practiced combinations against sides of beef long before the world ever heard of Rocky Balboa. Running out of savings, Frazier and his three children—Marvis, four; Jacqueline, three; and Weatta, fourteen months—scraped by on the money that his wife, Florence, earned at the Sears packing plant, and with help from well-wishers. So dire was the family's predicament that it became the subject of a Christmas Eve article in the *Philadelphia Inquirer*; the headline read: "Joe Frazier Faces Cheerless Yuletide—Hurt and Broke." WCAU, a local radio station, appealed to the public for money and toys. A ton of donations poured in, including, Frazier later wrote, $500 from one businessman.

Eight months later, on August 16, 1965, at Convention Hall in Philadelphia, Frazier made his long-delayed pro debut against Elwood Goss. Goss was supposed to fight Johnny Deutch, but when Roy Johnson, Frazier's scheduled opponent, did not show up, Goss took his place and promptly took a beating; the bout halted in one minute and forty-two seconds of the first round. One opponent soon followed another, including Abe Davis from Hartford, Connecticut, who entered the ring wearing sneakers because he had misplaced his regular shoes during the trip and couldn't squeeze into a pair of Sonny Liston's size 13s. No disrespect to the man, but it would not have mattered what shoes Davis put on that night; the "fight" lasted, mercifully, only two minutes and thirty-eight seconds.

Not every opponent was as clearly overmatched. Mike Bruce, from Westfield, Massachusetts, was able to knock Frazier to the canvas in the opening round. Frazier, his pride wounded more than his body, stormed back to finish Bruce in the third. Critics complained that Durham was bringing him along too slowly, but Durham knew his fighter better than the critics did. He knew his fighter needed work, tons of it, and in that respect he was really no different from countless other managers who select their prey with extreme caution, aware that one loss, one lucky punch, and their champ of the future, the ticket to their own fame and fortune, might be tarnished forever.

"The sin in those situations is putting a guy in over his head," suggested HBO boxing analyst Larry Merchant, who was the sports editor of the *Philadelphia Daily News* during the late 1950s and early 1960s. "It's built into the game to get some experience, to build the fighter up so that he is accustomed to dealing with the stuff that goes on. It's a lot like an actor who goes out to do summer stock and there is nothing wrong with the strategy of choosing matches that test but don't overtax their fighters as long as the opponent is trying to win, which is not always the case, because many of these guys know what they're there for. The fighter will tell you when he's ready by what he does."

Durham was not overly impressed the first time he saw Joe Frazier—at least not with his natural ability. Arms short, legs heavy, the 5-foot-11½-inch Frazier was no boxer in the purest sense. What did impress Durham was that Frazier, only eighteen, packed a nasty punch and worked extremely hard, and that he kept coming back to the Police Athletic League gym at Twenty-second and Columbia. Young fighters walked into the PAL gym all the time with grand designs of conquering the boxing world, but once they realized the sacrifices the sport demanded, physically and mentally, they walked out and never returned. Not this kid. He did not merely endure the rigorous training; he embraced it.

Every morning, Frazier jogged for three or four miles at Fairmount Park, put in his time at the slaughterhouse, and then went to the gym for two hours, where he jumped rope, hit the bags, and did sit-ups and push-ups. He became such a regular that he was given a key for the days he stayed late at work.

Frazier did not waste time. He knew he had wasted enough time already. "I felt disgusted about how sloppy I looked," explained Frazier, who weighed 220 pounds in late 1961. "At the same time, I was kicking myself for not acting on that dream of mine to be the next Joe Louis. Two years out on my own and what did I have to show for it? A big butt and no life to speak of. It was time to get serious." The hard work began to pay off. Frazier captured the Middle Atlantic AAU championship in 1963 and 1964. Then came Tokyo.

Joe Frazier arrived at the perfect time for Yank Durham. Beginning in the early 1950s, Durham managed and trained fighters such as Jerry Roberts, Bobby Coffer, and Gene Toran, but none of them became a champion. Fighting about a dozen times as an amateur, Durham, who grew up in Camden, New Jersey, dreamed about becoming a professional himself—until the biggest battle of his life, World War II, pretty much ended his dream as it ended many others. During an air raid in Liverpool, England, he broke both legs, fractured his skull, and busted his ribs. "We were getting ready for the invasion of France," he said. "I was a cook and we were getting the food supply together. This guy and I went out in a jeep to get a load of sugar." During the air raid, "I told him to stop so we could take cover. He stopped and I jumped off. I thought he was going to jump off, too, and I started across the road. The next thing I knew something brown ran over me."

After spending two years in hospitals, Durham gave boxing one last shot, but his body did not permit it. "I'll tell you about his fighting days what he told me," said his widow, Jane Durham. "He said, 'I thought white boys couldn't fight.' But a white boy kicked his butt." Durham became a welder for the Pennsylvania Railroad, leaving the house at 5 a.m., working till 3 p.m. While on call, he sometimes left in the middle of the night to repair the frozen tracks before the morning rush hour. Yet no matter how busy he was, he always found time for his fighters. "He was at the gym every day," his widow said, "even Sunday." Despite his dedication, by the early 1960s, Durham was nothing more than another trainer in another smelly gym, the years tolling, for his fighters and for him, and there was no reason to believe his story would come up with any other ending. "I don't think that he ever thought he would have a champ," Jane said.

Then came the day when Duke Dugent, who ran the PAL gym, brought Durham over to check out Frazier. Durham saw a man who knew precisely where he wanted to go and what he was willing to do to get there. "He came home one night," Jane remembered, "and said, 'I got a champ.'" Jane knew her husband meant what he said. She never heard him say anything like that about any of the other fighters he trained. "I won't tell you," she said, laughing, "what he said about a lot of them."

But did a welder for the Pennsylvania Railroad have the knowledge and the intuition about the sport and the soul to turn Joe Frazier into a champion? Would Durham know when to push him and, perhaps more important, when to pull him back? And could Durham and Frazier, individuals with distinct makeups, develop the trust in each other essential for their long and difficult journey ahead? Philadelphia was known for an abundance of great fighters but also for fighters who should have been greater. Some wore themselves out in intense sparring sessions, known as the gym wars. "The trainers pit their prestige against other trainers," said trainer Eddie Futch. "I noticed it as far back as 1942 when I started bringing fighters into the city."

Durham possessed a deep, booming voice that was impossible to confuse with anyone else's. "When he spoke," said Joe Hand, a member of the Frazier camp for years, "he sounded like he was hollering," and he often used the first person when talking to the press about his fighter. In 1970, when Durham boasted that he, meaning Frazier, was "the champ" and "beat them all," Ray Grody, who worked for the *Milwaukee Sentinel*, touched the trainer's face and cracked, "And look, not a mark on him either!" The fact that Frazier allowed Durham to speak in this manner was an example,

Hand said, "of how well Yank and Joe got along." Durham loved his men, but he was very tough on them. Once, when he became upset with a fighter he felt was not performing up to his potential, Durham, according to Hand, decided a little pain might be necessary to get his message across. Every time the fighter returned to the corner, Durham, with sharpened fingernails, stuck his hand inside the guy's mouth to retrieve the mouthpiece. The fighter, his gums bloodied, got the message.

No such tactics were necessary with Frazier. Frazier must have known he would never become the next Joe Louis unless he listened to his trainer. That did not mean he always agreed with him. "He used to think I was a damn fool," Durham said. "He'd say, 'Yank, it's crazy to walk right in there with a guy punching at me.' What I did was put him in the ring with a lot of fighters who didn't do anything but jab. I did a lot of it myself. I'd get in with him and back around, and I'd use my hands to point out the area I wanted him to stay in as he came forward. . . . He learned beautiful."

Frazier was dedicated to the point that the challenge for Durham was keeping him from training too strenuously. Frazier often wanted to go that one extra round with his sparring partners and never held anything back. He believed going too easy on them would become a habit he might repeat in a real fight. Durham was almost a second father to Frazier, who lost his dad, Rubin, to cancer in 1965. "Joe would do anything in the world Yank told him," Hand said. "Yank was in complete control of the situation. He had the ability, if Frazier was going to fight on December 10, to have him peak on December 10 and not a day sooner."

Even their differences worked in their favor. "Joe looked forward to going to church," said Stan Hochman, a former columnist for the *Philadelphia Daily News*. "Yank used obscenities and was earthy, and Joe kind of liked that aspect of Yank." Hochman once asked Frazier, who often read the Bible, how he could reconcile the teachings of the Lord with a sport in which one human being attempts to knock the living daylights out of another. "They are different things," Frazier told him. "One is belief, the other is a job you have to do." Frazier also enjoyed singing, forming a band named the Knockouts. Lester Pelemon, one of the members, said Frazier used to attend performances of his earlier group, the Soul Brothers Six, which did the original recording of the hit "Some Kind of Wonderful." For Frazier, singing became an ideal break away from the fight game. "We would drive to Boston, to Chicago. We'd drive everywhere. We'd sing all the way in the car," Pelemon remembered. "Singing was inspiration for Joe. He loved to sing."

On March 4, 1966, Frazier fought in a city other than Philadelphia for the first time in his pro career. He fought in *the* city, New York, in Madison Square Garden, known as the mecca of boxing. His opponent was Dick Wipperman from Buffalo. Wipperman was whipped from the opening bell, falling in five. Every time Frazier stepped into the ring, he was ready to absorb whatever punishment was necessary to inflict his own—the left hook, the popular weapon for many Philadelphia fighters, usually doing the most damage— which was certain to be more deadly. Frazier knew no other way to fight, and, with his lack of reach—only 73½ inches, less than Louis (76), Ali (80), and Liston (84)—there really was no other way. Ineffective from long range, Frazier, to maximize his power, needed to stand as close as possible to his opponent, "to breathe on his chest," as he put it. He believed that if you killed the body, the head would die, and he proved it repeatedly.

Frazier would often be compared to Marciano. In Frazier's autobiography, he agreed that they were both "undersized aggressors, convinced we were the tougher, stronger men." But he also pointed out their differences: that Marciano operated from a crouch while he bobbed and weaved, and that Marciano put people away with his right while "my haymaker was the left hand." A more appropriate comparsion was Henry Armstrong, the legendary fighter from the 1930s and 1940s who held titles simultaneously in three divisions: welterweight, featherweight, and lightweight. For Frazier, more victories followed in 1966—two in April, two in May, and one in July, no bout going longer than six rounds; in all, he scored 11 knockouts in his first 11 fights. On September 21, at the Garden, Frazier faced his most serious test, Argentina's Oscar Bonavena. Bonavena (21–2) was similar to Frazier. He, too, did not seem to care how often he was hit as long as he landed his own blows, and they were mighty. These two appeared likely to slug it out from the first bell to the last, longer if the rules had allowed.

They were men of great standing and privilege, men such as Thacher Longstreth, the president of the Philadelphia Chamber of Commerce; Arthur Kaufman, president of a prominent department store, Gimbels; Harold Wessel, a partner in the accounting firm of Ernst & Ernst; F. Bruce Baldwin, chairman of Horn & Hardart Baking Company; Milton Clark, head of a building maintenance firm; and Jack Kelly, brother of Princess Grace of Monaco. In late 1965, these men, several dozen at first, put together a syndicate they called Cloverlay—clover for luck, overlay meaning a good bet—to invest in Frazier's boxing career. They did not expect to get rich, and that was fine with them because they were already rich. They got involved partly out of civic duty, to help a local kid chase his dream, and partly for the special benefits they enjoyed in return. They were entitled to stop by Frazier's dressing room before a fight and pose for pictures afterward.

"The Frazier stock was called a cocktail stock," said Joe Hand, an early investor. "They would all go to cocktail parties, and say, 'Oh, yeah, I own a fighter.' Those type of people didn't own fighters in those days." Hand did not exactly fit the Cloverlay profile. He was a cop, and cops didn't get rich. Another investor was the *Philadelphia Daily News*'s Larry Merchant. "I just thought it would be fun to write about *my* fighter, the way managers talked about their fighters all the time," Merchant said. He sold his share for $2,000 when he went to work for the *New York Post*.

Frazier and Durham surely did not care what movitated the investors. All that mattered was that they provided financial backing in a profession that promised nothing and, more often than not, delivered less. In his debut against Elwood Goss, Frazier took home about $125, and he got that much only because of the tickets he was able to sell. When he was not working out at the gym, he was a janitor at the Bright Hope Baptist Church. The job did not pay much, but it paid off, leading to the deal with Cloverlay.

One day, Frazier's pastor, Reverend William Gray, introduced him to Baldwin, who closely followed the fight game and saw, in this powerful youngster, his chance to become part of it. Baldwin recruited a few of his friends to form the corporation, the stock selling for $250 a share. (When Frazier fought Ali in 1971, the shares were valued at $14,000 apiece.) Frazier signed a three-year contract with Cloverlay holding options for two additional three-year periods. He received a salary of $100 a week and 50 percent of his earnings in the ring—half to be added to his weekly salary, the other to be invested for him in a trust fund. The members received 35 percent, the other 15 percent going to Durham. If Cloverlay exercised its options, Frazier's share of the purses would increase to 55 percent in the second three years, 60 in the final three.

"The intention," Hand pointed out, "was that he would never be broke." The investors were smart, smart enough to know what they did not know. On boxing-related matters, they deferred to Durham and were not disappointed. "It was like the doctor telling you that you're going to need surgery," Hand said. " 'Okay, we're going to get the surgery.' We all depended on what he said. Yank knew every little dirty detail of the boxing business."

The members of Cloverlay believed in Joe Frazier. The members of the fourth estate weren't always so sure. On a personal level, the reporters liked him but did not get close to him. Some of the fault belonged to Frazier. "He wasn't a verbal guy," said Phil Pepe, the boxing writer for the *New York Daily News*. "Ali was a dream. You didn't even have to ask Ali a question. You just ask him one and he goes on and fills your notebook. Joe was not like that. You had to pull it out of him, whatever you could." Frazier, at first, according to Philadelphia columnist Stan Hochman, "didn't feel comfortable around strangers." He was seen as a decent and honorable man who always tried his best. They admired his tenacity, his lack of fear, his left hook, but at times did not afford him as much respect as he deserved. Frazier, the skeptics said, relied too much on his left. Frazier was too easy to hit. Frazier couldn't knock a guy out with a single punch. The skeptics said a lot of things over the years. Such cynicism from the media is as much a part of boxing as the punching bag.

"It's not like any other sport where you're competing against the best people all the time," Larry Merchant explained. "You can be very excited about a fighter and skeptical at the very same time. 'Wow, that was a terrific fight and a great performance, but who was the guy he fought?' You don't know in boxing whether what you're looking at is an illusion. There was skepticism about the last guy who had fought in that style, Marciano. And there are always people out there who are true nonbelievers, because if you're a nonbeliever, you're more likely to be right in the long run than if you're a believer. Even with George Foreman, who looked so imposing, like what a heavyweight champion was supposed to look like, there were skeptics. He was matched more carefully than Frazier. They were afraid to put him in with Quarry."

Early in the Bonavena fight, it appeared that the nonbelievers just might have been right about Joe Frazier. In the second round, Bonavena sent him to the canvas with a right hand to the chin, the first time Frazier hit the deck since his second fight, against Mike Bruce, twelve months earlier. He rose at the count of five, but a left hook quickly put him on the floor again. With about a minute left in the round, Bonavena tried to finish him off—a third knockdown, under New York State rules, would automatically end the fight—but Frazier hung on until the bell. He recovered, but about the eighth round he mentioned to Durham he was getting tired. "I told him he better get rested, get back out there and fight because he still didn't have it won," Durham said. "He responded."

Frazier escaped with a split decision, going the distance for the first time. Coming close to defeat may have helped him recognize a few things he needed to work on. Durham told him to bring his arms in close and put his legs together "and go in there punching. You can't pick off punches, you got to move your head, bob and weave, slip punches, and keep coming." Those in the Garden that evening also learned something. "That was the fight where everyone said, 'Okay, Joe Frazier is for real,'" Merchant said. "Oscar was a very tough fighter who fought all the top guys of his time. You need exceptional will and strength to fight in that style, and he showed that he had it against Bonavena."

Two months later, Frazier went to Los Angeles to oppose Eddie Machen. Machen, after handing Jerry Quarry his first loss in July, prevailed in a 10-round decision two months later over Scrap Iron Johnson. Machen was crafty, and there wasn't a style he hadn't encountered in his prior sixty-one fights. The only opponent to knock him down was the ex-champion, Ingemar Johansson. Some wondered whether Durham was now rushing his fighter, but, again, he was not deterred. "When he made up his mind," his widow said, "nobody was going to change it." Eddie Futch, the respected west coast trainer, told Durham that Frazier could handle Machen. Frazier felt the same way and was looking forward to the challenge. "I was in a hurry to get to the top," Frazier wrote, "where the money and the glory were, and figured serious competition would get me there quicker and overcome whatever reservations the critics had about Smokin' Joe."

Machen got in a few good licks, including a hard right in the eighth round just when Frazier appeared in control, but Frazier absorbed them and responded with his own, which Machen could not absorb; the fight was halted in the tenth. Frazier was not the most skillful defensive fighter in the division, but as Durham said, his offense *was* his defense. "That was the turning point of Joe's career," said Bruce Wright, Cloverlay's attorney. "It took a lot of courage to take that fight." Machen was done after fighting Frazier. He never won again. "I'll never forget Machen afterwards," Futch recalled. "He couldn't get over how hard Joe hit. 'With everything,' he told me. 'Arms, elbows, wherever he hits you, it hurts. You guys don't need to teach the guy anything about defense. Just get him ready and turn him loose.'"

On February 21, 1967, Frazier put away Doug Jones in the sixth round. Durham had shortened the arc of Frazier's left hook for more power and to help his punches reach their target sooner. Frazier was also extremely effective with the jab and the right-hand uppercuts he threw in the second and sixth rounds when Jones protected himself against the left. "He's like a leech," a Jones handler explained. "You can't get away from Frazier. This guy is Murder Incorporated. Jones, the poor devil, had to change styles every round. Frazier just took the fight away from him. There was nothing he could do."

Frazier was already, in fact, being mentioned as a future opponent for Ali, perhaps even by the end of the year. Durham, however, brushed aside such speculation. "I don't need Clay right now," Durham said. "He wants me now, but when I take the fight it will be a war between equals. Right now Joe is still learning. Tonight he graduated from high school, and I want him to go to college before he takes on Professor Clay." That day would come soon enough. Until then, there were more lessons to learn—in training camp, in the ring, in life. Frazier was only twenty-three. He had been fighting professionally for a mere eighteen months.

On April 11, Frazier scored a fifth-round technical knockout over Jeff Davis in Miami Beach. In the second round, he scored with a straight right. Davis wobbled. In the third, he nailed Davis with left hooks to the head and body. A left hook in the fifth sent Davis to the canvas. He got up at the count of eight, but with blood streaming out of both nostrils, and the fight was stopped by the referee Jimmy Peerless. Then came Houston and the Ali suspension.

Suddenly, everything was different. Suddenly, all Frazier had to do was prevail over the other seven contenders in the World Boxing Association elimination tournament and the heavyweight championship, and the spoils that went along with it would belong to him. First, however, came the fight with Scrap Iron Johnson in Los Angeles. Johnson became only the second opponent to go the whole way against Frazier, but Frazier won an easy 10-round decision to remain on track for his title shot.

There would be no title shot for Frazier, not yet. Durham declined the WBA invitation. The move was perhaps the shrewdest he ever made. By separating his fighter from the pack, he contributed to the growing aura surrounding Joe Frazier, the sense that of the heavyweights in the post-Ali period, he seemed the most worthy to succeed him. Part of this motivation was that once the tournament came to an end, seven of the eight combatants would have fallen, while his man would still be around, unscathed. At that point, the lone survivor—Ellis, Quarry, Terrell, whoever—would have to come to *him*, because no champion could be fully accepted by the press and the public unless he defeated Frazier.

On May 10, Cloverlay's board of directors voted unanimously to back Durham's recommendation. They believed in him and watched their investment grow. They were not going to stop believing in him now. Cloverlay also objected to the provision that the winner's ancillary rights—income earned outside of ticket sales—would be owned for two years by Sports Action, the group putting the tournament together. Merchant believes there were other factors that influenced Durham. "He wasn't entirely positive about Joe having to fight some of those guys, like Terrell, who was six-foot-six and could, presumably, stay away from him and give him trouble," Merchant claims. "I was disappointed. I felt that if Ali was out of the picture, a tournament was the sporting way to decide who should fill the vacancy, but at the same time, I understood why his management saw it differently. They wanted to be in control of his destiny."

With the top contenders committed to the tournament, Durham matched Frazier against George Chuvalo on July 19 at the Garden. Chuvalo was no artiste. Compared to Chuvalo, Frazier was a Rembrandt in the ring. Ali dubbed Chuvalo "the Washerwoman." "He punches like a woman who's washing clothes," he said, but Chuvalo was, if nothing else, durable, going the full 15 rounds against Ali and Terrell. In 62 bouts, Chuvalo had never been knocked down. After dropping a decision to Bonavena in 1966, he won twelve fights in a row, all by knockout, only two opponents lasting past the third round. Frazier was the overwhelming favorite, but some questions were fair to ask: Would he lose patience if Chuvalo did not fall in the early rounds? What if Chuvalo connected with his powerful right?

The answers came swiftly, conclusively. Chuvalo again did not hit the deck, but, for the first time, he lost by a technical knockout, the end coming officially in the fourth, when the fighter's right eye was almost completely shut, and the referee, Johnny Colon, stopped it. Chuvalo had to undergo surgery for a fracture under his eye. "Another punch," Chuvalo said in 2006, "the doctor told me I would have been blind." The triumph drew praise from Red Smith, the *New York Times* columnist. Ali has faced quality opponents, Smith wrote, "but he has never been introduced to a full-grown heavyweight who combines Joe's speed and punch." Three months later, Frazier dispatched Tony Doyle in the second round, and, in December, required only two more to put away Marion Connors. Frazier went six for six in 1967, five fights ending within six rounds. The Durham strategy was paying off. The other contenders were dropping one by one in the tournament, Durham's man still standing, more imposing than ever.

Next for Frazier, on March 4, 1968, was Buster Mathis, all 243½ pounds of him. Even so, Mathis, who once tipped the scales in the 300s and had been taught by the unconventional trainer Cus D'Amato, was *not* imposing, his victories coming against the likes of Charley Chase, Waban (Tugboat) Thomas, and Tom Swift. Safe to say, the Mathis résumé, while spotless (23–0, 17 knockouts), was somewhat inflated. Except one name stood out, a loser in two decisions during their amateur days, the final of the 1964 Olympic Trials at New York's World's Fair the most significant: Smokin' Joe Frazier. Frazier relished the opportunity for payback. He was convinced the decision in New York was wrong.

"All that fat boy had done was run like a thief, hit me a peck and backpedal like crazy," Frazier wrote. So dejected was Frazier after the setback that he briefly considered quitting the sport until Durham, and the Police Athletic League's Duke Dugent, persuaded him to join the U.S. squad as an alternate. It worked out better than he could have imagined. When Mathis broke his hand, ironically, by hitting Frazier in the head during an exhibition in San Francisco, Frazier took his place. A few weeks later he took the gold. In the semifinals, Frazier prevailed over his Russian opponent but busted his left thumb. He did not tell his coaches or teammates about the injury. "When they offered to X-ray it, I said no. I wasn't about to blow my shot at the gold by having some medical officer discover a fracture and scratch me from the competition," Frazier explained. In the final bout, using his right hand a lot, he won a very close decision over Germany's Hans Huber.

Revenge was not the sole motivation for Frazier. At stake against Mathis was the heavyweight championship, not the WBA version (Jimmy Ellis and Jerry Quarry would settle that a month later in Oakland) but a championship nonetheless, one administered by the very influential New York State Athletic Commission. Only four states (six, eventually)—New York, Massachusetts, Maine, and Illinois—agreed to recognize the winner, but four was more than enough. Madison Square Garden, shut out of the WBA bonanza, could surely benefit from a marquee match to make a statement—and a buck, of course. The Garden was also searching for a heavyweight to headline the first boxing card in its new $43 million building atop the Penn-Central railroad station between Thirty-second and Thirty-third streets, fronting Eighth Avenue.

Frazier was the ideal choice. He put forth a total effort every time he stepped between the ropes, and, unlike another heavyweight from that period, he was not a polarizing figure. "In the Garden's mind, Joe Frazier was a solid American, a really good guy, and Ali was not," said the *Times*'s Robert Lipsyte. "This guy would not fight for his country. You forget what a dangerous character he was of his time. Harry Markson [the head of the Garden's boxing department] would not even introduce him as Muhammad Ali." (When, in March 1965, he introduced him as Cassius Clay before the Luis Rodriguez–Holly Mims fight, Ali, as promised, walked out of the arena, receiving a lot of boos.) New York boxing fans loved to watch fighters who hit hard, and few in the sport in the late 1960s hit harder than Frazier. "In terms of style, he was the black Dempsey, the black Marciano," Merchant said. "That's what moves fans. That's what puts asses in seats."

Frazier was not overly concerned with Buster Mathis. Mathis was composed of flesh and bones, susceptible to the same set of weaknesses, physical and mental, that afflicted everyone insane enough to take up this line of work that left many penniless or impaired, or both, before the age of forty. One day, about two weeks before the fight, George Kalinsky, the Garden's official photographer, showed Frazier a close-up he had taken of Mathis, the sweat pouring down his cheeks. Kalinsky thought it was a terrifying portrait. Frazier saw something else. "You're not looking at power," he assured Kalinsky. "You're looking at fear. He's afraid of me." As the fight approached, it became clear that however Frazier fared against Mathis, or for that matter the winner of the Ellis-Quarry duel, if the match could be made, the title, in the opinion of many experts and fans, would still belong to the man who had never had it taken away from him in the ring. Several militant black protest organizations announced that they would picket outside the Garden on fight night.

"To us, and to millions of other blacks at home and throughout the world, Muhammad Ali is the world's heavyweight champion," said Lincoln Lynch of the United Black Front. "He is still the greatest."

Frazier did not allow himself to become distracted. Few athletes could concentrate on the task ahead of him as well as Frazier could. "Those black radicals could say this and that," he wrote. "It didn't matter. I'd fought for this opportunity. I'd punched and got punched. And with my body and blood, I'd paid the price." As for Ali, Frazier knew already how he would go after him if he ever got the chance. "I remember being with Joe watching Ali fight on TV," said Kalinsky, who believes it was the second Ali-Cooper bout in May 1966. "Joe only had one focus. He wanted to be in the ring with Ali. Joe said, 'I can take this guy. It's no big deal. He's fighting a bunch of bums.' I said, 'Well, what would you do?' He said, 'I would just pound him in the body, then get him in the head and he will go down.'" His chance would not come for nearly five years. Until then, Frazier could do nothing, except beat whoever was put in front of him, and wait.

Mathis, a skillful boxer for his size, captured the early rounds, but as Frazier would point out in his book, his opponent was now in the big leagues, "pros," where two grown men go at it for 10 or 12 or, if necessary, 15 rounds, and one man, however nimble, cannot run forever from the other. Mathis slowed down in the seventh, and, from then on, he belonged to Frazier. The end, caused by a left hook, was vicious, as it often must be: Mathis on the canvas, his face bloody, his eyes empty, his chance of a title gone for good. He began to rise at the count of eight but was clearly out of it, seizing the top rope to steady himself. After the referee Arthur Mercante wisely stopped the fight, Durham and Frazier embraced. Less than three years since his first professional bout, Joe Frazier was a champion. Yank Durham told his wife back in 1962 that it would happen someday, and that day had arrived. Durham possessed the knowledge and the intuition. He knew when to push his man and when to hold him back. The two trusted each other, and it changed their lives.

"After Mathis, I was willing to fight anybody," Durham said, "Clay, Quarry, anybody who would put on gloves. Joe had come to the point where he himself knew he could handle anyone." Buster Mathis was never a major factor again in the heavyweight division. "I thought he had a chance because Mathis had a good punch," Jose Torres said. "But he started getting hit, and he could not adjust to the pain when he got hit. He never learned how to take those punches with grace."

A month later, after Ellis outdueled Quarry, the stage was set for Ellis and Frazier to unify the title, but the two would not face each other for almost two full years. In the interim, Frazier fought four times. Two were mismatches. He knocked out Manuel Ramos in the second round, although Ramos nailed him with a hard right on the side of the head. Ten months later, he knocked out Dave Zyglewicz. Zyglewicz did not hurt him with a punch of any kind. The fight was over in ninety-six seconds. In between Ramos and Zyglewicz came a second battle with Bonavena, on December 10, 1968, at the Spectrum in Philadelphia, the first time Frazier defended his title in his adopted hometown. The city of Philadelphia, however, never fully adopted him. Only about 7,000 fans showed up. Even blacks did not seem to embrace Frazier. "He was not one of the guys that you could always catch hanging out at Broad and Girard or Twenty-second and Columbia," said J Russell Peltz, a boxing promoter in the city for nearly forty years. "He would always get in his car and drive back to where he lived [in the suburbs]. The black community saw that. He distanced himself from the city when he became a pro."

Frazier became friendly with the Philadelphia police commissioner, Frank Rizzo, who would be elected mayor in 1971. Rizzo was known as a strict law-and-order man. In August 1970, the police raided the offices of the Black Panther Party. Those arrested were ordered to strip and stand naked in front of cameras, and a photo of the scene appeared the next day on the front page of the *Philadelphia Daily News*. "Frank Rizzo was probably the most disliked person by black people ever in Philadelphia," Joe Hand said.

Another factor hurting Frazier's relationship with the African American community, according to Hand, was his association with Cloverlay. "Most of the investors were white, so people would always relate to Joe as a white guy," Hand added. The poor turnout for the Bonavena fight upset Frazier, but given the high ticket prices—the best seats went for $50, the highest ever for a boxing card in Philadelphia—the decision by the locals to stay away may have been driven more by economics than by any lack of affection toward one of their own.

The second Frazier-Bonavena fight was similar to the first. Bonavena did not knock down Frazier this time and did not deserve the decision but took advantage of every opening and won four of the last five rounds. Frazier was in bad shape afterward. His right cheek and right eyebrow swelled. His right hip was sore. Blood drooled from a cut under his lower lip. A rumor spread that his jaw was broken; it was not. For the first time in twenty-two bouts, Frazier was forced to go past the eleventh round. Afterward, he was asked if he was tired. Frazier laughed. "Man, are you kidding?" he replied. He had spent six weeks in training camp, his longest stint to date. He had sparred for about 150 rounds and boldly predicted he would knock his opponent out to make up for his subpar showing the first time. Yet despite Frazier's failure to back it up, there was no cause for any concern. In forty-two previous fights, nobody had knocked Bonavena out. "Bonavena was a guy I couldn't crack," Frazier wrote. "He had a style that for me was like oil and water."

One fan at the Spectrum was particularly unimpressed. Of course—how else would Muhammad Ali react? It was "not a true championship fight," said Ali, who sat in the tenth row. "They were just swinging away." He tried to enter Frazier's dressing room after the fight but was stopped by the guards. "That's all right," Ali said. "I just wanted to wish Frazier luck and tell him I am going to whop up on him." Ali could not possibly know, in late 1968, whether he would ever fight again or go to prison or remain in exile for another year or two. It seemed very clear, though, that if he was permitted to fight again, and if he regained his title, the day would come when he would have to face Joe Frazier.

Through cameo appearances—in Atlantic City, he crashed a Frazier concert—and interviews, Ali played his part magnificently. Nobody in the history of boxing—of any sport—was a more creative and unabashed self-promoter. He made sure he and Frazier were linked in the public consciousness as often as possible, setting up a conflict of personalities (and, later, unfairly, visions of America) that could be settled only one way, the way men always settle these things: with their fists. Frazier did his part, as well. "I'd like to button his big mouth once and for all," Frazier said in June 1969 while training for his upcoming duel with Jerry Quarry at the Garden. "I think the public is fed up with his fussin' and fumin.' What kind of a man is this who don't want to fight for his country? If he was in Russia, or some place else, they'd put him up against the wall. He walks around like he's one kind of a big hero but he's just a phony, a disgrace." The victory over Quarry was Frazier's fourth successful title defense.

In September, Ali alerted a Philadelphia radio station and newspapers that he would show up a few hours later at the PAL gym ready to rumble with Frazier. Word got around town fast. After Ali arrived, hundreds tried to squeeze into a gym that was supposed to hold only a few dozen, dozens more spilling into the surrounding streets, stopping the rush-hour traffic. The sudden rush of bodies caused a ring post to be bent. Sergeant Vince Furlong told the crowd, and the combatants, that there would be no fight on this day. Ali suggested that he and Frazier take it outside, to Fairmount Park, about a mile away. He hopped into his red convertible and took off. "The crowd followed him like a Pied Piper," Furlong said. "There never was a sense of danger, just mob excitement." Frazier stayed behind. "Here I am," Ali told the people at the park. "Haven't had a fight in three years [actually, two and a half], twenty-five pounds overweight, and Joe Frazier won't show up. What kind of a champ can he be?"

Looking back, the entire episode certainly seems staged, but it put the fighters exactly where they wanted to be, in the news, though Frazier, according to former *Sports Illustrated* writer Mark Kram, felt that Ali went too far. "By not joining Ali in the park," Kram wrote, "Joe felt silly, used, an object of ridicule and diminished in stature." The headline in the next day's *Philadelphia Inquirer* read: "Ali and 10,000 Fans Disappointed, Frazier Skips Battle in Park." Ali and Frazier met the same day to tape the nationally syndicated *Mike Douglas Show*.

"Six weeks, that's all I would need to get back in shape," Ali said shortly before going on the air. "Every time you'd breathe," Frazier said, "you'd be breathing on me because I'd be right on top of you." After the show, they tussled on the street, each restrained by his entourage, although not before a right from Ali landed on Frazier's shoulder and another struck his manager. "You crazy mothafucka," Durham said. Were they serious or merely playacting? It did not matter. Ali and Frazier were cultivating interest in a battle that, as the months dragged on, became the match every fan of the sport could not wait to see. "If the showdown ever comes, it would be the biggest thing in the history of boxing," Ali said. "Whole countries and nations would be watching and taking sides. It would be a Holy War, the good against the bad." He did not have to specify, of course, which fighter he felt represented the good.

On February 16, 1970, one showdown finally did come: Frazier versus Ellis. It would be no holy war by any stretch, but, for the first time since Ali was stripped of his crown in April 1967, only one man would hold the most hallowed individual prize in sports.

Boxing no longer commanded the same spot in the country's imagination that it did during earlier decades, when only baseball was more popular, but the owner of the heavyweight championship, as long as he was deemed sufficiently worthy, remained a larger-than-life figure. "It has to do with the intrinsic feeling of man against man and the implicit feeling about the raw courage it takes to do that," Merchant suggested. "When the guy was ordinary, when it was Jack Sharkey, it did not mean all that much. When it was extraordinary, when it was Jack Dempsey or Joe Louis, it could not have meant more."

In 1965, Jimmy Ellis was an unknown middleweight with three defeats in his last four fights who could not line any up any future opponents. He talked about quitting, but his wife, Mary, talked him out of it. Mary woke up with him, at four-thirty some mornings, to drive the car in the dark and deserted streets of Louisville while he jogged two or three miles before he showered, ate breakfast, and left for his job as a concrete finisher. On occasion, he tapped on the car window to be sure Mary did not accidentally run him over when she nodded off for a few minutes. After he put in his eight or nine hours at work, Jimmy put in a few more at the gym. When he got home after the long day, Mary took his shoes off and fixed him a nice dinner and ran a hot bath. "He was just wore out," she said. "He went to bed and was ready for the next morning." Jimmy and Mary made these sacrifices in hopes of earning a better life for themselves and the kids they kept having, one after another, until there were six. Mary was a very spiritual person, as was Jimmy, the son of a Baptist minister. Mary must have believed in her heart that all those early mornings she waited in the car for him to finish his workout would pay off someday. "James, you don't need to quit," she told Jimmy. "You're a good fighter. Please don't quit." She knew her husband needed a new trainer, so she came up with the idea of writing a letter to Angelo Dundee and signed Jimmy's name. Jimmy went along. He knew Ali from their amateur days in Louisville. They competed on a local boxing show, *Tomorrow's Champions*. Jimmy even beat him once. The letter read, "I am thinking of quitting boxing, but before I do, I would like one more shot to see if I could make it. I'd like to sign with a good manager in New York IF you do not think you have the time to handle my career. I hope you will be able to help me . . . P.S. H-e-e-e-e-l-p."

The letter worked. Dundee agreed to train Jimmy at the Fifth Street Gym. "I read [Angelo's response] to him, and his eyes just opened up," Mary said. "He was very excited." It was a risk for Jimmy to forgo a secure job and take off for Miami Beach, leaving Mary and the children in Louisville, but this was his chance, probably the last, to make it big. Mary cooked about ten biscuits for Jimmy every morning to fatten him up. Dundee said he needed to move up in weight classes, where he could make some real dough. "He ate and ate and ate," said Mary. "He loved maraconi and cheese and cornbread." Dundee gave him $200 a week to be a sparring partner for Ali. Jimmy sent $175 of it to Mary. "I just fine-tuned him," Dundee said. "He had a lot of talent. I just put the talent in the right direction." From May 25, 1965, when Ellis knocked out Joe Blackwood, through the end of the decade, he did not lose a single fight.

The turning point came when he fought Johnny Persol in the Garden on March 22, 1967, on the same card of Ali's bout with Zora Folley, the last before the suspension. Persol was supposed to handle Ellis on his march toward a shot at the crown. Ellis handled him. In the first round, with a lunging left hook followed by a right to the jaw, Ellis sent Persol to the deck for his third straight first-round knockout. "They put us in a dressing room which was a boiler room," Ferdie Pacheco said. "I told Ellis, 'Let's keep working so it looks like you've done five rounds by the time you get in there, jump on his ass and let everything fly in the first round. If you don't get him, you're going to leave him in worse shape.' Ellis was ready. He was so fucking ready, he would go through the wall. Afterwards, Angelo says, 'You know what, we've got us a heavyweight.'"

In the WBA tournament, Ellis was an underdog in every match. After Jimmy outpointed Jerry Quarry to win the title, he and Mary finally bought their first house, a two-story colonial in the east section of Louisville. They were so excited they slept on a mattress on the floor until they picked up their bed. All those early mornings and the biscuits Mary fed Jimmy paid off. "He probably got more out of his talent than any fighter ever," said Dave Kindred, who wrote about Ellis for the *Louisville Courier-Journal*. "I don't think anybody thought he had any kind of a chance in that tournament."

Five months later, Ellis opposed ex-champion Floyd Patterson in Stockholm. The fight went the distance, and Patterson nearly won; some believe he actually did. Ellis didn't fight once in 1969. Dundee indicated it was because of a broken nose suffered in the Patterson fight and because of matches that were canceled for one reason or another. Ellis certainly wasn't in any rush to face Frazier. "Was there anybody in the world," Pacheco said, "including his mother and his wife, who did not think that Frazier was going to run right through Ellis? Frazier was a lion. He was a legitimate heavyweight. I mean, he was a piece of iron. We had a built-up guy that we pumped up with air. He was not real. He was a middleweight." According to Pacheco, the strategy was to "cash in before Frazier catches us. We were running down the street hoping that Frazier doesn't get us while we fight anybody that shows up."

At one point, Ellis agreed to put his title on the line against Dave Zyglewicz for $80,000, not an especially large amount for a heavyweight title bout; he earned $125,000 for the Quarry fight. On the other hand, Ellis would not exactly be facing Jack Dempsey. Zyglewicz launched his career by answering an ad in *Ring* magazine placed by Hugh Benbow, the manager of Cleveland Williams, seeking "boys from 18 to 23 years old that weigh around two hundred pounds and six feet tall who want to become scientific boxers and make a lot of money." After Zyglewicz responded, Benbow mailed him a bus ticket to train at his gym in Texas. "Jimmy, this is not a fight," Pacheco told Ellis. "This is like a one-round execution.

This guy is awful. Put the $80,000 in the bank and it will keep your family fed for five years." The plans were in motion until Ellis, according to Pacheco, talked the idea over with Shotgun Sheldon, one of his sparring partners.

"You're not really going to fight Zyglewicz," Shotgun said.

"Why not?" Ellis asked.

"Man, you're giving away your title for $80,000," Shotgun explained.

"What are you talking about?" Ellis wondered.

"Think about it," Shotgun went on. "It's Houston where they are all white sheriffs down there. And the referee is white and the boxer is white. You think you're going to knock that boxer out? If you knock him out, they will disqualify you."

The more Ellis thought about it, the more he realized Shotgun knew what he was talking about. He decided not to take the Zyglewicz fight. Frazier did, winning easily. "Frazier knocked him out," Pacheco said. "Was that worth $80,000? You bet your ass it was. It was like picking up candy."

Ellis stayed away from competition for seventeen months; that was clearly not the smartest way to get ready for Joe Frazier. "You can't get in the best shape laying off that long," Dundee admitted. "Activity is what fine-tunes a fighter." During the same seventeen months, Frazier beat up on Ramos, Zyglewicz, and Quarry and went the distance against Bonavena—a total of 25 rounds. Yet, as usual, in preparing for Ellis, Frazier did not take anything for granted. He began training in Miami Beach in the middle of the winter but shifted his headquarters to the Concord resort at Kiamesha Lake in upstate New York to get out of the heat and better preserve his strength and stamina. He sparred for more than 125 rounds. While in New York for the final week, he jogged almost every day in Central Park from Fifty-ninth Street to One-hundred-second Street on the East Side. Frazier wanted to whip Muhammad Ali more than any human being on the planet, but he did not know when or whether that chance would ever come, and it certainly would not come if he did not take care of Jimmy Ellis first.

Ali was not content to let Frazier and Ellis grab all the head-lines. He kept talking about retirement, although nobody who knew him believed for a second that he really meant it, and when he offered to hand over his championship belt in the ring to the Frazier-Ellis winner, he was merely drawing attention to the fact that he was *giving* the belt away, that no one ever *took* it from him.

The Garden wisely said no thanks. "How can you give away something you don't have?" asked Garden matchmaker Teddy Brenner. "You have the belt but you don't have the title." Ali, in any case, did not sound like a man who had put the sport behind him. "When Frazier and Ellis climb in that ring Monday," he sug-gested, "everybody knows that somewhere out there in the streets is someone who can toy with both of them. Who are they? One of them used to be my sparring partner. The other is a flat-footed bull who moves like a plowhorse. . . . The people aren't going to let me retire in their minds. The fans won't be at ease about accepting a new champion because they know I'm not too old to fight." On assignment for *Esquire*, Ali watched the fight via closed-circuit at the Arena in Philadelphia. He predicted Ellis would knock Frazier out in the eighth round.

Frazier was listed as the 4–1 favorite in New York City, but even among some who witnessed his maturation over the previous four years, the view persisted that he was no lock. The Philadelphia columnist Stan Hochman wrote about Ellis's swift, lean legs and ability to dart from side to side, and how Frazier tended at times to forget about bobbing and weaving when chasing his opponent. Hochman suggested that Ellis could knock Frazier out as early as the second round. Among Ellis's nine prior victims, four fell in the opening round. At the same time, nobody had ever put him away, as a heavyweight or a middleweight. Only Rubin "Hurricane" Carter knocked Ellis to the canvas, and that was way back in 1964.

The string of quick knockouts was noteworthy, but, in Joe Fra-zier, he was dealing with an adversary much more resilient than those who went down. Ellis was so concerned with Frazier's fire-power that he and Dundee briefly worked out on the day before the fight at the Felt Forum, a smaller auditorium inside the Garden complex. Wearing street clothes, Ellis took off his shirt, put on gloves, and practiced a defensive move to neutralize Frazier's left hook. Ellis seemed to be in excellent condition, but that was apparently not the case. He asked Pacheco to fly to New York several days sooner than scheduled. Pacheco was swamped with patients but came anyway. "What's happening?" he said when he saw Ellis. "I can't lift my arm to comb my hair," Ellis told him. "I think I hurt my shoulder in training." Pacheco knew there was little he could do. Ellis had injured his rotator cuff, which normally requires five or six weeks to heal. The smart move would have been to postpone the fight, but it was the largest payday in the fighter's career. Pacheco gave him cortisone shots typically used on horses. "I had him ready for the Belmont," he joked.

The first round was a lot like other first rounds in Frazier fights. "The first round, I'm a little tight," he once explained. "That's when you'll see the other guys doing his thing." Ellis was doing his thing, moving from side to side, scoring with left jabs and hard rights to the head. Ellis liked to jab and punch in combinations. However, none of the shots slowed down Frazier, not for an instant, and that was when Jimmy Ellis must have sensed that he was in for a difficult evening. If he didn't, more signs came the next round when Frazier landed a series of left hooks to his head. Ellis was no longer standing as tall as he had in the first round. So much for those last-minute preparations at the Felt Forum. Ellis tried to hang on to Frazier to clear his head, but Frazier pulled away. The strategy was to sneak right hands over the jab, but it was not working.

The third round was even more one-sided. Another left stunned Ellis. When Frazier returned to his corner, he was smiling. Frazier smiled a lot. Few prizefighters in history have derived as much pure enjoyment from demolishing the body and spirit of another living creature as Smokin' Joe Frazier did. "There wasn't a feeling much better than seeing that look in the big guys' eyes when I'd unload on them. That look said—oh, shit, so this is what fighting this little son of a bitch is gonna be like. Sure I smiled through that mouthpiece. It felt damn good to be a giant killer. I loved being under those bright lights, performing. It was what I was meant to do—what the Lord had in mind for me." He unloaded against Ellis and did not receive much resistance.

"Sissy, you can't hit," Frazier told him. "I took everything you can throw. You got nothing." Frazier was not the only one who knew the end was coming soon. So did the photographers, who edged forward on the ring apron, ready to shoot the deciding blow. In the fourth, Frazier went after the body. He then pounded Ellis with a left hook to the chin that sent him to the floor, his face on the canvas. Ellis somehow got up at the count of eight. Pacheco wished he hadn't. "There was nothing I could do but pray that it was over soon," Pacheco said. "There was no way we could win." Later in the round, another left dropped Ellis again. He rose at nine this time. He was saved by the bell.

Dundee tried every means possible to revive his fighter in the one minute between rounds that always goes by too fast in dire moments like this. He put ice on the back of his neck and down his trunks. He threw cold water in his face. He gave him smelling salts, pinched him, and banged on his knees. But this was not Muhammad Ali versus Henry Cooper. There was no cut to enlarge in his glove to give his fighter more time, and besides, more time would not have made a difference anyway, not against Frazier. Ellis stared ahead, a blank look on his face, a beaten fighter if there ever was one. Dundee then did the only humane thing he could as a trainer, and as a friend who cared deeply about a husband and a father of six. Ellis could lose his life if Dundee let him back in there against an opponent who would not show any mercy, and why should he? When Ellis tried to get up from his stool, Dundee held him down to stop the fight, which went into the books as a fifth-round technical knockout.

"He wasn't there," Dundee recalled. "How do you send a guy out when he doesn't have his faculties?" Afterward, Ellis could only remember the first time he hit the floor. Mary hugged her man in the dressing room. She was grateful for Dundee's compassion. She and Jimmy, still in one piece, could return to their home in Louisville. The fight drew 18,079 spectators for a gross gate of $645,997, a record for an indoor heavyweight title bout. Frazier and Ellis each pocketed more than $300,000.

Frazier was euphoric. He leaped into Yank Durham's arms as soon as the fight was stopped. He danced around the ring, singing "Free at last, free at last." At last, he was, indeed, the only official world heavyweight champion, but Joe Frazier was not free and could never be free until he beat the man who was still the true champion in the minds of many fans. "He could never lick Clay in a million years," Dundee said. "Clay would have slapped him all over the joint. He'd never find him."

Ali was impressed with Frazier's performance, though as usual he responded with a performance of his own. At the Arena, before the lights went back on, he shadowboxed on the runway that circled the floor. When he got to the parking lot, he stood on the hood of a car like a candidate, which is what he was, campaigning for a chance to reclaim his crown. Fans climbed over nearby hoods to get as close to him as possible. "I want Frazier," Ali told the crowd. "I'm starting my comeback now. This town is too small for both of us." Coming back was not a decision Ali could make entirely on his own. The only ones with the power to put him in the ring were the real politicians, and they were not ready to let him return just yet.

Frazier made plans for an extensive vacation. He would hit the road with his band and his bike, the blue Harley Davidson Electra Glide motorcycle he purchased for $2,500, which caused great concern among the folks at Cloverlay but afforded him great pleasure. Cloverlay, Frazier wrote in his autobiography, went "absolutely nuts when I crashed the sucker in Philadelphia and then a second time down in Beaufort." Stan Hochman said that when Frazier trained in New Jersey and wanted to ride his bike to the shore, Cloverlay made up a story that motorcycles were banned on the Atlantic City Expressway and "asked me to go along with it and tell Joe it was illegal." Durham took a more fatalistic approach. "The more people tell him not to, the more he'll do it," he said.

"He's young and he's got to get it out of his system. You know how young automobile drivers are. After a while, they steady down. It's all part of growing up."

Frazier would also spend time with his wife and five kids and three dogs at his six-bedroom house on two acres in Whitemarsh, just outside Philadelphia. The days of relying on strangers to enjoy Christmas were long gone. Soon enough, he would defend his title against an opponent Durham would choose with the same wisdom he chose the others.

Joe Frazier had come so far, so fast. In 1961, he was an overweight teenager pounding sides of beef. He was not on track to become the next Joe Louis. In 1970, he was the heavyweight champion of the world. From Ellwood Goss to Jimmy Ellis, he beat everyone placed in front of him. The critics were wrong. Durham was right. His offense was his defense. The right hand was not as good as the left, but it was more than good enough. He could take any punch from anyone, and he never backed off. Frazier was exactly what he always dreamed of being—the best.

4

The Tune-ups

By the time Leroy Johnson secured Ali's license in Georgia, discussions were already under way with Frazier's next opponent. Who would it be? George Foreman, the 1968 Olympic hero who recorded his sixteenth straight victory on the same evening Frazier defeated Ellis? Foreman, only twenty-one, was not ready. Former champion Floyd Patterson? Patterson, thirty-six, according to the Garden matchmaker, Teddy Brenner, was not willing. Oscar Bonavena? Frazier beat him twice. In the end, the choice was the light heavyweight champion Bob Foster.

Foster, who grew up in Albuquerque, New Mexico, developed his boxing skills in the air force. He was in more than a hundred fights, losing only three. In 1958, Foster went to Waukegan, Illinois, to try out for the U.S. squad in the Pan American Games. During those memorable days, another candidate for the team kept tapping on everyone's bunk in the middle of the night, boasting that he was going to whip them all. The kid was Cassius Clay. Foster thought Clay was harmless at first but soon began to find him annoying. One day he decided to teach him a lesson. "You can't beat me," Foster fired back. Clay insisted he could. The two took off for the gym a few blocks away to settle the argument.

"I spanked his little butt," said Foster proudly. "He couldn't punch, and if I fought a guy who couldn't punch, I would just

90

walk right into him. It was all for fun." Foster became so highly regarded that when his tour in the air force was about to expire, the other three branches of the military also made offers to obtain his services for their boxing teams. Foster chose the army because its commanders vowed to make him a master sergeant within three months of his discharge, and to move him and his wife and their four children to Fort Campbell, Kentucky. After a couple of months, however, Foster took off. "If I was that good, hell," he reasoned, "I might as well get out and make some money." In March 1961, in his first pro fight, he knocked out Duke Williams in the second round.

For the first eighteen months, fighting was easy for Foster—9 straight wins, 5 knockouts, each within 4 rounds. After that, fighting stopped being easy. In October 1962, Doug Jones, whom Foster knew from the air force, put him away in the eighth round. On July 10, 1964, with only seven days' notice, Foster was knocked out in the seventh round at the Garden by Ernie Terrell, who outweighed him by almost 20 pounds. Foster hung in there until a right to the chin from Terrell ended his chances. "I never should have fought him," Foster admitted. "He was the number one heavyweight contender and I was not even rated." Then why *did* he fight him? Foster answered without hesitation. "I had four kids, and nobody in my division wanted to fight me," he explained. "I had to take what I could get." On December 6, 1965, again on short notice, he opposed Zora Folley, dropping a 10-round decision, though the evening was not a total loss. "I learned how to fight fighting Folley," Foster said. "He was a good boxer. I probably hit him four or five times in the ten rounds."

Unfortunately, whatever he learned he could not put to use anytime soon. Still, he needed to make a living, so he worked the eight-to-four shift at the American Machine and Foundry in York, Pennsylvania, which made bombs. "I was earning $600 a week," Foster said. "That was good money back then. One thing my mother always taught me: 'I don't care what you do in your lifetime. I want you to always keep yourself a job.'" At least the work was not dangerous. "We just made the shell," he said. "We didn't load them."

Either way, Foster assumed his boxing career was kaput. Then one day a friend told him he would set him up with a new manager. Exactly one year after his loss to Folley, Foster was back between the ropes, knocking out LeRoy Green in the second. Soon there were more fights, four in five months, and more victories. Not a single opponent lasted beyond the third round. On May 24, 1968, Foster finally landed a shot at the light heavyweight title. If there was ever the slightest doubt in his mind that he would prevail, it went away when he saw his opponent, Dick Tiger, the light heavyweight champion, for the first time in person. "I looked at him and I thought, 'There is no way in the world this guy is going to beat me,'" Foster said. "'He is too small.'" Foster was right. There was no way. He knocked Tiger out in 4 rounds. It was only the second time since Tiger started his career in 1952, a span of 78 bouts, that he was knocked down and the first time he was knocked out.

From July 1968 through June 1970, Foster went 11 for 11, only three matches lasting past the fifth. Few men hit harder in any division than Foster. Nonetheless, was that a good enough reason to put him in the same ring with Smokin' Joe Frazier? Foster could not cope with heavyweights Ernie Terrell and Zora Folley, and neither was as lethal as Frazier. History was also against Foster. Seven previous light heavyweights (Jack O'Brien, George Carpentier, Tommy Loughran, John Henry Lewis, Joey Maxim, Archie Moore, and Billy Conn) had failed in their attempts to become the first from their class to win the heavyweight championship. Foster was not fazed, by the opponent or the odds. He stood to earn over $100,000 no matter how he fared, which was a long way from $600 a week making shells.

The fight was set for November 18, 1970, at Cobo Arena in Detroit. Detroit was supposed to be a great sports town, but it never got too excited over this event. Frazier was admired, but Frazier was not adored. A few days before the fight, Joe Falls, a columnist for the *Detroit Free Press*, asked the man on the street for his opinion of Frazier. The responses were most revealing. "He's in football, a coach I think," one woman suggested. "I'm sorry but I don't know who Joe Frazier is," another person replied. "I'm from out of town." The press did not get too excited either; many focused on the upcoming college football game between rivals Michigan and Ohio State. Two days before the bout, the *Detroit News*, the city's other major daily, did not print a single story about Frazier or Foster. The fight's press agent, Murray Goodman, was so frustrated by the lack of coverage that he took out paid advertisements in the local papers. Ultimately, only about 6,300 fans showed up at the 12,000-seat arena, the second smallest crowd for a heavyweight championship bout in modern times. (The lowest was 2,434 for the 1965 Ali-Liston rematch in Lewiston, Maine.) Promoters blamed the poor turnout on a General Motors strike that had hurt the local economy, although it hadn't prevented more than 9,000 from attending a closed-circuit showing of the Ali-Quarry fight a few weeks earlier.

One person who took the fight very seriously was Joe Frazier. Spending about five weeks at Vacation Valley, a resort in Pennsylvania's Pocono Mountains, he trained longer for Foster than for any prior opponent, sparring for about 175 rounds. For Mathis and Quarry, he went 100, for Ellis, 110. Frazier was also recuperating from a broken ankle he had suffered in April during a split on stage while appearing with the Knockouts at Caesar's Palace in Las Vegas. According to his friend Lester Pelemon, Frazier did not stop the performance. "Joe was tough," Pelemon said. Frazier could not afford to take Foster lightly. As Mike Bruce proved in Frazier's second bout, when he sent him to the canvas, any opponent could inflict damage at any moment, and this would be the worst moment of all. With the successful Ali comeback in Atlanta, one more win and Frazier would have done his part in securing the fight he and everybody yearned for, the fight of the century.

Despite giving away 21 pounds—Frazier weighed in at 209, his third heaviest in 26 bouts—Foster was confident. He was almost 5 inches taller and enjoyed a 5½-inch advantage in reach. In the opening round, he got in some good licks on Frazier while moving efficiently from side to side. "I had him," Foster said. "He tried to box with me in the first round, jabbing and moving, but his arms ain't that long. That's how I hit him with the right hand." He respected his opponent but he did not fear him. He did not fear anyone. "The only thing he can do is knock you out," Foster said. "He can't eat you." Frazier was flustered. While he knew Foster was certainly no bum, he also knew he was no Baryshnikov. Foster hurt him.

"When the fight was over, for some reason, it was just Joe and I in the hotel room," recalled Joe Hand, the Cloverlay administrator. "I had never seen him drink before, but there was a bottle of liquor in the room, and he took a lot of it. 'My ear hurts me so bad,' he said."

The solution came, as did so many over the years, from Yank Durham. Between rounds, he told his fighter he was holding his left hand too low. Frazier, he said, also needed to move in closer to Foster.

In the second round, Frazier followed Durham's advice, and no more advice, or rounds, became necessary. A hard left put Foster on the floor the first time. He barely stumbled to his feet at the count of nine. Frazier was hoping the fight would be stopped. He knew Foster was badly hurt and could offer no defense, and he knew his own power. Yet when the referee Tom Briscoe did not stop it, Frazier went back to work. "There's a man out there trying to take what you got," Frazier once said. "You're supposed to destroy him. He's trying to do the same to you. Why should you have pity on him?" Another left put Foster down for good. He didn't get up for almost a minute while his handlers worked over him. "You know what's coming," Foster recalled, "but it still gets to you before you think it's going to get to you." Afterward, Foster, like Ellis, could remember only one of the two knockdowns. While Frazier demonstrated his superiority once again, some fans in the balcony served as a reminder that the real challenge remained ahead of him.

"Ah-lee, Ah-lee, Ah-lee," they chanted.

Ali saw the Frazier-Foster bout on closed circuit at Municipal Auditorium in Atlanta. He was in town as the guest of Leroy Johnson.

"I want Joe Frazier," he screamed before throwing a few punches. "Is Joe Frazier this fast? Can he do anything about this? I'll show him who the heavyweight champion of the world is." First things first. Ali did not fight for forty-three months, but after a triumphant return against Jerry Quarry, he agreed to fight for the second time in only forty-three *days*. His opponent would be Oscar Bonavena, one of only two boxers (Scrap Iron Johnson was the other) to last the distance against Frazier, which he did twice, in 1966 and 1968.

Bonavena was the perfect choice for Ali's second post-exile contest. Bonavena would make him work harder than he did in only nine minutes against Quarry, yet he was not likely to beat him and sabotage what promised to be the most lucrative payday in boxing history. "We brought in Oscar," Pacheco said, "because he was such a tough guy with Frazier and we wanted to see if Ali could handle a tough guy who would sit there and take his punches." There were moments in Atlanta when the deposed champion looked more like an old Ali than the Ali of old, and an old Ali would be in tremendous danger against a battle-tested Frazier still very much in his prime. Since March 22, 1967, Ali had gone only 3 official rounds compared to Frazier's 67. "He needed a strenuous fight," Dundee maintained. Ali agreed. "I want to know within myself if I still have it, if I'm still champ."

The fight was to be held at Madison Square Garden, Ali's first in the building above Penn Station. Ali was never the Garden favorite that Frazier was. Of Ali's first thirty fights, the Garden hosted only three. He made his debut February 10, 1962, against a southpaw named Sonny Banks, and it was not an inspiring performance, to say the least. Banks stunned Ali with a left hook in the opening round, sending him to the floor for the first time in his career. Ali recovered, putting away Banks in the fourth. On March 13, 1963, however, Ali was fortunate to escape with a 10-round decision over Doug Jones after predicting he would knock him out in four. Ali was actually trailing until he rallied over the last three rounds, although not everyone was convinced he rallied enough. When they heard the decision, many fans chanted in unison: "Fix, fix, fix . . . fake, fake, fake." After capturing the crown from Liston in 1964, of his nine successful title defenses, only the final one, against Folley in 1967, was staged at the Garden.

His return to the mecca of boxing represented a significant political triumph for Ali. New York was the first place that officially put him out of work. The New York State Athletic Commission took away his crown only an hour or so after he failed to step over the line in Houston. The WBA banishment came the same day. Ali's lawyers attempted to regain his license in New York, but in December 1969, federal judge Marvin E. Frankel ruled that "the commission was well within the bounds of rationality when it concluded that the conviction and five-year sentence in this case justified refusal of the 1969 application." Ali's lawyers did not give up. They compiled a list of more than ninety convicted felons in the state who were allowed to box despite their convictions, with offenses that included desertion from the military and assaulting an officer. On September 14, 1970, Judge Walter R. Mansfield found the records "astounding" and ruled that the commission's suspension was "an intentional, arbitrary and unreasonable discrimination . . . not the even-handed administration of the law which the 14th Amendment requires." Ali took a day away from training for the Quarry fight to apply for his license. The commission chose not to appeal the decision and accepted his application. Ali was free to fight in New York.

The fight with Bonavena was scheduled for December 7. A worse date could not have been chosen. The most famous draft dodger in the United States was going to fight on the anniversary of the day that the Japanese bombed Pearl Harbor. The outrage generated among veterans came as no surprise. Among the offended was Neil W. Kelleher, a Republican assemblyman from Troy, just outside Albany, who, in a telegram to New York City mayor John Lindsay, called the match "a disgrace to the people of New York State." Kelleher joined the navy two days after Pearl Harbor and served three years on a destroyer in the South Pacific. "December 7 has never left my mind," he said in 2006. Herbert R. Rainwater, the national commander of the Veterans of Foreign Wars, asked veterans to boycott the fight, saying it was "an affront to the memories of American soldiers entombed on the U.S.S. *Arizona*." Efforts to change the date were unsuccessful, the commission claiming that it would result in "utter chaos." Tom Kenville, who worked in publicity at the Garden, said that the building, which opened in early 1968, was booked with an event almost every night of the year to "pay off the debt to build it." In December, the NBA's Knicks and the NHL's Rangers, for instance, played home games at the Garden.

Bonavena, nicknamed "Ringo" because he wore his long, dark hair similar to the Beatles' Ringo Starr, marched to his own drum. He was disqualified in the final match of the 1963 Pan American Games for biting his opponent, Lee Carr, on the chest. His behavior was erratic outside the ropes, too. "To make fights with this guy was just terrible," according to Don Majeski, an agent for boxing promoters and managers. "He would pull out of fights, or threaten to pull out, unless he got more money. It was always problematical for everybody who ever dealt with him." Teddy Brenner claimed he took an extra $5,000 from the Garden box office to guarantee that Bonavena would keep his commitment to fight George Chuvalo in June 1966. In the fall of 1970, as the Ali-Bonavena bout approached, Brenner remained anxious. "I didn't sleep nights," he later wrote. "I was worried about what Bonavena would pull."

Few questioned the Argentinian's will in the ring. "He was just a little rock of stone," Majeski said. "He would have his hands sort of spread out when he would come in, bob and weave a little bit, and had like a low center of gravity so you couldn't really knock him out with a flush blow. He would sort of smother your punches so you couldn't really land well." Bonavena, boxing historian Bert Sugar said, "didn't lead with a hand. He led with his chest. He was the most awkward thing you ever saw. He had no balance."

Oscar Bonavena was not the first prizefighter from his small country to find success. In 1923, Luis Firpo, known as the Wild Bull of the Pampas, nearly upset Jack Dempsey at New York's Polo Grounds to become the first Hispanic to win the world heavyweight championship. After Firpo was floored seven times by Dempsey in the opening round, he unloaded with a smashing right to the jaw that knocked his opponent through the ropes, crashing into a group of writers who helped him back into the ring. Some have argued that Dempsey should have been counted out because he did not get up on his own. Even so, the staggered champion was perhaps one solid punch or two away from going down for good, but Firpo, befitting his nickname, was wild, and the danger passed. In the next round, Dempsey regained control and knocked him out. Nonetheless, Luis Firpo became a hero back home as the man who had knocked down the great Jack Dempsey. Another star in Latin America was Pascual Perez, a flyweight who was his country's first world champion in the mid-1950s. While Bonavena never became an elite fighter, he was very popular in Argentina.

Bonavena fought his first eight pro bouts in the state of New York, winning all of them, seven by knockout, three in the opening round. The fighters he defeated were closer to pretenders than contenders, but winning was sure better than losing, and, besides, the checks didn't bounce. He was guided in the early days by Charley Goldman, Marciano's trainer. Goldman, in his late seventies, predicted Bonavena would also win a title someday if given the opportunity. "He's learning faster than Rocky did and he is faster with his fists and his feet," Goldman said. "And like Rocky, he's a natural puncher with both hands. He's the greatest natural heavyweight I've ever seen."

Maybe so, but Bonavena was not destined to end his career undefeated like Marciano. The first setback came February 26, 1965, in a 10-round decision to Zora Folley. So much for the bright lights of New York. His next bout was in Argentina and so were the next 12 after that. He won them all, except when he was disqualified in the eighth round against Jose Giorgetti. A month later, when the two squared off again, Bonavena was awarded the decision. Back in New York, after he beat the favored Chuvalo, came the first loss to Frazier. Bonavena went home once again, winning his next nine fights before he was invited to participate in the WBA elimination tournament. In the quarterfinal match, in Frankfurt, against German Karl Mildenberger, a 4–1 favorite, Bonavena knocked him down four times and took a unanimous 12-round decision. He lost in the semis to Jimmy Ellis. From December 1967 to December 1970, he fought only once in the States, the second confrontation with Frazier. Entering the duel with Ali, Bonavena was 46–6–1.

In his corner for the Ali fight was Gil Clancy, one of the most respected trainers in the business. Clancy guided Emile Griffith to five titles in the middleweight and welterweight divisions. Aware of Bonavena's reputation for being difficult, Clancy didn't come aboard immediately when the fighter first asked him. Once Bonavena agreed to give Clancy half the money up front, he signed on. "I never had one bit of trouble with him at training camp or anyplace else," Clancy said. "He did his job every day." Clancy advised Bonavena to stay in the corner and try to lure Ali into chasing him, which would presumably neutralize his superior quickness. From that vantage point, his fighter could score with body punches.

"My idea is an appeal to Clay's pride," Clancy said. "He claims to be the champion and he boasts about how the power of his punch has improved. He won't want to look bad in front of all his admirers, so I'm figuring he'll have to go after Bonavena, which means changing his own style." Ali was not concerned. If Bonavena remained a stationary target, he figured, he would not have to expend nearly as much energy, and his opponent would become more vulnerable to the jabs he would unleash before quickly slipping out of hitting range. Dundee assembled the game plan. "I had Jimmy Ellis in with the guy," he said. "You couldn't time a shot on him. You had to hit him with that big, heavy jab."

Three days before the fight, Ali sparred for 12 rounds, which was not how boxers normally prepared so close to the opening bell. In camp, Ali allowed his sparring partners to pound away at his body. He believed the punishment would strengthen his ability to absorb blows in the future and help him slip away and retreat. Ferdie Pacheco did not buy into Ali's reasoning. "We had sparring partners who could punch," Pacheco said. "He had a tremendous body. *How* tremendous? His kidneys are completely shot. I told him [years later], 'The kidneys are a very delicate set of filters but if you keep smashing them, those filters start disintegrating.'"

Outside the ropes, he was the Ali of old, attempting to convince the public there was genuine animosity between him and his adversary. Ali called Bonavena "the bull" and promised he would be "mine in nine." Bonavena went along, referring to Ali as a "black kangaroo" and ridiculing him for evading the draft. "Why you no go in the army? You chicken? Chick, chick, chick." He even borrowed a page from the Ali playbook, predicting that the former champion would fall in round 11. The Garden sold out, producing a live gate of $650,000, a record for a nontitle bout. Top Rank Inc., the promoter, lined up about 150 closed-circuit outlets across the nation.

The afternoon of the fight was bizarre, even for Muhammad Ali. The typical fighter goes to the weigh-in ceremony in the late morning and returns to his hotel to rest and focus on how he plans to knock the other guy's brains out before he knocks out his, Survival 101. After the weigh-in—he checked in at 212, Bonavena, 204—Ali went for a walk. In Manhattan! In the middle of the day! In December! Budd Schulberg, who spent the day with him, wrote that Ali purchased an overcoat at Saks Fifth Avenue and a few tapes at Sam Goody for his wife, Belinda, before finally heading back to the hotel.

"He walked around, stopped, and talked to people," Schulberg said. "He was like a tourist, window shopping, bumming along on his own pace. It was amazing. I had never seen anyone so cavalier. It was typical Ali. Angelo was anxious but Angelo knew that he couldn't change Ali. Ali was Ali." The night became even more bizarre. On his way to the Garden, after only one block, Ali stepped out of his giant black limo to take a less luxurious form of transportation, dragging along members of his entourage, the shepherd tending to his flock once again. "He said, 'Let's go on the subway with the people,'" Gene Kilroy said. "No one ever did that to go to a fight. All the people were yelling, 'Ah-lee, Ah-lee.' He fed off that."

Shortly before 11 p.m., the fight started. Early on, Bonavena landed a few left hooks, although two were below the belt, which resulted in warnings from referee Mark Conn. When the bell rang, Conn told the other judges, Joe Eppy and Jack Gordon, that the infractions meant Bonavena was not eligible to be awarded the first round. In the third, Ali connected with several combinations. He scored points but looked slow and sluggish. "Where is that boxing?" asked Howard Cosell, anchoring the closed-circuit telecast. "Where is the speed of hands? One wonders if Ali is hurt. Strange thing to see, ladies and gentlemen. You've not seen Ali like this before." Angelo Dundee had probably never seen Ali like this, either. "I was givin' him hell cause he was letting the guy take charge, instead of moving," Dundee said decades later. "The rhythm wasn't there. The bounce wasn't there."

Nor was the banter, perhaps the clearest indication that he was not the same Ali. During one break, Herbert Muhammad, his manager, left his ringside seat and climbed the steps in Ali's corner. "I told Muhammad to get serious," Herbert said. Dundee was not surprised to see Herbert Muhammad show concern. "Poor Herbert use to die a thousand deaths on the fights," Dundee said. Pacheco was not feeling much better. "Let me tell you, halfway through that fight, I was thinking, 'This guy [Ali] is so not ready," Pacheco said. "Bonavena is there to be knocked down and he ain't doing it. And he's not going to do it because he can't do it. Because he's tired." Round nine arrived, Ali's chance to come through on his prediction and make the crowd, and the press, forget what they had seen so far. He got in a few good shots, but Bonavena got in a few of his own, and when the bell rang, the fight was far from over.

Oscar Bonavena was not Jerry Quarry. He did not cut easily. He did not adopt the wrong strategy. He kept lunging forward, throwing punches from every angle, as awkward as ever. Round 11 arrived, Bonavena's chance to make good on his prediction. He landed a solid right to Ali's head. Bundini Brown shouted "Dance and box!" and "The world is watching!"

Yet, on this unexpected night, even Brown could not help Ali pull out the old magic. He wasn't floating and he wasn't stinging. Over the next few rounds, neither man inflicted any significant damage. During Round 14, some of the 19,417 spectators began to boo loudly, and who could blame them? They paid good money—

ringside seats went for $75—for *this*? The fighter who called himself the greatest of all time was having trouble against an opponent with six losses and a draw. Then came Round 15, finally, mercifully. Ali had gone this far only twice in his career. The first was against Chuvalo in 1966, when he did everything he could to put him away. "Good God, we hit that guy five thousand times," Pacheco said. "It was just that Chuvalo could take anybody's punch . . . *anybody*." The second was against Terrell in 1967, when Ali did everything he could to keep him on his feet. He wanted Terrell to absorb as much punishment as possible for insisting on calling him Cassius Clay. "What's my name?" Ali shouted between punches. "What's my name?"

Against Bonavena, Ali, despite his poor showing, was well ahead on the judges' cards entering the final three minutes, and Gil Clancy knew it. He told his fighter he needed to knock Ali out. Bonavena tried, but when his jaw got in the way of an Ali left hook, he was the one who went down. The boos turned into cheers. Ali was the greatest again. Bonavena was on his feet at six and took the mandatory eight count, but another left and right from Ali seconds later sent him back to the canvas. He rose at seven. "Can you continue?" the referee asked. Yes, Bonavena said, nodding. He did, although not for long. Ali, who never went to a neutral corner, a mistake by the experienced Mark Conn, knocked Bonavena down for the third time with just under a minute to go in the round. Conn waived his arms, invoking the three-knockdown rule, which automatically ended the fight. Ali raised his arms. The final two minutes were impressive, but not nearly impressive enough to wipe out the first forty-two.

"When he knocked him out in 15, it caused people to think, alas, there was no problem after all," Pacheco said. "There was a problem. It took him 15 rounds to knock him out. It was a *big* problem." One problem was that Ali did not take his opponent seriously. "The night before the fight with Bonavena," Ali admitted months later, "I stayed up until 6 a.m. with some friends in Harlem. We were talking about my fight with Joe Frazier. That's how much attention I paid to Bonavena." Dundee offered a similar assessment. "Every day in the gym, he'd talk Frazier," Dundee said. "I finally had to show him Bonavena's picture. This is who you are fighting, I told him."

Nonetheless, Ali's unblemished record was still intact, and so were the plans to fight Frazier. The New York papers were soon filled with speculation. Will it be at the Garden or the Astrodome in Houston? Will it be as early as mid-February? These were legitimate questions, but there was one question that did not come up in the days after the Bonavena fight, and, given Ali's listless performance and his inactivity—only 18 rounds in 45 months—it was perhaps the most legitimate of all. Was Muhammad Ali truly ready to take on Joe Frazier? The reason nobody mentioned it can be summed up in the one word that trumps any other in the callous world of professional boxing: money.

"Everybody wanted their money now," Pacheco said. "Don't fuck with it. We got it now. Let's get the money. Let's go, let's go, let's go." Waiting was too risky. If, for example, Ali were to lose his next fight—boxing, like any sport, was not immune to major upsets—the payday with Frazier would be gone. Contributing to the sense of urgency was the lingering fear that, any day, the Supreme Court would decide not to hear Ali's appeal, and he would head to prison. Pacheco claims he made a case for a few more fights before Frazier, but nobody would listen. "You have to remember something," Pacheco said. "I was just a doctor. I wasn't there as a boxing maven." The *Times*'s Robert Lipsyte was more understanding. "He probably could have used a little more time," Lipsyte said, "but here was a guy who was denied doing what he wanted to do for three and a half years, and all of a sudden, it opened up so he went for it."

Frazier was probably more anxious for the fight than anyone. Ten months since disposing of Ellis, he was still not "free at last." Frazier watched the Ali-Bonavena fight on closed circuit from the Monticello Raceway, about 90 miles away, where his group was performing. He told the press it was a boring fight and that Ali was fortunate to prevail. "I only cared that he'd won," Frazier later wrote, "making him eligible to get what he had coming from me."

Yank Durham was also ready. "Joe Frazier's here," he told Ali during a party after the Bonavena match. "If Joe Frazier dreamed he was here," Ali responded, "he better wake up and apologize. You tell him he's in trouble. Do you really believe you can whip me?" Replied Durham, who was never intimidated by Ali, "In six. Honest, I'm so sure of it."

And so 1970 drew to a close, the first year of a new decade much like the end of the last, with a nation fractured at the core, and little relief in sight. Peace in Southeast Asia was not at hand, as Secretary of State Henry Kissinger would say nearly two years later. Yet in the small, inconsequential universe of professional boxing, at least, the matter of which fighter could rightfully be considered the superior heavyweight was finally going to be settled. Muhammad Ali and Joe Frazier were deserving champions, undefeated, two of the best in history, but each still had something to prove, to the fans, to the press, and to themselves. Each needed the other.

5

Jack, Jerry, and the Deal

They were men who knew the boxing business inside and out and men who did not, yet smart men, all of them, who recognized the record-setting potential of an Ali-Frazier showdown. The classic duels of the past—Johnson versus Jeffries, Tunney versus Dempsey, Louis versus Schmeling—made good money in their day, but strictly from the live gate, the amount spent by fans purchasing tickets. By 1970, there was a way to make more money in promoting prizefights, a lot more, and these men were eager to take advantage.

This way can be traced back to the evening of June 15, 1951, when Joe Louis took on Lee Savold at the old Garden. This duel was not a classic. Savold was thirty-five, his best days behind him. The same was true, sadly, for the beloved Louis, thirty-seven, in the ring for the seventh time since he came out of retirement. The Brown Bomber put his opponent away with a left hook in the sixth, his fifty-fifth and final triumph by knockout. Four months later, Marciano retired him for good. The Louis-Savold bout was the first aired on closed-circuit television, at eight outlets in six cities: Washington, Chicago, Cleveland, Pittsburgh, Baltimore, and Albany, New York. About 22,000 fans paid 50 cents to $1.30 per ticket, generating additional revenue for the fight's promoters. In 1955, the Marciano–Archie Moore title bout produced $1,125,000 in closed-circuit revenue. The 1962 Liston-Patterson match brought in a record $4.5 million, with 600,000 seats sold at 247 outlets.

Promoters no longer needed to fill large outdoor facilities, as was the case when about 80,000 attended the Louis-Schmeling rematch at Yankee Stadium on June 22, 1938, the fight of the century—until March 8, 1971. As the closed-circuit technology evolved, the idea became to put as many asses in as many seats in as many facilities as possible. Only 5,000 fans showed up at Municipal Auditorium (its capacity) in Atlanta for Ali versus Quarry, but the fight was a financial success because it was shown at approximately 200 venues across the country. Ali versus Bonavena sold out in 18 locations in the New York metropolitan area alone. If that many people paid to catch Ali in two nontitle bouts against inferior opponents, then surely even more would turn out to see if he could retrieve his crown from Frazier. Those hoping to promote the fight reportedly included Sonny Werblin, the former owner of the New York Jets football franchise, who teamed with *Tonight Show* host Johnny Carson; the General Electric Company; Top Rank's Bob Arum and Fred Hofheinz; and Harry Markson and Teddy Brenner from Madison Square Garden. The fight to land the fight promised to provide nearly as much intrigue as the fight itself.

Soon after the Ali-Bonavena fight, Markson and Brenner boarded a train to Philadelphia on a Sunday morning to present a formal proposal to Yank Durham and Joe Frazier. Markson and Brenner knew the fight game as well as anyone. Markson started as a sportswriter for the *Bronx News*, joining the Garden in 1933 to work in publicity. He learned from one of the best, Mike Jacobs, who promoted the Louis title fights, including the much-anticipated rematch against Billy Conn in 1946. Five years earlier, Conn took Louis, the champion since 1937, to the thirteenth round.

One lesson Markson picked up from Jacobs was that setting ticket prices did not always result from a thorough analysis of the marketplace. After Louis-Conn II was made at Yankee Stadium, a columnist asked Jacobs how much he figured to charge for ringside seats: $40, $60, $80, or $100. Jacobs said he was not sure. The columnist wrote that Jacobs was considering $100, higher than any previous fight. The next day, money orders and cables arrived from people seeking tickets at $100 apiece. "He hadn't planned to charge $100," Markson said, "but when he saw the response, he realized it was the proper price." Markson did not make enemies as many did in his corrupt business. "He was honest and dignified," said the *Times*'s Dave Anderson. "You never had the feeling that he was trying to scheme you." Brenner, a Garden fixture since the late 1950s, was regarded as the premier matchmaker in the business. "He created the phrase 'styles make fights,'" said Bruce Trampler, a matchmaker for Top Rank in Las Vegas. "He could see the fight before it happened."

Markson and Brenner maintained a distinct advantage over their competition. Nothing in the sweet science rivaled the tradition of Madison Square Garden. The first Garden opened its doors on May 31, 1879, at the corner of Fifth Avenue and Twenty-third Street in lower Manhattan. In 1890, a new version, boasting the world's largest indoor swimming pool and a roof garden, replaced the original. Among the dignitaries on opening night were the Whitneys, J. P. Morgan, General William Tecumseh Sherman, and Stanford White, the Garden's architect. White was an incorrigible playboy who spent the last evening of his life in a building he designed. He made the mistake of fooling around with the wrong woman, actress Evelyn Nesbitt, the wife of millionaire Harry Thaw. On June 25, 1906, during a performance of the musical reveue *Mamzelle Champagne*, Thaw shot White three times in the head from point-blank range. The court case became widely known as the trial of the century and was chronicled in the 1981 film *Ragtime*, featuring the final screen appearance of Hollywood icon James Cagney. The Garden moved uptown to 50th Street and Eighth Avenue in 1925, and finally, in 1968, to its present location atop Penn Station.

The first big heavyweight fight in the Garden took place on July 17, 1882, between John L. Sullivan and Tug Wilson from England. Nobody was tougher in those days than John L. Sullivan, and he knew it and so did everyone else. Sullivan promised Wilson $1,000 and half the gate receipts if he was still on his feet at the end of four rounds. The overmatched Wilson, as the story goes, resorted to every possible tactic to avoid a knockout. He held. He clinched. He fell to the floor twenty-four times. The following day's account in the *New York Times* described the action: "He (Sullivan) pounded Mr. Wilson over into his corner, and was, to all intents and purposes, bent upon beating Mr. Wilson into a state of insensibility before the close of the first round." Nonetheless, after 4 rounds, Tug Wilson was still standing and, presumably, received his reward. A year later, Sullivan took on another British fighter, Charlie Mitchell, prevailing in three rounds when Alexander Williams, a police captain, called a halt "just short of murder." The Sullivan legend continued to grow. In 1884, he was arrested during the second round of a bout with Al Greenfield for "cruel and inhuman manner, outraging decency, shocking humanity, and tending to corrupt public morals." Sullivan soon fought again, but boxing in the Garden lost its influence in the ensuing years, with numerous fights held at neighborhood clubs in New York.

The Garden resurfaced as a major stage in the 1920s due to the marketing talents of George Lewis "Tex" Rickard, who promoted the 1919 title bout in Toledo, Ohio, between Jess Willard, the conquerer of Jack Johnson, and Jack Dempsey; Dempsey prevailed. Rickard helped secure passage of a bill, introduced by Democratic state Senator Jimmy Walker, to regulate boxing in New York. The city's elite started to embrace it, including Anne Morgan, the daughter of J. P., who even took part in the promotion of the lightweight battle between Benny Leonard and Richie Mitchell. In 1924, Rickard was involved in raising money for the construction of a new Garden, with six millionaires pledging $1 million apiece. The first fight in the third Garden took place on December 11, 1925, between light heavyweights Paul Berlenbach and Jack Delaney. In the 1930s, after Rickard died from an infected appendix, Mike Jacobs took over. By the end of the decade and throughout the 1940s, the best in the sport fought in the Garden: Henry Armstrong, Sugar Ray Robinson, and Joe Louis, who successfully defended his crown eight times there. Friday night became known as fight night. "You congregated in front of the Garden," historian Bert Sugar recalled. "It was just the place to be."

In 1957, however, Judge Sylvester Ryan ruled that the Garden, along with the International Boxing Club, had taken part in a conspiracy in restraint of trade and monopolized fights in violation of the Sherman Act. The IBC was forced to break up. Between 1952 and 1967, when Ali knocked out Folley, no heavyweight title bouts were staged in the Garden. Nonetheless, in the fall of 1970, in the minds of many, it remained boxing's most hallowed ground.

Markson and Brenner benefited from a relationship with Frazier and Durham dating back to the Wipperman fight in 1966. The Garden, along with the New York State Athletic Commission, gave Frazier the opportunity to capture a title for the first time when he prevailed over Buster Mathis on March 4, 1968, and staged his unification bout with Jimmy Ellis two years later. The Garden also made Frazier a rich man. He collected more than $400,000 for fighting Quarry, and over $300,000 for fighting Ellis. That was a lot of money in the late 1960s and early 1970s, but Markson and Brenner surely knew that they would need to offer a lot more to snare him this time. Durham made it clear that he and Frazier were going to follow the money, and who could blame them? Durham toiled for many years in a Philadelphia gym before the sport paid him back, and there was no guarantee that anything close to this kind of windfall for a single fight would ever be within his grasp again. Frazier was not a kid anymore. He was to turn twenty-seven in January 1971, and with the way he approached his job, in the ring and in camp, a lengthy career was not very likely.

Markson and Brenner met with Frazier and Durham at the Cloverlay gym on Broad Street. This was no time for small talk. This was the time for zeroes, lots of them. Their offer was a guaranteed $1.25 million to each fighter against 35 percent of the live gate and the ancillary income, which encompassed the closed-circuit revenue. "Yank, Joe, Harry Markson, and I sat down . . . with yellow pads and pens," Brenner recalled. "Joe started to write it down. Yank started to write it down. But they couldn't put the commas in the right spots.

They kept writing the numbers but the commas kept going in the wrong places." The commas were, eventually, put in the proper places, but the two Garden envoys went back to New York without a deal. Nothing was wrong with their offer. Their offer was extremely generous. Only there was a better one on the table.

Born in Hamilton, Ontario, on October 25, 1912, Jack Kent Cooke grew up with big dreams. When he was thirteen, he overheard his father, Ralph, who sold picture frames, and a few friends discussing their recent commissions. One salesman mentioned how he was raking in $50 a week. Most teenagers would have been impressed. Not this teenager. "Wait until I'm your age," Jack blurted out. "I'll be a millionaire!" A few years later, the stock market crashed. The Cookes were not affected as severely as some families, but they were not spared either. While the family held on to its house in a comfortable part of Toronto known as the Beaches, Ralph Cooke lost a lot of his savings and his job. He left home to sell encyclopedias door to door, traveling all the way to western Canada. He was gone so often that, according to family lore, the neighbors kiddingly referred to his wife, Nancy, as "the rich widow down the street." The impact of the Great Depression on their ambitious child was large, and lasting. "To the day he died, he was very cautious," said Jack Kent Cooke's son, John. "He was not impulsive. He gave the impression that he would do things quickly but in fact they were well reasoned out."

In 1934, with his bride, Barbara Jean Carnegie, and $50 he borrowed from his dad, Jack Kent Cooke took off in a 1930 Ford Roadster to sell the *New Educator Encylopedia* in western Canada for $39.95 a set. Like father, like son. Their journey of well over a thousand miles was often difficult. One night, in the province of Saskatchewan, the rain came down so hard that their car got stuck in the mud. They went to sleep, and it was not the first time they spent the night in their Roadster. The next morning, hungry and broke, they walked into the nearest town, Verigin, population less than 300. While Jack went in search of a sale, his wife hung out in the kitchen of the only hotel. The hours went by, slowly, torturously. She smelled the wonderful pies and bread being prepared for the hotel guests but was not offered a single piece. Jack did not fare much better.

"I saw the local grain elevator operator and the local minister and the local doctor, whoever the hell I thought might have a $5 deposit on a perfectly dreadful set of encyclopedias," he said. "But all I got were post-dated checks. I couldn't use them to get my car unstuck." As evening approached, Jack was running out of potential customers. When school finally let out, he spent more than two hours with the local principal. He even went to his house and watched as the principal's wife, who was flashing Jack dirty looks, put her husband's dinner on the table. The perseverance paid off, as it would pay off countless times in the decades ahead. The principal handed Jack five dollars, which must have seemed like a million at that moment, to leave him and his wife alone. The money was enough for Jack and Jeannie, as he called her, to buy gas and sandwiches and get their car out of the mud. Jack later said that day was when he hit bottom.

In 1936, he started working for Colgate-Palmolive in northern Ontario. He was making pretty good money in those days, but he definitely wasn't going to make his first million selling soap. One day, without an appointment, Jack tracked down Roy Herbert Thomson, who owned a newspaper and several radio stations in Ontario, to ask him for a job. Thomson said there was nothing he could do, but Jack won him over. He could sell anything, especially himself. Thomson hired him to manage a radio station he was buying in Stratford. The job was perfect for Jack, who loved music. When he was a boy, he and his mother spent nights listening to the radio. He took lessons in the clarinet, saxophone, and piano. In high school, he formed a twelve-piece band, Oley Kent and His Bourgeois Canadians, which was available for parties, dinners, cruise ships, and weddings.

In his new job, Jack was no longer on the bottom, although times were still tough. With the radio station in the red, he didn't accept a salary the first few months and often slept in his office.

"Jack and Roy Thomson hardly had a pot to pee in when they first started," said Jim Lacher, Jack's former treasurer in Los Angeles. "Jack used to tell me that he and Roy didn't have enough money to buy lunch. They would go and have a cup of soup and then ask for ketchup and then ask for saltines. They would fill up on saltines and ketchup." Gradually, under Jack's guidance, the station started to make money. He was on his way. Before too long, Thomson asked him to manage three other stations. In 1944, at the age of thirty-two, he became the youngest radio station owner-operator in Canada. Two decades after he overheard his dad and the other salesmen, the first million was his, and more would come, although, like many who lived through the Depression, he appreciated the value of every cent.

"He was staying at the Waldorf-Astoria and wanted to have a party for the press," said Don Fraser, who worked for him in Los Angeles. "He says, 'Don't get the liquor from the hotel. They charge too much.' So I had to get beer from one place, vodka from another."

In 1951, Jack bought the Toronto Maple Leafs baseball team in the Class AAA International League. The Maple Leafs doubled their attendance in his first full year. He tried on several occasions to acquire a major league franchise for Toronto but did not succeed. In 1959, Jack made a bid for a TV license but was turned down. A year later, he moved to northern California and became a United States citizen. He played golf at Pebble Beach, but a life of leisure was not for Jack Kent Cooke, then or ever. "That was a dopey idea, retiring," he later admitted. He missed the action. "He often said to me, 'Doing a business deal, David, is better than fornication,'" writer Dave Kindred said.

Jack became involved in the cable television industry, which was beginning to take off, and owned a 25 percent interest in the NFL's Washington Redskins. In 1965, he paid a record $5.175 million for the NBA's Los Angeles Lakers and, months later, spent $2 million to acquire the new hockey franchise awarded to Los Angeles, the Kings, after promising to build a new arena, which he named the Forum, and which cost him another $16 million. With its white Romanesque columns, the place became known as the

Fabulous Forum, and nothing Jack Kent Cooke did in his professional life ever gave him more pride. Bud Furillo, the late sports editor of the *Los Angeles Herald-Examiner*, said that Jack once told him, "Bud, when I fly into Los Angeles International, over the Forum, I feel like Sir Christopher Wren who built St. Paul's Cathedral. This is my monument, Bud.'" John Kent Cooke said that his father asked the airlines to mention the Forum whenever their planes flew directly over, "and, by golly, a lot of the pilots did."

Jack Kent Cooke demanded from the people who worked for him as much as he demanded from himself, which was a great deal. "There were intercoms in the offices," ex-Lakers publicist Stu Zanville said. "You'd see people jump six feet up when he called them. With everything going on in his life, he still read every word of my release. I was impressed—and terrified." Chick Hearn, the legendary radio and television play-by-play announcer for the Lakers, once told Don Fraser, "If you last a year, you will be with him as long as you want." Of course, lasting a year was the hard part.

"When I went to work for him, he had hired and fired seven treasurers in two years," Lacher remembered. Lacher somehow lasted almost thirty years. His secret? "You just didn't argue with Jack," he explained. "If he made a rash decision, I would say, 'Jack, is that really what you want to do? How about trying it this way?' He would always listen to me." Alan Rothenberg, Jack's attorney, also got along very well with his boss, although he acknowledged, "with him, you were either friend or foe. There was nothing in between. There was very little gray in his world." John Kent Cooke offers no apologies for the way his father conducted his affairs. "Some people can't take the pressure and when things were not done right, dad would let them know it," Cooke said. "On the other hand, when it was done right, he would be profuse in his praise."

The call came in mid-December. Jack Kent Cooke and Jerry Perenchio would meet soon. There was not much time.

Andrew Jerrold Perenchio was born on December 20, 1930, in Fresno, California. At a critical period in his life, Jerry, too, learned about loss. His father, A. J., was co-owner of the Sunny-side Winery, one of California's oldest wineries. Starting at age twelve, Jerry received an allowance of $150 a week, and, at fifteen, he was sent to the prestigious Black-Foxe Military Institute in Los Angeles. In his senior year, he was voted the school's "biggest showman and promoter." After Jerry enrolled at UCLA, however, the world he knew and relied on ceased to exist. His father, report-edly, squandered most of the family's money with deals that back-fired. "I'm busted, I'm broke—no more allowances," he told his son. Jerry did not forgive his father for years. "He had to put him-self through college," said Jacquelyn, his former wife, "and I don't think he ever forgot it. It hurt him that he didn't have his education paid for by his dad. He had gone to private schools. He had gone to Black-Foxe. He had gone to all of this. All of a sudden, nothing was there for him."

Jerry started over, forming a company, Party Management, which booked bands for fraternity parties from UC-Berkeley to San Diego State. By the time he graduated in 1954, Jerry later claimed, he was grossing $500,000 per year. After college, he joined the air force, where he became a jet pilot and flight instructor, but the mil-itary was only a detour. In 1958, Jerry started working for the talent agency Music Corporation of America, where he found his mentor, company chairman Lew Wasserman, arguably the most powerful man in Hollywood. Wasserman kept the stars in the spotlight, the agents in the shadows, and the press in the dark. He didn't give interviews, and one day neither would Jerry.

"He admired him terrifically," Jacquelyn Perenchio said, "and credited him with his real training and discipline." In less than two years, he became one of MCA's vice presidents. "His clients didn't have to call," she said, "because always he knew what was expected. He went to every opening of every show." Shelly Saltman, who worked for years with singer Andy Williams, said Jerry was unique in the amount of attention he paid to his clients, who over the years included some of the biggest names in show biz: Marlon Brando, Elizabeth Taylor, Richard Burton, Jane Fonda, Glen Campbell, Henry Mancini, and Williams.

"I was with him when Andy did his first appearance in England," Saltman said. "There are a lot of agents who are order takers who just do the job and show up. Jerry sold his clients. He was a master at turning negatives into positives." In the summer of 1962, Jerry faced one of those negatives when the Justice Department filed an antitrust suit against MCA, contending it was a talent agency and a production company. MCA was forced to break up. Jerry started over again. By 1971, his share of Chartwell Artists, named after the estate belonging to his hero, Winston Churchill, was reported to be worth close to $2 million. Like Jack Kent Cooke, Jerry Perenchio knew how to put deals together. When he found out that Caesar's Palace in Las Vegas, in which he was an investor, was looking for a buyer, Jerry, according to his then wife, Jaquelyn, flew from Las Vegas to Miami to meet with Clifford Perlman, who owned a restaurant chain with his brother, Stuart. Jerry, Jaquelyn said, earned a finder's fee of about $800,000.

In late 1970, he went to London on business. Among the messages he received from his office in Los Angeles was one from Frank Fried, a Chicago music promoter who often booked Williams and Mancini. Jerry returned the call. Fried told him about a recent meeting with Herbert Muhammad, who asked if he was interested in bidding for the rights to the Ali-Frazier fight. The meeting was arranged by Gene Dibble, Fried's neighbor in Chicago, who was friendly with Muhammad and the other Black Muslims handling Ali's business affairs. Fried declined, but informed Muhammad he knew others who might be interested, prompting the call to Los Angeles. Jerry had gone to Atlanta for the Ali-Quarry fight and watched the Ali-Bonavena duel on closed circuit in Los Angeles. "I knew right away I wanted it," Jerry said. "This was the sort of thing I'd been training 20 years for."

Jerry wasted no time. He told Don Loze, Chartwell's executive vice president, to put $250,000 into the company account, allowing him to write a check when the time came. The Ali and Frazier camps would need to know that Jerry was a serious player. Loze spent the night putting together a chart of the company's potential cash flow. The next morning, he went to City National Bank in

Los Angeles to seek a loan, but he had to wait while the bank president, Bill Olsen, working his last day before going on vacation for the Christmas holidays, wrapped up other business. Just then, Henry Traub, Loze's friend, who was also one of the bank's major depositers, walked in to give Olsen his Christmas present. He brought Loze into Olsen's office. "Bill," Traub suggested, "why don't you talk to Don? It's obviously important." Olsen agreed. After Loze told him he needed the money for the Ali-Frazier fight, Olsen asked him the questions any bank president would ask someone borrowing $250,000. Loze gave the right answers and got the loan.

The loan was only the first step. Still ahead was the difficult task of raising the $5 million required to prevail over the Garden, Sonny Werblin, Top Rank, or any other competitors who might surface. Jerry, from London, and Loze, in Los Angeles, began working the phones. Spending $16,000 on long-distance charges, Jerry ran the idea by more than seventy people, reportedly including Aristotle Onassis. Finally, Loze said, a call to an L.A. investment firm led to a stockbroker named David Stern, which led to the appointment with Jack Kent Cooke. "Jerry had a list of things he wanted to say to him," Loze said. "He wrote all of them down." The meeting at the Forum was pivotal. Jerry was looking for someone to say yes, and soon, though according to Jim Lacher, he made what could have been a terrible mistake before the meeting began. "He was about an hour late," Lacher said, "which you did not do with Cooke." Fortunately for Jerry, Jack was very interested in promoting the fight and did not make an issue of his tardiness. (Jack later informed reporters that his group, in fact, had approached Angelo Dundee about securing the rights to the fight several weeks before he received the call from Jerry.)

The meeting went very well. "He'll do it," Jerry told Loze. Jack was excited, too. A spectacular event such as Ali versus Frazier deserved a spectacular setting, and he knew just the place.

So did Fred Hofheinz, whose family owned the lease to the Astrodome. The Astrodome held a number of advantages over the Forum and the Garden. The Forum and the Garden could only sell about 20,000 seats apiece. The capacity of the Astrodome was about 70,000, which meant that the live gate could reach $2 million for the first time ever. Texas also did not impose a tax on the ancillary income, which was expected to hit $4 million at the time, resulting in a savings of about $200,000. Finally, Ali had enjoyed a lot of success in the Dome. On November 14, 1966, he stopped Cleveland Williams in the third round in what many boxing experts considered his most dominating performance to date. More than 35,000 fans showed up, the largest crowd in history for an indoor fight. Three months later, Ali toyed with Terrell. Houston, of course, was also where Ali refused to step over the line, which cost him his crown. How ironic would it be, indeed, if Houston turned out to be where he won it back.

The offer from Hofheinz and Arum, who promoted the Ali-Bonavena fight, was similar to the Garden's. Not surprisingly, so was the response, this time from Herbert Muhammad, who, Hofheinz claims, told him that if he and Arum were to raise their offer to a guaranteed $2.5 million for each fighter, with no payoff on the back end, they would have a deal. Hofheinz talked it over with his father, Judge Roy Hofheinz. "Son, what do you want to do?" the elder Hofheinz asked. His son was not sure. He went to see a banker, who told him that the necessary funds were available, but ultimately, "I got cold feet," Fred Hofheinz acknowledged. "Five million dollars sounded like a lot of money. It was a dicey thing, particularly for a guy like me who was really not a part of the long-term history of the sport." Complicating his decision was that his father was ill and spending a lot more time in Florida. "I wasn't going to sit there," Hofheinz went on, "and put $5 million worth of the family money on a deal and have everybody in my family wondering what the hell I'm doing when my dad was sick."

Hofheinz was in the Garden on the night of the fight. His seats, which came courtesy of Ali, were only a few rows from the ring. At times, his mind drifted to what might have been if he had not gotten cold feet. "I kicked myself for a long time," Hofheinz said. "Bob and I both regret it. We could have done it. We had the money to do it." Also dropping out of the talks was Sonny Werblin and

Madison Square Garden. Arum, who went on to make a fortune promoting Ali, Oscar De La Hoya, and numerous other champions, said, "Once Jerry put $2.5 million out there for each fighter, it was case closed. That blew everyone's mind. No fighter had ever made anything like that in the history of boxing, not Jack Dempsey, not Gene Tunney, not Louis, nobody! Two and a half million dollars was the equivalent of a guy getting thirty millon dollars today."

Jerry Perenchio and Jack Kent Cooke were not home free yet. When Jerry offered a $250,000 deposit during one meeting, it raised concerns that he did not have the rest of the $5 million. In addition, because Chartwell was not officially licensed to promote prizefights, the deal could not be consummated without a third party. The third party turned out to be the Garden. For a guarantee of $500,000, the Garden locked up the rights to 30 percent of the live gate, which was expected to surpass $1 million, as well as a cut of the closed-circuit proceeds in the states of New York and Illinois. The arrangement was not exactly the kind of windfall that Harry Markson and Teddy Brenner had in mind when they boarded the train to Philadelphia, but it sure was better than being entirely shut out of the most lucrative fight in the sport's history. Both the Frazier and the Ali camps suggested to Jerry that he bring the Garden into the equation. Once the money was right, Durham insisted the fight be held there, which was fine with Ali and his handlers. The Garden was an established entity in the boxing community. Jerry Perenchio was not. Jerry phoned Jack to tell him the news.

"I'm disappointed it won't be in the Forum, Jerry," he said. "But I want the fight anyway. I think we're going to have a lot of fun." Jack was compensated by the clause in the contract indicating that the Forum would host the rematch for a guarantee to each fighter of $750,000 against 25 percent of the profits. If the first fight lived up to its billing (and there was no reason to believe it would not), a second within a year, maybe two, seemed almost automatic. Ali and Frazier were only in their late twenties and were certainly not going to earn more money fighting anyone else.

The deal was done. Well, not quite. The Garden, as the licensed promoter responsible for paying Ali and Frazier within twenty-four hours after the fight, asked Jack to submit a $4.5 million letter of credit. Jack was offended. Of course he was good for the money. He was one of the richest men in the whole country. If he was not good for the money, nobody was. At this point, Jack reportedly hesitated about going ahead with his investment, deciding to sleep on it. "It was a great risk, and Dad was quite right in waiting," John Kent Cooke said. The next morning, Jack agreed to give the Garden its precious guarantee.

"He had gone to his ranch near Bakersfield for the weekend," recalled Freddie Dale, Jerry's business partner. "We chartered a plane and flew an auditor out there to get his signature on the papers." Jack later indicated he had not been close to backing off. "I wanted them to squirm a little, nothing more and nothing less," he insisted. About 10 a.m. on December 30, 1970, a $4.5 million letter of credit from Chase Manhattan Bank arrived at the Garden. Shortly afterward, Ali and Frazier signed their contracts. Now, finally, the deal was done, the fight of the century set for Monday night, March 8, 1971.

Around noon, the members of the fourth estate began to assemble at Toots Shor's restaurant in Manhattan for the official announcement. Toots Shor's was a gathering place for famous athletes and celebrities. Sinatra was a frequent visitor, as was DiMaggio. When Yogi Berra joked "Nobody goes there anymore, it's gotten too crowded" he was referring to Toots Shor's. Ali arrived first. "I'm the real champ," he declared as he made his way past dozens of people outside the restaurant. Frazier showed up about five minutes later. Ali was in top form. When Jerry estimated the gross potential between $20 and $30 million from the live gate and the ancillary income, Ali stood up, looked at his rival, and remarked, "They got us cheap. Only five million out of 20 to 30. We've been taken."

Ali promised that if he were somehow to lose, he would crawl on his knees to Frazier in the middle of the ring and call him "the greatest." The fight, the ex-champ proclaimed, was big "not because of Joe Frazier. Joe Frazier never wrote no poems. Joe Frazier never did no shuffles. Joe Frazier never did no predicting. Joe Frazier don't even answer no questions." Frazier did not attempt to match Ali's wit. He knew this was one exchange he could never possibly win. "Let him do the talking," he suggested. "I'll do the fighting." Ali, with his usual clowning, according to Frazier, even messed up his jacket. "Sit down and shut up," he finally told Ali, who shot back, "This is your first title fight. It is my 13th." Years later, in a rare interview he did with HBO, Jerry Perenchio described the emotions he witnessed that afternoon. "I was sitting right next to Joe Frazier," he said. Ali "was putting Joe down something awful, telling how ugly he was, and Frazier was as hard as a rock and I could feel his muscles rippling as he was sitting there, getting angrier and angrier. Finally, Frazier got up and he looked at Ali, glaringly, and he said, 'I will be there.'"

Soon there was nothing more to be said, not even by Muhammad Ali. The reporters left to meet their deadlines. A story like this comes along once in a lifetime, if that, and they were the fortunate souls entrusted to tell it. They would tell it for a full two months, from every conceivable angle, until the March evening when their words would not matter anymore, when only two men could write the story and they were in the ring. Ali and Frazier left, as well. The campaign they had waged for years was finally giving them exactly what they wanted and needed, then and forever: each other. Among the last to depart Toots Shor's, almost certainly, was Jerry Perenchio, only ten days into his forty-first year. No longer was Jerry just the agent coming to every premiere obediently to serve his star clients. He was now one of the stars. The end of 1970 was a day away. The city that never sleeps was going to sleep even less, with parties everywhere to usher in 1971. There was much to celebrate and much to plan. The fight of the century does not come along every year.

6

The Show

In January 1971, Neal Marshall and Art Fisher were in the studio putting together a variety show for Henry Mancini one evening when Fisher's agent, Jerry Perenchio, who was also the executive producer, paid a visit. Perenchio was not in a very jovial mood, to say the least. He and Jack Kent Cooke had just returned to Los Angeles from a meeting in New York with ABC Sports president Roone Arledge, who arrived quite late, as Marshall remembers being told, failing to afford his distinguished visitors from California the proper respect.

"Do you guys think you can do this?" Perenchio asked Marshall and Fisher.

"Do what?" Fisher responded.

"Can you give me a first-class production of Ali-Frazier?" Perenchio asked.

Fisher did not hesitate. Art Fisher was not the hesitating type.

"Yes," he answered.

That was all Perenchio needed to hear. He went to ABC first, presumably, because the network of Howard Cosell and *Wide World of Sports* was known for producing the best boxing telecasts in the business. That was no longer the issue. "I can't wait to make this call to Roone Arledge to tell him who my production team is," he declared, according to Marshall, who became accustomed to this aspect of Perenchio's personality. "Perenchio was a fearless guy, especially when it came to business." Marshall said.

Once he and Fisher, thirty-seven, were safely alone, Marshall, twenty-eight, told him what had been racing through his mind from the moment his friend said yes to Perenchio. "Art," Marshall asked, "do you have any idea what we're doing?"

"No," Fisher said. "Do you?"

The two laughed nervously, and while they were filled with doubts up until the very day of the telecast, they did not share these doubts with anyone but each other, deciding that what they did know about producing a major television event was far more important than what they did not know. They knew how to stage an entertaining variety show, and that was a start. From a technical standpoint, almost every challenge they faced in producing entertainment specials applied in this case. How do we light it? How do we make it sound right? What colors do we use?

One of the first challenges was choosing a strong broadcast team. Marshall favored Cosell, who was more famous than ever with the debut a few months earlier of ABC's *Monday Night Football*, as the lead announcer. "Cosell," Marshall felt, "had become the voice of boxing, a larger-than-life figure." Maybe, but in Perenchio's opinion, and that was the opinion that mattered the most, the voice of boxing was also a voice that did not know when to stay silent. Perenchio and actor Burt Lancaster, one of his clients, arrived at the same conclusion while attending the Ali-Bonavena closed-circuit screening. "The people there were shouting, 'Shut up, Howard. Let us watch the fight.'" Lancaster said. "It was like he thought that he was the object of their interest. He imposed his personality on them." The complaint was not without merit. Cosell was loquacious—the kind of fancy word he loved to throw out—during the telecast, going on and on about how Ali was not performing like the Ali of old. Marshall believes that another reason Perenchio did not hire Cosell was that he was still angry over how he and Cooke had been treated by ABC.

"This was Jerry's way of saying to ABC and to Roone Arledge that they didn't do business the right way so he did not want any part of their organization," he said. Marshall continued to lobby for Cosell until an adamant Perenchio, in the middle of taking a steam, finally shot back: "You want him, *you* pay him." In his 1973 autobiography, *Cosell*, the broadcaster addressed the criticism from Lancaster. "I'll say this for Burt," Cosell said. "When he did the telecast, he didn't talk too much. But that's about all I can say for him. . . . We've become friendly since that bout. We've had dinner together on a couple of occasions and we have laughed about the promotion and the ploy in my direction."

To what extent Muhammad Ali or anyone in his entourage made a similar appeal on Cosell's behalf to Perenchio or Cooke is uncertain, although it is fairly safe to assume an effort was made. Few stood by Ali during the exile as passionately as Howard Cosell. Still, he did not call Ali's triumphant comeback in Atlanta, and now he would not be calling Ali's most important fight ever. In his book, Cosell took the high road. "I'm in my fifties now," he wrote, "and I couldn't care less whether I do an event or not. I learned long ago that sometimes you prosper by not doing something—you might even be missed—and that life doesn't begin or end with a telecast of a sports event." That may very well have been Cosell's attitude upon reflection, but at the time, according to Robin Thaxton, Perenchio's former stepson, he did not take the rejection very well. Thaxton claims that he was walking through the lobby of the St. Regis Hotel in New York several weeks before the fight when he heard Cosell ranting about Perenchio.

"He was drunk," Thaxton said. "He was putting on a performance. I went upstairs and told Jerry; we were getting ready to go for dinner. We went downstairs. Cosell had sort of calmed down by then; he was off to the side talking to somebody. Jerry walked by, nodded his head and said, 'Hello, Mr. Cosell.' Howard didn't say a godamn line. He just walked right out."

In early March, outraged that a rerun was not scheduled to air on national television, Cosell complained, "no group ever acted so defiantly of the public interest than the promoters of this fight." ABC claimed that the price to carry it, at reportedly about $600,000, was roughly ten times the standard rate. Perenchio contended that an offer was never made, although another Chartwell official said that one was submitted but merely to make the fee so unreasonably high that the only way to watch the fight would be on closed circuit or when a planned documentary was released. In any case, Cosell, who picked Frazier to win, was in the Garden on March 8, as a spectator.

If not Howard Cosell, then who? The answer was Don Dunphy. In the opinion of many boxing diehards, Dunphy, not Cosell, was the true voice of the sport. He had anchored the radio broadcast of the first Louis-Conn fight on June 18, 1941, from the Polo Grounds in New York. Dunphy was almost late for the big night. He was stuck in a traffic jam on 125th Street, a mile and a half away, and did not arrive at ringside until about twenty minutes before the opening bell. Dunphy called the fights every Friday night for nineteen years on the popular *Gillette Cavalcade of Sports* series before he made the transition to television. "If anyone was going to make comparisons to Max Baer or Joe Louis," said Shelly Saltman, who worked briefly with Dunphy, "he was the guy. He was *there*." On radio, he was known for his rapid-fire delivery. "I felt I was compelled," Dunphy explained, "to describe every action, every movement and that meant I had to keep up a steady stream of words."

Another challenge for Perenchio and his advisors was to select an expert analyst. That expert was Burt Lancaster. *Burt Lancaster?* What the heck did Burt Lancaster know about the nuances of the sweet science? The only fights he was familiar with took place on sound stages. Lancaster, who had played a boxer in *The Killers*, knew enough, as it turned out. Besides, it did not matter whether Lancaster was a boxing expert. He was Burt Lancaster. He was a movie star. From the start, Perenchio wisely recognized that this was a spectacle more than a sporting contest and that every decision must be viewed in that context. "This was a guy who saw the biggest possibilities in everything he did," Marshall said. "In his mind, this was a mega-event and he was going to treat it like a mega-event every single day."

Dunphy and Lancaster did not hit it off at first. "The rhythm between us just wasn't there," Dunphy wrote in his 1988 autobiography. "Like a boxer against a slugger, it was a bad match." Marshall provided a more detailed explanation. "Don's big issue," he said, "was that bringing in Burt was against the sanctity of boxing. Burt was from a totally different planet. He was Jerry's guy. Don came to me once and said, 'Neal, why can't it just be Archie Moore [Moore, the former light heavyweight champion, was the third member of the broadcast team] and me?' I said, 'Don, this event has transcended boxing.' He kind of nodded his head and said, 'That's what they said when [Sugar Ray] Robinson fought [Jake] LaMotta.' Nothing transcended boxing for Don Dunphy. In Don's universe, boxing was bigger than show business." Dunphy learned to coexist with Lancaster. "In terms of how he was professionally," Marshall said, "Don Dunphy was a dream. He would take the stuff you gave him, glance at it, and then it was like he had rehearsed it for hours. That's how fast he was."

Burt Lancaster was no Don Dunphy. Lancaster was used to working in scenes and doing extra takes when necessary, but in live TV there are no extra takes. Fortunately, with the plan devised by Marshall and Fisher, the actor did not have anything to worry about. Instead of opening the show with live interviews of the fighters in their dressing rooms, they chose to tape them in advance. They realized there would not be enough time for Lancaster and Moore to do the interviews and return to their seats at ringside before the fight got under way. Lancaster was assigned to interview Ali. Moore took Frazier. "On the night of the fight," Marshall said, "when Don Dunphy says, 'Live from Madison Square Garden,' we did that hours before. Don, the traditionalist, didn't like it at first. 'Neal, this is a live event, you can't do this,' he said. At the end, he thought that it was the greatest thing that he had ever been involved in. He kept nudging Lancaster, 'They made me a movie star. They made me a movie star.'"

A few days before the fight, Lancaster asked Marshall to meet him in his suite at the St. Regis. "I need something to say in Ali's dressing room," Lancaster said.

"Okay, let's talk about it," Marshall suggested.

"No, I want you to write something," Lancaster told him. "Meet me back here in an hour. I want to see what you've got."

Marshall jotted down three or four lines.

"He sat down there with those three or four lines for an hour and 45 minutes," Marshall remembered. "He walked around the room looking for the character that was going to be the interviewer."

Finally, Marshall came up with a suggestion. "You're J. J. Hunsecker [the gossip columnist Lancaster portrayed in *Sweet Smell of Success*, the 1957 film co-starring Tony Curtis]," Marshall said.

"That's what I was looking for," Lancaster said.

Lancaster worked hard. He scanned hours of film, made publicity appearances on television, and visited the two training camps. Lancaster put the observations, statistics, and historical data he gathered into three loose-leaf notebooks. He was, essentially, preparing to portray another character, a boxing commentator, this one in real (not reel) life. "I found him nothing but an articulate man who worked his craft and studied it," Shelly Saltman said. "He was nervous. He had never done this before. Everyone knew him as an Academy Award–winning actor [for *Elmer Gantry* in 1960] and he did not want to look foolish." Even so, Dunphy was adamant that Lancaster speak only between rounds. The actor went along. "I don't think Burt, during blow by blow, had any inkling to go near a microphone," Marshall said. "Burt knew what he was up against. I once said to Don, 'If you have any inkling to talk to anybody, Archie Moore is the guy you want to talk to, and he said, 'absolutely.'"

Marshall and Fisher were full of suggestions, although many ran counter to boxing's staid establishment. One idea was to change the color of the canvas from white to a more television-friendly color. Marshall, along with Bill Klages, the lighting director, went to see Harry Markson at the Garden. Marshall was in the middle of a long technical explanation about how a white canvas in the Ellis-Frazier bout caused a projector breakdown when Markson told them he had heard enough.

"Boys," Markson said, "you have your problems and I have my problems, and one of the things that has fallen to me is that I am now a protector of the great traditions of boxing. The tradition of boxing is we have a white canvas."

Marshall and Klages went back to Markson to see if he would accept gray as a compromise, but the shade he went with was still not suitable for them. Without telling Markson, Klages experimented with a darker version, but even that failed to solve their problem. In the end, Marshall figured that Markson would be so preoccupied with more pertinent matters on the night of the fight that the last thing he would pay attention to was the color of the canvas. On the afternoon of March 8, Marshall told members of his crew to stamp rosin in the canvas to darken the color.

"What the hell are you guys doing?" a few Garden representatives wanted to know. "Look," Marshall pointed out, "this will ensure that if a cornerman pours water in the ring, there will be no slippery spots." The Garden reps fell for it. "We were desperate guys," Marshall explained, "and these were desperate measures." If Markson did notice any difference, he never uttered a word about it to Marshall. Marshall and Fisher also hoped to put a tiny microphone on the referee, but Edwin B. Dooley, the chairman of the New York State Athletic Commission, rejected the idea. He also turned down their request to mike Angelo Dundee and Yank Durham. "It was a case of Art and me being seen as two Hollywood guys always trying to make this into some kind of entertainment spectacular," Marshall said. "They were right. Our obligation was to the people in the theaters."

While Marshall and Fisher concentrated on the telecast, Perenchio and the promotional company he formed, Fight of Champions, worked on booking the event in as many outlets across the country as possible. At the press conference in December, Perenchio calculated that if he and Cooke were to sell about 70 percent of the estimated 1.5 million available seats, at an average of $10 per head, they would earn $10.5 million plus revenue from foreign sales and "other things we hope we can execute." After paying $5 million to Ali and Frazier, and money for expenses, Fight of Champions would still generate a tidy profit of $2 million or

$3 million. "You've got to throw away the book on this fight," Perenchio insisted. "It's potentially the greatest single grosser in the history of the world. It's like *Gone With the Wind*."

Perenchio suggested that closed-circuit tickets might go for as much as $25 or $30 in some affluent markets. When Bob Arum heard these figures, "My first inclination was to say that the guy is crazy. Nobody would pay that. Up to that point, closed-circuit seats sold for $5 or $10. Closed circuit did not have definition. The equipment was shitty. I would not have possibly thought to charge $25." Members of the boxing establishment were of the opinion, according to Arum, that Perenchio was a "schmuck who is going to blow his cookies." Perenchio did not seem overly concerned about what other people said. What did they know? This "schmuck" had outfoxed everyone before in landing the event and appeared ready to outfox everyone again.

For starters, unlike the standard 50–50 split between the promoter and distributor, Perenchio insisted on a 65–35 breakdown, even more lopsided in some areas of the nation. "What we have here is the Mona Lisa," Perenchio said about the fight. "You expect us to sell it for chopped liver?" Perenchio did not back down when any of the old-time boxing promoters, such as Lou Handler in Detroit, resisted this new way of doing business. In hopes of forcing Perenchio to lower his demands, Handler rented the 12,000-seat Cobo Hall for the night of March 8 before reaching an agreement with Fight of Champions. If Perenchio did not budge, the arena would stay dark. "He won't get the split he's asking," Handler asserted. "The profit motive moves all of us, but there's no reason we should be lining the pockets of Mr. Perenchio and Mr. Cooke."

The ploy was not successful. The Michigan territory was sold to an exhibitor who intended to screen the fight at several smaller venues. Exhibitors were required to guarantee half of the gross for a capacity audience. Fight of Champions kept the guarantee, or received a percentage of the final take, whichever amount was higher. Another new twist was doing business with the concert promoters Perenchio and his people had dealt with for years. "I know how to book Andy Williams into Salt Lake City," he said. "Well, this fight is like booking Andy Williams into 500 Salt Lake Citys all at once." These promoters possessed the resources to put up the guarantee and were generally more experienced in publicizing and hosting major events. "They knew how to put asses in seats," said Saltman, who worked on worldwide promotion for the fight. "Boxing guys were one-dimensional."

Marc Berman, who secured the rights to San Diego, said marketing the Ali-Frazier bout was easier than getting the word out about the top musical acts. "There was so much television exposure, and stories in the sports section," Berman pointed out, "that all you had to do was put it on sale and run a couple of ads." Instead of just selling individual cities, Perenchio packaged entire states, or regions, which they referred to as territories. High-profile figures in sports and entertainment got involved. Danny Kaye was part of a group that purchased the rights to Oregon, Washington, and Utah. Andy Williams, the singer Sergio Mendez, and owners of the Phoenix Suns basketball franchise lined up fourteen midwestern and southern states. Baseball pitcher Dean Chance bought four locations in West Virginia, while hockey star Bobby Orr landed Quebec, Ontario, and Winnipeg.

The territories were valuable. One day, according to Saltman, a stranger came in to see Freddie Dale, who was in charge of booking the territories. The man opened up his attaché case, and inside were wads of $100 bills. "It was like one of those scenes from a movie," said Saltman, "where you see them exchange money for illegal contraband. 'I got one million dollars here,' the guy said. 'I want the state of Louisiana.' Freddie said, 'I'm sorry. It's already sold.'" Some, it seems, did not react too well to missing out on the opportunity. Perenchio, his former wife said, received death threats. "We had to have a New York policeman practically live with us for the last two weeks," Jacquelyn Perenchio remembered. "He was in the hotel all the time and went everyplace with us. When Jerry's son had to have new shoes, he had to go with him."

The soliciting was not restricted to the United States. From their base in Manhattan, Dale and a few others made calls all over the world. They hoped to cover a lot of ground in only a matter of

weeks. Days before the fight, they had lined up thirty-five countries, though only England and Canada would show the event on
closed circuit. The rest would see it via satellite on home television. At times, the negotiations were not easy. Don Loze thought
he was about to close a deal with a company in Mexico until, at the
last moment, it fell apart. "What if one of those things [projectors]
breaks down?" the company's president asked. "We'll have a riot on
our hands." Fortunately for Loze, another company filled the void.

Breakdowns were a major concern in the States as well. Probably nobody was more worried than Barry Burnstein. Burnstein was
in charge of guaranteeing that the closed-circuit venues across the
country received the proper video equipment, and that the equipment worked. "Is there a projector there, you ask yourself," said
Burnstein. "Is there a projectionist? The whole week before the
fight, your stomach turns. . . . I have dreams about it—when I'm
awake and when I'm asleep. I dreamed about a projector falling off
a truck. I dream the projector fell out of an airplane and I try to
reach out and get it." His company took every precaution, testing
equipment at venues throughout the country. "I bleed when it just
doesn't come through at all," he went on. "No picture whatsoever.
It happens in a small percentage of cases."

The hookup was pretty elaborate. The picture was to go by
cable from the Garden to the telephone company on Sixth Avenue,
and then by microwave relay to a telephone building in another city,
where it would be transferred by cable to the specific location. Two
auxiliary generators were made available to protect against a power
failure at the Garden. "If the A.T.&T. building blows up downtown," said Lou Falcigno, director of operations, "we'll be all right.
There is an alternate line going to another A.T.&T. building."

As March 8 approached, some began to question whether Perenchio would turn the profit he had said was possible during the
press conference on December 30. "He is the ebullient theatrical
booking agent," a *Wall Street Journal* reporter wrote, "who may,
once he totals up expenses and receipts, wish he was in the fight

instead of financing it." The *Journal* referred to his failure to persuade sponsors to pay the $400,000-per-minute price he requested for between-round commercials during the telecast, twice as much as corporations spent for ads during the recent Super Bowl. Perenchio counted on interest from the tobacco industry, which was prohibited from advertising on television. "It was a false assumption on their part that we have money to throw around like that," a cigarette company official said.

Perenchio eventually gave up the concept. He said he needed to sell about 1.1 million seats to break even, which, despite the unprecedented hype the fight generated day after day in the print and electronic media, was no sure thing. He was also facing over $50 million in lawsuits while more than twenty auditoriums were being withheld from potential bidders due to Ali's draft conviction. Nonetheless, Perenchio cited the $7 million in guarantees locked up, and was confident that the fight would draw extremely well. "I don't think he ever sweated it," Shelly Saltman said. "If he did, as a good commander of the troops, he never let us know."

Jack Kent Cooke also put up a brave front—in public, that is. "There's no risk here," said Cooke, who estimated that he and Perenchio would take home about $750,000 after taxes. "We've got our money back already." Cooke was to receive 60 percent of the profits, Perenchio, 40 percent. In private, however, Cooke was very concerned, according to Jim Lacher, his treasurer. "You've got to remember," Lacher explained, "Jerry had no experience in promoting a fight. He had no experience in promoting sports. He promoted concerts, but there's a lot of difference between rock concerts and sports." Lacher said Cooke dispatched him to New York in February to monitor the situation. The foreign rights, he said, "weren't doing too well. He also had an awfully tough time selling in the Midwest. I would confer with Jack three or four times a day."

Cooke started to feel more comfortable, according to Lacher, as the big night crept closer, but he did not take any chances, buying insurance in case there were equipment breakdowns. "What would have happened if something went wrong with the uplink out of Madison Square Garden?" Lacher pointed out. "What would happen if all the places are dark across the whole country?" The people with perhaps the most to lose were the local promoters, who would not be able to recoup the money they spent up front if the turnout was poorer than they expected. Many pinned their hopes on the tendency of boxing fans to buy tickets at the last minute.

Perenchio capitalized on every opportunity. "We're business people," he insisted. "We intend to make money out of this. We're not in it for the exercise." His plans included a feature-length documentary, and hawking such souvenirs as the fighters' gloves, trunks, and shoes. "If a movie studio can auction off Judy Garland's shoes," Perenchio reasoned, "these things ought to be worth something, too." His sense of proprietorship landed him in a bitter disagreement at the Fifth Street Gym about a week or two before the fight with Richard Durham, the collaborator in Ali's autobiography. Durham and Ali had been meeting with an independent filmmaker about making their own documentary. Ali was lying on the rubbing table when Perenchio and Durham, an African American, who was not intimidated, got into it.

"This ain't no plantation deal," Durham insisted. "You don't get the house, the field hands, and all the cotton for that two and a half million." Perenchio, who reportedly had invested about $500,000 in his documentary, did not hold back either. "We got a contract for *this*," he said, pointing to Ali's chest.

In another example, when the Mutual Broadcasting System announced plans to broadcast round-by-round recaps on the radio, Perenchio's lawyers sought an injunction, arguing that it was an invasion of property rights and unfair competition. "Jerry's feeling was that in order to get people into the theaters, you had to make any type of access on any other level impossible," Marshall said. "If you're interested in watching this event, here is the only way that you can do it. I was in a meeting when someone said, 'Jerry, it's a *recap*,' and his feeling was that if there was one person who, because he knows he can get a recap, is not going to buy a ticket, then that's one ticket that we just lost.'"

Several days before the bout, state Supreme Court Justice Edward T. McCaffrey ruled that Mutual could air the bulletins, but only if they were fifty words or less and did not claim to be a blow-by-blow account. The promoters appealed but were not successful. They also wanted a guarantee that if a radio broadcast of the fight to U.S. servicemen in Vietnam was pirated to parts of the world where promoters had signed exclusive contracts, they would receive $250,000 in damages and a right to sue the Armed Forces Radio and Television Service if it affected their overseas commerical receipts. During negotiations with Pentagon officials, Perenchio and Cooke backed off, although because of the existing arrangements, only soldiers in South Vietnam and perhaps several other outposts were guaranteed to hear the broadcast.

Perenchio deferred to nobody—nobody except Mr. Jack Kent Cooke. "He would have to come out to Cooke's ranch and Jerry hated that," Jacquelyn Perenchio said. "It was belittling to Jerry. He made him trek way out some place by helicopter when he could have done it in town just as easily. There was nothing that Jerry could do. He was beholden to him. The business he was in, where he had to be at the beck and call of people he agented, he was used to it. It didn't kill him."

Later, when Cooke came to New York, he occupied a suite at the Waldorf Astoria and, essentially, held court. "Jack was a master of grand entrances," Marshall said. "When you sat down to meet with him and Jerry, there was no doubt about who the focal point of attention was. As far as Jack was concerned, this was his baby even more than Perenchio's. Jack could keep track of a lot of stuff going on, was extremely articulate, and loved the sound of his own voice."

In one memorable meeting, Cooke asked Marshall and Fisher for a rundown of the production. They told him about an opening film, interviews with Ali and Frazier in the dressing rooms, and their plans for using the slow-motion technology. Next, they went through the broadcasters. Cooke was not pleased.

"Where's Chick Hearn?" he asked. "What's Chick's job going to be?"

Marshall and Fisher were stumped. Hearn, Lakers' announcer, was not slated to be part of the telecast. Fisher wisely suggested that

Hearn could anchor the weigh-in ceremony, solving one problem. Cooke also wanted to know about the six ringside seats belonging to the promoters. The seats, Fisher told him, were reserved for Dunphy, Lancaster, Moore, a hand-held cameraman, and an engineer. Cooke did the math. "Who gets the other seat?" he asked. "Frank Sinatra," Fisher said. Perenchio explained that Sinatra was taking pictures for *Life* magazine. Cooke did not love the idea.

"If I want a photographer," he said, "who isn't just a sports photographer . . . then I could pick up this telephone right now, and I would get you Avedon or I would get you Karsh of Ottawa. But if you said to me, 'Get me a photographer,' I doubt very much I would pick up this phone and dial information and say to the operator, 'Sweetheart, I need a photographer, see if you can find me Frank Sinatra.'" Despite Cooke's reaction, the seat went to Sinatra.

How *did* Frank Sinatra wind up with a ringside seat to the fight of the century? Jim Mahoney, Sinatra's longtime publicist, claims it was his idea to have him take the photos. Knowing his boss was planning to attend the fight, Mahoney phoned Tommy Thompson, a *Life* writer who had done several pieces on Sinatra. Thompson, according to Mahoney, ran it by his editors, who signed off. Neal Marshall, however, believes that the impetus may have come from Sinatra's friend Lancaster, who hoped to exchange a seat for singing lessons that would help him prepare for his role in an upcoming revival of the Broadway musical *Knickerbocker Holiday*. Sinatra, in any case, was determined to do a good job. George Kalinsky, the Garden photographer, was in his office one day when Joe Acquefreda, the head of security, walked in.

"Joe says, 'I have somebody who wants to meet you.' I look up and it's Frank Sinatra," Kalinsky recalled. "He said, 'I hear you're the greatest photographer. I want you to teach me all you know about photography in five minutes.' He was trying to be funny." They went to lunch in midtown and talked for three hours. Kalinsky suggested that Sinatra use a wide-angle lens and set his camera, a Nikon, at a certain distance so he would not have to spend much time on focusing. "Make sure you feel the atmosphere," Kalinsky said.

*   *   *

About two weeks before the fight, Robin Thaxton said, Perenchio asked if he wanted to go with him to see Cooke at the Waldorf. "He's going to take me to the woodshed," he warned his stepson. "We're running over budget and he's pissed about the money we're spending. I'll go over and take my whippin' and pay my penance to Mr. Cooke and we'll just keep on going." At the Waldorf, Thaxton remembered, "the butler answered the door and brought us in. Cooke was sitting in Chinese silk pajamas like on a throne at a large table. There was a guy who had a calculator and his job was to punch the numbers that Jack ran off and give Jack the correct answer. The only problem was that Jack would give him the numbers and then give him the answer before he could hit the button. This guy was a nervous wreck. 'You shouldn't be spending this money,' Cooke was saying. 'You're being negligent in how you're going about this, spending money outside of what our agreement was.'"

Cooke threatened, according to Thaxton, to seize control of the whole enterprise. Perenchio, he said, threatened him right back.

"You might find it very difficult to complete the operation of this not knowing what we know," Perenchio allegedly told Cooke. "The link might not hook up right. We could have technical difficulties beyond belief." (Don Loze claims that Fisher and Marshall came to his hotel room the night before the fight asking for money to pay off workers. Otherwise, he said, he was told they were going to cut the cables in the morning. "I didn't give them anything," Loze said. "I didn't have any money to give them.") As Thaxton sees it, "Jack overplayed his hand and Jerry didn't fold. I remember Jerry talking to my mom and saying, 'I can't believe it. Jack actually tried to take this deal away from me.' Nothing ever transpired after that. Jack came to the party my mother had before the fight and was very gracious."

Nobody could take this deal away from Andrew Jerrold Perenchio. Cooke invested the money but Perenchio invested the time and energy to make the evening of March 8, 1971, at Madison Square Garden a show that people would never forget. The days went by fast. From the initial press conference to the fight covered less than ten weeks. "We're like a guy in an orchard," he said, "with only a limited amount of time to pick the fruit. We can only get at the lower branches." Freddie Dale and his associates were busy lining up territories. Neal Marshall and Art Fisher were busy setting up the telecast. Perenchio was busy with everything else. "Jerry could go on four hours sleep," Thaxton said. Many questions remained: Would there be any breakdowns? Was the satellite going to work? Would enough people come to the theaters? What would the weather be on fight night?

"You can only do so much," Perenchio told his stepson in the final days. "You just have to hope this is all going to come off."

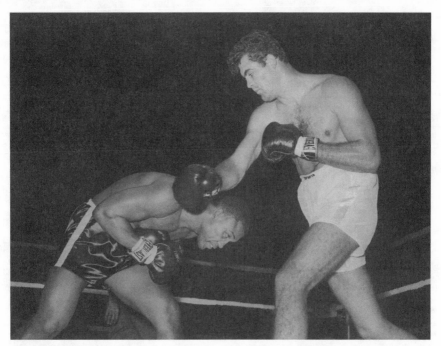

Joe Frazier faces off against Tony Doyle in the first round of their 1967 fight in Philadelphia. Frazier put Doyle away in the second, advancing his record to 18–0.

Joe Frazier pounds away at Marion Connor in the first round of their scheduled ten-round bout at the Boston Garden in 1967. Frazier won by a technical knockout in the third.

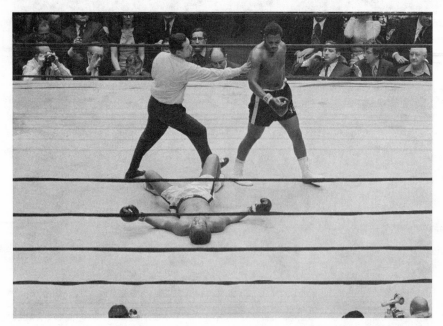

Joe Frazier heads toward the neutral corner after knocking Jimmy Ellis to the canvas for the second time in the fourth round of their 1970 unification title bout at Madison Square Garden. Frazier prevailed when Ellis failed to come out for the fifth round.

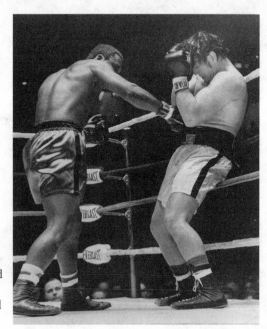

Oscar Bonavena covers up against the ropes in his 1968 confrontation with Joe Frazier in Philadelphia. Frazier absorbed a lot of pounding but was able to outduel Bonavena for the second time to retain his title.

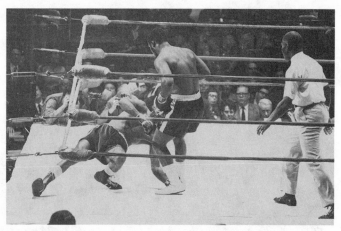

Bob Foster begins to fall from a powerful Joe Frazier left hook in the second round of their 1970 heavyweight championship bout in Detroit. Frazier knocked out Foster in his last tune-up before encountering Muhammad Ali.

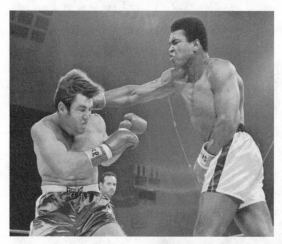

Muhammad Ali connects with a right to the jaw of Jerry Quarry during their 1970 confrontation in Atlanta, Ali's first fight since he was stripped of the title. He won by a third-round technical knockout.

Muhammad Ali knocks down Oscar Bonavena during the fifteenth round of their December 1970 heavyweight duel at Madison Square Garden.

Muhammad Ali raises his arms in triumph during the fifteenth round of his 1970 heavyweight bout with Oscar Bonavena in New York.

Joe Frazier signs autographs for fans before the start of a Sunday afternoon workout for his bout with Muhammad Ali.

Muhammad Ali signing autographs for fans. On the far right is Georgia state senator Leroy Johnson, who helped make Ali's comeback fight in Georgia possible.

Joe Frazier knocks down Muhammad Ali in the fifteenth round of the fight of the century at Madison Square Garden. It was the only knockdown of the fight.

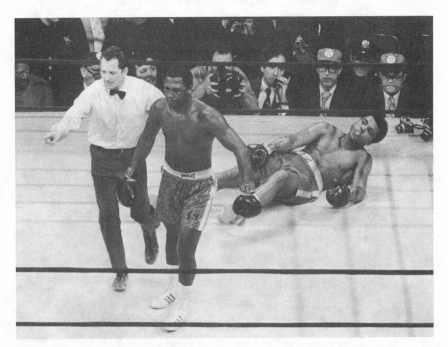

Referee Arthur Mercante directs Joe Frazier to a neutral corner after Frazier knocked down Muhammad Ali in the fifteenth round of their historic duel. Ali was up in a hurry.

Muhammad Ali and Joe Frazier retreat to their respective corners after the final round of their remarkable fight. Frazier was declared the victor on all three judges' cards.

Joe Frazier, still the heavyweight boxing champ of the world, hides a swollen left eye behind dark glasses.

Joe Frazier sitting in front of a huge mural showing him knocking down Muhammad Ali in their 1971 fight.

7

The Countdown

In January, Muhammad Ali and Joe Frazier, at long last, met in the ring—to pose for publicity shots with George Kalinsky. In the time since Ali and Frazier saw each other at Toots Shor's, the most significant development had not come out of either camp; it had come from court. On January 11, a spokesman for the Supreme Court announced that the justices would review the case of *United States of America v. Cassius Marcellus Clay*, probably in April. Gone was the one scenario that would have canceled the fight, perhaps for good.

For Ali, the announcement was the latest in a succession of promising news to emerge from the courts. In June 1970, the Supreme Court, in *Welsh v. the United States*, modified the rule that objecting to military service must be based on religious belief, determining that moral and ethical reasons are sufficient if they are "deeply held." Three months later, the Mansfield ruling paved the way for Ali to regain his license in the state of New York. Ali was not in the clear just yet, but the possibility of him serving time seemed more remote than ever. "It was a little pressure waiting for the Supreme Court decision but I thrive on pressure," Ali said. "The one thing on my mind and the only thing now is Joe Frazier." Frazier's response was not much different. "The only thing I care about is that [Ali] is there to fight me," he said. "After that

I couldn't care what he does or what happens to him. All I want is to have him there so I can beat him to a pulp."

The Supreme Court's decision to hear his appeal came a few days after Ali agreed to an exhibition bout on January 21 against sparring partners Bunky Akins and Rufus Brassell in Dayton, Ohio. The Morehouse College exhibition eight weeks before the Quarry fight went over so well that Angelo Dundee apparently saw no harm in another. Perenchio saw a great deal of harm and vowed to do something about it. Too much was at stake to risk a major injury to his prized investment. He informed the Ali camp that the contract the fighter signed prohibited him from any ring appearances in public prior to March 8. Strong words were not sufficient. Robin Thaxton claims that his stepfather dispatched him to Dayton to extricate Ali out of the deal. Perenchio later said he paid $10,000 to halt the proceedings. Thaxton said similar payoffs were necessary to abort other Ali exhibitions.

"I don't even know if Jerry knew they were legit but he wasn't taking any chances," Thaxton said. Nonetheless, Ali was not deterred. Weeks later, he agreed to an exhibition against Jimmy Ellis, set for February 23 in Miami Beach, only thirteen days before he was to face Frazier. "I need a good competitive workout and I need to get the feel of the crowd," Ali told reporters. Neal Marshall was in a meeting with Perenchio when the promoter first heard of Ali's intentions. "Jerry said, 'What the hell is he thinking?'" Marshall recalled. Perenchio even threatened to sue Ali.

"The man is driving us nuts with his crazy ideas," he said. "I heard a lot about how unpredictable he was before I got into boxing. Now I'm beginning to learn about him first hand. Well, he'll find out quickly that he is going to do things my way or he won't be getting that two and a half million." Perenchio prevailed again. The fight against Ellis was called off, although the fact that Ali had agreed to the tune-up in the first place suggested that perhaps he was not as confident as he claimed. Ali and Ellis, actually, fought briefly, according to Dundee, who was away in Georgia for a family funeral. "I called the gym at the time I knew he'd be working out," Dundee said, "and when the phone is answered, all I hear is shouting. I ask what's going on. They tell me Ali and Jimmy are in the ring. Fortunately, it only lasted one round. Some of the other guys around the gym got in and stopped it."

The phones at the Garden did not stop ringing. Within ten days of the December 30 press conference, about 800 mail orders arrived, including one from Cloverlay for 2,400 tickets. Harry Markson called it the biggest ticket rush since the Louis-Conn fight in 1946, when Mike Jacobs charged $100 for ringside seats. Markson was charging a record $150, although, according to Teddy Brenner, he was angry with himself for not selling the prime tickets for $250. On January 25, shortly before 7 a.m., three hours ahead of schedule because so many people were waiting in line, the Garden opened its box office to sell the remaining 4,000 tickets, which went for $20, $40, and $75. In two hours, every ticket was gone. The line had begun to form about 3 p.m. the previous day. During the night, the temperatures dipped near the freezing mark, but, bundled in blankets, engaged in discussions about the fight and its social implications, people did not leave.

"Everyone was very friendly," said college professor Philip Sigler, who, accompanied by his wife, Marcy, was the first to arrive. The crowd, he said, was mostly pro-Ali.

In charge of Garden publicity back then was John Francis Xavier Condon, who doubled as its basketball public address announcer. Condon was one of the most creative PR guys in sports. In June 1969, he came up with the idea of installing a boxing ring in Times Square, along with a Dixieland band, to promote the Frazier-Quarry fight. An estimated lunchtime crowd of 4,000 watched the two boxers in separate sparring sessions, the stunt drawing coverage in the tabloids and on TV. He was a master at feeding the vultures, aka the working press. "He would whisper things in your ear," said the *Daily News*'s Phil Pepe, "and let you know what was going on so you wouldn't get beat." However, in the weeks leading up to Ali-Frazier, Condon was feeling a little constrained. In addition to the 19,000-plus seats on the main floor, the 3,400 tickets for the closed-circuit screening at the Felt Forum were also sold out. For once, taking a columnist to lunch to drum up publicity would serve no purpose.

"They've immoblized me with no more seats to peddle," Condon complained. "Yank Durham is now screaming for a black referee. I could have made a big thing out of that. Now let Durham shout into a vacuum. Who needs him?" Thousands of seats were still available, but they were for arenas far away from Gotham, with the revenue from their sale, except in Illinois and New York, going into the pockets of Jerry Perenchio and Jack Kent Cooke, and not Madison Square Garden. Tom Kenville, who worked for Condon, was typing a press release one day when Harry Markson approached. "What are you doing *that* for? Markson asked. "We don't have any tickets to sell."

In early January, the Garden began to receive requests for credentials from media outlets in the United States and throughout the world. Within several weeks, roughly 1,500 applications poured in; only about 600 were granted. Ultimately, writers and broadcasters representing 26 countries showed up at the Garden, including Moshe Lehrer from *Maariv*, a newspaper in Israel. Lehrer had had no plans to make the long trek to New York until he had a conversation with his eighty-year-old mother. "Moshe," she said, "who's going to win the fight?" If his mother cared that much, he figured, he needed to be there. Also assigned to cover the fight were three of America's most prominent writers: Norman Mailer (*Life*), William Saroyan (*True*), and Budd Schulberg (*Playboy*). Approximately 135 ringside seats, according to Kenville, were set aside for the wire services, dailies, and magazines, including at least a half dozen for *Ring*. "That was because Nat Fleischer [the publisher] and Harry went back to the '30s," Kenville explained.

The remaining members of the fourth estate were scattered throughout the Garden, including in the upper-level press box. "We had to put all the British press up there," Kenville said. "Unfortunately, you could not really see much. You had to have binoculars. There was one old English writer, I remember, who did not mind at all. 'That is all right,' he said. 'I did not come to report the fight, just to write about it.'" Condon could be stern, if necessary. When a photographer for the *Village Voice*, a New York City weekly, kept pestering him for a credential, Condon slammed the door in his face. He could also be soft. A journalist called one day from the Upper Peninsula of Michigan to say he was going to be in New York the week of the fight for another event and wondered if there was an extra ticket available. Normally a request from such a tiny newspaper would be automatically rejected. "Put him up in the top, what the hell," Condon told Kenville. "At least he'll be in the building." Condon worked sixteen hours a day for a solid two months, becoming a target for people who felt they were not properly accommodated. "I have been called prejudiced toward whites, prejudiced toward blacks and just about every unflattering name in the language," he said. Those he turned down included antiwar activist Abbie Hoffman, representing the *Evergreen Review*, a literary magazine.

Frazier and Ali met for the photo shoot at the Cloverlay gym on North Broad in Philadelphia. George Kalinsky started the session by shooting the fighters in separate profiles in the ring, Ali first. Moving around with Ali, Kalinsky asked him to throw a flurry of punches toward the camera but stop just short of hitting the lens. "I want you to make believe I'm Joe Frazier," Kalinsky told Ali. "My camera is going to be able to get the emotion and feeling of Joe Frazier on you." After the first two shots, the photographer realized that Ali "was able to miss my camera or my face, whatever he was aiming at, by a quarter of an inch. I thought that was incredible precision. We went a whole round. After the round, he put his arms up in victory, doing the 'I Am the Greatest' routine." The same precision was not the case with Frazier. "I may have lasted seven seconds with him," Kalinsky remembered. "I was afraid that he was going to hit me—and Joe was the one I knew really well!"

He then asked Ali and Frazier to pose nose-to-nose against a wall adjacent to the ring. He dabbed water and vaseline on their faces to make the shot realistic. "Ali, make it look like you're in the ring," Kalinsky suggested. "*I'll* make it look like it's in the ring," Frazier interjected. After Ali landed several light jabs, Frazier socked him with a left to the midsection. Ali fell against the wall, which prevented him from hitting the floor. "You son-of-a-bitch, you can really hit," he said. "You better believe it," Frazier said, "and that's the way it's going to be on the night of the fight. You are going down."

At that moment, Kalinsky felt he knew precisely what was going through his friend's mind. "Joe was so enamored with the fact that this was Ali," he said. "They were, finally, in the same ring together. Joe had to show Ali who was the boss." When the session began, only Kalinsky, Ali, Frazier, their handlers, and Condon were in the gym, but the news quickly spread, and soon hundreds of fans had assembled outside. Condon notified the city fire and police departments as a precaution. "We actually felt the building shake, there were so many people around it," Kalinsky said. After the shoot ended, Ali was heading for the exit when Kalinsky issued one final request. "When you go out, can you go around to the window and ham it up a little bit?" he asked. Ham it up a little bit? Muhammad Ali? Ali would not be Ali if he did not ham it up, a lot, at every opportunity. When Ali reached the window, he opened his mouth wide while Frazier stared at him from the other side. The picture captured the contrast between the two personalities, and it has been reprinted numerous times over the years. Ali hopped into his Rolls and took off.

Ali began training in mid-January at the Fifth Street Gym. He weighed nearly 230 pounds, about 15 more than he planned to be against Frazier. In his first spirited workout, Ali sparred 6 rounds with three different partners. He played to the audience, as always, but recognized that he was in for some rigorous days ahead. "Ain't my *lungs*," he said. "They all right. It's in my *muscles. They* get tired. Ain't like when I was a young man. Now I'm older, gonna be twenty-nine." Even so, he was the same Ali outside the ropes. "He [Frazier] can throw all the punches he wants; he's not in there with an amateur. He's in there with the best professional and the fastest in the history of the whole world," Ali declared. "No, I'm not putting Joe Frazier down. I'm just telling the truth. Liston was the greatest thing that ever was until I beat him. Then they called him a bum." When a local television reporter arrived for an interview, he was greeted by the esteemed poet T. S. Ali: "Frazier will catch hell. From the start of the bell. Then we'll jump out. And take on Howard Cosell."

Inside the ropes, the poet once again let himself be a punching bag. He felt that absorbing punishment from his sparring partners prepared his body for the shots that Frazier would administer, and nobody in his corner was about to convince him otherwise. Dundee, at least, persuaded Ali to shelve his idea of setting up headquarters near the new home he had purchased in Cherry Hill, New Jersey. During training, Ali stayed at Octagon Towers, an upscale Jewish retirement home near the beach. "The Jews, at first, were scared shitless of Ali's group," Ferdie Pacheco said. "They didn't realize they were boxers, not gangsters." As usual, it did not take Ali very long to ingratiate himself with the new crowd. When his stay ended, the residents gave him a farewell party with a cake that showed a victorious Ali in the ring standing over his hapless victim.

Miami Beach was a long way from New York and its constant distractions. Of course, in those days, in the life of Muhammad Ali, Pluto would not have been far enough away from the spotlight. "There is one word," Pacheco said, "that fit the whole time preparing for Frazier: frenzy. It was a boxing frenzy. It was a publicity frenzy. It was everything going too fast at the same time, everybody showing up at one time. Everybody was kissing his ass and he was eating it up. Training was mostly a publicity stunt. He trained a little bit and then he talked a lot." At the same time, he admitted, "I don't see how he could have done it any other way. He was rejoicing at being the number one guy in the country, in the world! It wasn't good, but that's the way it was."

The basic strategy mapped out by Dundee was for his man to dance in the early rounds while flicking his familiar left jabs to keep Frazier at bay. After about six or seven rounds, Ali then would come off his toes to become the aggressor. "I can't wait to see how Frazier will react to backing up," Dundee said. "The whole key to the fight is my guy's jab. When he starts to land it, everything else falls in place."

With Ali, working on his body was always only one part of his preparation. He soon went to work on another part, the psyche— *Joe Frazier*'s psyche. Ali began to portray Frazier as an Uncle Tom, a pawn of the white Establishment, while he was the one who could truly identify with the suffering of black people in the United States and all over the globe. Ali claimed that he was fighting for a cause while Frazier was fighting for a check, and that Frazier was too ugly and too dumb to be the heavyweight champion. "I know what's going to happen the night before the fight," Ali said. "That Joe Frazier, he's gonna get telephone calls and telegrams from folks in Georgia and Alabama and Mississippi saying, 'Joe Frazier, you be a white man tonight and stop that draft-dodging nigger.'"

Ali delivered the line with a laugh and rolled his eyes, but by attacking Frazier's legitimacy as an advocate for his own race, he demeaned his opponent, and he did it over and over again, like a candidate who had found his stump speech. Some have argued that Ali was merely attempting to promote the fight, as usual, and disrupt Frazier's concentration. "I never took it seriously," HBO's Larry Merchant said, "and I don't think Ali really thought Frazier was an Uncle Tom. I just think he thought it would provoke him, though I could see how Frazier, being the target, thought differently." Even so, this was one fight that did not need Ali to promote it. The fight easily sold out. Besides, he and Frazier were guaranteed $2.5 million apiece no matter how many spectators showed up at Madison Square Garden or watched on closed-circuit TV.

The attacks were also inaccurate. Unlike Ali, Frazier did not publicly empathize with the plight of fellow blacks. He did not mingle with the well-known black activists of his day, such as Whitney Young, the Reverend Ralph Abernathy, the Reverend Jesse Jackson, Coretta Scott King, and Julian Bond, or the well-known black entertainers, such as Sidney Poitier, Bill Cosby, and Diana Ross.

Frazier was friendly with Philadelphia police commissioner Frank Rizzo, an enemy to many African Americans. But Frazier, even more than Ali, suffered from racism in his youth. When he was fourteen, a white boy called him a nigger. Frazier beat him up. His mother told him that if he couldn't get along with white folks, he would need to leave home, which he did a few years later, heading first to New York and then to Philadelphia.

Pacheco urged Ali to let the issue go. "You do not need to do this," Pacheco told him. "He's a black man like you are." Ali understood, but told Pacheco, "I like to get under his skin." Writer Dave Kindred believes that Ali's fears prompted the Uncle Tom references. "I think Frazier scared Ali more than anybody ever," Kindred said, "and that was why he was so mean, so contemptible in the things he said about him. Ali's moments of panic came out as mean-spirited stuff always when he was most afraid." Veteran columnists such as Dick Young and Jimmy Cannon, always wary of Ali, criticized his treatment of Frazier, while the younger members of the pack gave him a pass. "He was such good entertainment and gave them such good quotes," explained Thomas Hauser.

Joe Frazier did not give Ali a pass, then or ever. He rightly pointed out the hypocrisy of being labeled an Uncle Tom by a black man whose trainer was white. In his autobiography, Frazier called it a "cynical attempt by Clay to make me feel isolated from my own people. He thought that would weaken me when it came time to face him in that ring. Well, he was wrong. It didn't weaken me, it awakened me to what a cheap-shot son of a bitch he was." While Ali might have been fighting for a "cause," so was Frazier. His cause was to provide for his wife and children, which was every bit as noble as any principles Muhammad Ali ever espoused. To be sure, Frazier made the situation worse for himself by always referring to Ali as Clay. "Only those who were bigots, rednecks, hardliners, continued to call him Clay, almost as an insult," former *Today Show* host Bryant Gumbel explained decades later, "and when Frazier chose to do that, to a lot of African-Americans, it was kind of like, 'Hey, who you siding with here? Take a look in the mirror.'"

*   *   *

Frazier set up camp on January 21 at the Concord, a resort in the Catskill Mountains about ninety miles north of New York City, where he had trained for seven of his previous fights. The cold weather suited him perfectly. He was not in camp to entertain the public and the press with his comedic talents and social theories. He was in camp for one reason, to prepare his body and his mind for the most important night of his career. His sparring partners, who included Don Warner, light heavyweight Ray Anderson, Billy "Moleman" Williams, and a very talented heavyweight from San Diego named Ken Norton, paid the price for Frazier's dedication. Generally, before Frazier fights, "guys would come into camp and the first week there, they would beat Joe up so bad, I'd feel sorry for him," said Lester Pelemon, who assisted with the workouts. "By the second week, Joe would come around and we would have to send for more sparring partners." After warming up with music blaring in the background, Frazier went after them with every weapon he possessed. From the day in the early 1960s he walked into the Police Athletic Gym, his last chance to be the next Joe Louis, he knew of no other way to prepare. One afternoon, while giving Warner a ride home, Cloverlay's Joe Hand casually asked if he was coming back to the gym the next day. "I can't come tomorrow," said Warner, a towel with a bag of ice wrapped around his mouth. "I need a while for my gums to be straightened out." When Warner put the towel down, Hand got a closer look at the damage. "His teeth were so loose," Hand said. "They were like a little kid's teeth ready to fall out. Frazier would just beat the hell out of him."

Norton, who two years later would upset Ali and break his jaw, was no ordinary sparring partner. There were moments when Norton held his own with the heavyweight champion, but there were also moments when he did not. "He kind of got smart with Frazier in one sparring session," recalled Ed Casey, a former heavyweight from New Bedford, Massachusetts, who hung around the champion's camp for a few days. "Frazier hit him with a left hook just to show him that he was the boss. They blew the whistle to end the round. He hurt him." Outside the ropes, however, Frazier was a different man. Stan Hochman, the *Philadelphia Daily News* columnist, said Frazier allowed his sparring partners to beat him when they shot craps at night. "The way he would lose was by taking even odds at making a ten or a four when he would have been getting 9–5 or 2–1 or whatever the odds were," Hochman remembered. "I used to think, 'What is this man doing?' It was his way of giving the partners money to soften the damage he had done to them in sparring, and Yank went along with it."

As devoted to his craft as Frazier was, the loneliness of training camp got to him on occasion, just as it gets to everyone. Early in his career, he killed a lot of the boredom by phoning his friends and family. "Joe used to run up these tremendous phone bills," Hand said, "hundreds and hundreds of dollars. I was the guardian of the money, and I would say to him, 'You got this freakin' phone bill.' He said to me, 'Would you rather have me on the street seeing my friends or would you rather me talk to them?'" Hand did not bring it up again. Frazier later spent much of his spare time strumming his guitar. No matter how he distracted himself, the longer Frazier was in camp, the more irritable he generally became, Hand said. "I went to see him in Atlantic City before one fight and he was being really arrogant," he said. "I said, 'I'm gone.' He said, 'Now, you wait a minute. I want to ask you, when was the last time that you got laid? I've been in training camp for a month.' He was so grumpy. There were never any women around the camp."

In early February, when a 17-inch snowfall prevented Frazier from doing his roadwork, camp was moved to the Cloverlay gym in Philadelphia. The storm provided a welcome excuse. Frazier was not pleased with the icy, slippery ground. Instead of being able to stop along his route to shadow-box, he was forced to keep running to stay warm. The sweat from his face froze on the whiskers of his chin. Back home, he began his daily run around 5 a.m. and went for about five or six miles. Three weeks into training, Frazier was down from 220 to 215 pounds, with about another 10 to go. In sparring sessions, he concentrated on cutting off the ring, a tactic he figured to employ against a retreating Ali. He watched films of Henry Armstrong, who was a master at this strategy. It certainly worked against Ray Anderson, a speedy 173-pounder. "He catches up with me every day," Anderson said. "And if he can catch me he sure as hell can catch Ali. When Joe gets in close there's no way to stop him. When you cover your body with your elbows and fore-arms he belts you on the chin. . . . There ain't no way out. You get to a point where you say to yourself, aw, what the hell's the use?'"

One day, Anderson, who was not wearing headgear and a mouthpiece, was smacked on the upper lip by a Frazier left hook. He required three stitches and was done for the rest of camp. Replacing him was another nimble light heavyweight, Paul Car-doza, from New England. Less than a week earlier, Cardoza had knocked out Sixto Martinez (Morales) in the fifth round in Provi-dence. Cardoza, who weighed about 175, soon discovered the dif-ference between Sixto Martinez and Smokin' Joe Frazier. It did not hit him in the ring. It hit him hours later, at dinner. "As I lifted my fork," Cardoza said, "my arms and shoulders hurt awful. Joe was on your butt, moving, moving, punching. I don't care if Ali had gotten five guys, each of them taking a round with him. There was no way that he was going to have partners who would have toughened him up to get him in the kind of shape that Joe was getting into."

Norton told Cardoza he was giving Frazier too much respect by not throwing jabs, but Cardoza was not concerned with respect. Cardoza was concerned with survival. "I'm moving to get the hell out of the way," he told Norton. Perhaps even more impressive than Frazier's work ethic and lethal left was his unwavering sense of belief in himself. Ed Casey was in the dressing room when Fra-zier walked in one day. "It was just me and him," Casey recalled. "He took off his robe, got completely naked, and got on the scale. After he weighed himself, he said, 'That's right where I want to be.' He asked me, 'You're a fighter, right?' I said, 'Yeah,' and he said, 'Are you ever going to be the heavyweight champ?' I looked at him and my mouth hung open. 'I'd like to be,' and he said, 'Man, you have to change that attitude. You have got to say that you are *going* to be the heavyweight champion of the world because if you don't have that attitude, you don't belong in the game.' He put on his robe and out he went."

Frazier planned to pound away at Ali's midsection in the early rounds, knowing that Ali's tendency was to lean back to protect his precious face. Once the body punches took their inevitable toll, Frazier assumed, Ali would try to cover up, exposing his head. Frazier adhered to the boxing axiom "You kill the body, the head will die." He was going to do exactly what he did against everyone he ever fought, from Elwood Goss to Bob Foster, which was to apply unrelenting pressure. "That's what wears them down as much as punches," Frazier insisted. "I'm gonna keep him running more than he ever did, worrying about getting hit. He's quick when he stops to throw a jab or combination, but he has to stop to do it. That's when I'll be ready to lay it on him."

Assisting Durham was Eddie Futch. Futch was the sport's preeminent closer, typically showing up for the last few weeks of camp to provide the words of wisdom that could mean the difference between winning and losing. He took up boxing in Detroit during the 1920s. In 1933, Futch captured the city's Golden Gloves tournament. Although he was only a lightweight and was outweighed by 70 pounds, Futch sparred on many occasions with another Motor City boxer, Joe Louis. He said Louis used to tell him that if he could hit him, he knew he could hit anybody. "I had to devise ways and means of not getting killed," Futch said. He became a trainer after a heart murmur ended his fighting career. In 1958, one of his fighters, Don Jordan, won the welterweight crown. In 1966, Futch told Durham that Frazier was ready to take on Eddie Machen. The victory was one of the most pivotal in Frazier's career.

"If Frazier ever listened to anybody more than he listened to Eddie Futch, he was very wrong," Dave Kindred said. "Eddie Futch was by far the smartest guy I was ever around. He understood fighters. He understood psychology. He understood strategy. He knew everything." Futch spoke softly, but the message got through loud and clear. "If you didn't want to work, it was your call," said Freddie Roach, who was trained by Futch in the 1970s and 1980s. "But he wouldn't put up with that. He would just leave." Of course,

Futch did not have to worry about Frazier's level of commitment. Frazier, for instance, rubbed rock salt and water into his scalp, face, fists, and forearms to toughen his skin against cuts.

As much as Futch contributed, Durham was firmly in charge. Durham, whose share of the $2.5 million purse would be $375,000, made sure nothing interfered with his fighter's preparation, including the pesky members of the press.

"I would call Yank up to see about sending reporters from New York down there and he would say, 'nobody today' or 'nobody this week,'" the Garden's Tom Kenville recalled. "He would say, 'Those goddamn Philadelphia writers are here every day.' Remember, Yank and Joe were not working on a percentage. It was always best to have a fighter on a percentage because then you could say, 'If you don't work with the press and they don't get the stories in the paper, you don't sell tickets, you're not going to make that much money.' But every time we would get on our high horse about wanting more press down there, somebody in the Frazier camp would say, 'They can write whatever they want but it won't put more people in the seats.'"

One day, the artist LeRoy Neiman stopped by to watch Frazier work. "Yank said to me, 'Who is that guy that's in here?' Joe Hand remembered. "'He sketches,' I told him. He said, 'I don't give a fuck who he is. I don't want him here.'"

Durham was just as stern with members of his own race. When a local black group picketed outside the Cloverlay gym in February to call for a boycott of the fight, complaining of high ticket prices for the closed-circuit screenings and that not enough African American promoters had been given territories, Durham told the protestors to take up their concerns with Jack Kent Cooke.

"I still feel the same way I did before," Durham said. "I told white groups. I told black groups . . . if you want the fight, come up with the money." Two weeks before the fight, he fired Don Warner, Frazier's sparring partner for about four years, after Ali claimed that a spy was calling him every night to report on his opponent's condition. "I've been suspicious of Don Warner for two weeks now," Durham said. "You have to look for things like that in a fight like this." Three decades later, Warner's guilt remains in doubt.

"Don Warner was not a spy," Joe Hand claims. "He had gone to a couple of Muslim meetings and that didn't sit too good. They figured every Muslim was on Ali's side." Stan Hochman, who covered the story for the *Philadelphia Daily News*, said he began to have "second thoughts about my role in the episode but I never confronted Yank about whether the thing was genuine or not."

Either way, Warner, who had been earning $375 a week, was suddenly out of work. He filed a lawsuit against Cloverlay, Durham, and Frazier. His attorney, Leon Silverman, said in 2006 that after Ali gave his deposition in 1974, which, he said, supported Warner's innocence, the case was settled out of court in the neighborhood of $35,000. According to one newspaper account, Warner claimed that he received crank phone calls and that someone threw rocks through a window of his home.

On Wednesday, March 3, Frazier and Ali appeared separately for their routine pre-fight physicals at the Felt Forum. The New York State Athletic Commission's Edwin Dooley kept them apart to avoid a repeat of the scene from the press conference at Toots Shor's and a verbal altercation that had taken place between Ali and Bonavena in December. Frazier, wearing green velvet trunks under a leopard-print mini-robe, arrived first about 12:30 p.m. The exam took ten minutes. Dr. A. Harry Kleiman asked Frazier to touch the floor and his hips and lift his hands straight up, which he quickly did twenty times. Frazier's pulse was faster than normal, but that seemed to be no real concern.

The only negative news came when Dooley informed Frazier that he was required to shave off his beard before the fight. Frazier hoped to keep it on since he planned to tour with his band, and the beard was part of the persona he projected onstage. (In his autobiography, Frazier wrote that he was feeling fatigued about four or five weeks before the fight. He said his family physician, Dr. J. Finton Speller, told him he was suffering from high blood pressure. "Maybe it wasn't the ideal setup—to be fighting the biggest fight of my life with a body that was under siege," Frazier admitted.

"But there was no way I was going to postpone the fight. I'd waited all my life for this chance." Once his workouts ended, Frazier said, he took shots of vitamin E and vitamin C to maintain his energy level. Even so, according to Thomas Hauser, "There were serious conversations within the Frazier camp about calling the fight off. If it hadn't been Ali, they probably would have called it off.")

After the physical, Frazier projected another persona, one of the fearless champion. "I don't think this fight will go more than ten rounds," he told hundreds of reporters and photographers. "I think it's going to be bad for him. I really do." About an hour later, Ali arrived. When John Condon introduced him as the "former heavyweight champion," Ali took the cue like the actor he was. "*Former* heavyweight champion of the world!" he screamed before entering the ring. "What do you mean former? I even look like a champ. I'm tall and slim. He's ugly. How you gonna have two champs? He's the alternate champ. I'm the real champ." With Frazier gone from the premises, Ali asked: "Was he smoking? He's smoking too much, gonna get cancer. Get TB. How's he gonna fight if he smokes?"

Ali delivered more one-liners than Henny Youngman.

Dr. Kleiman: "Is there any reason you shouldn't fight?"

Ali: "Only reason I shouldn't fight, that's if Joe Frazier don't show up."

Dr. Kleiman: "Have you been to a doctor in the last few weeks?"

Ali: "Nothing I can talk about . . . no, I'm just joking."

Dr. Kleiman: "Is there any other information you can give us?"

Ali: "About what?"

Dr. Kleiman: "Your physical condition?"

Ali: "Would you stop the show if I had a sore toe? Now would you stop all of this if I said I was hurt?"

Dr. Kleiman: "Please open your mouth and say . . . "

Ali: "You mean I got to open my mouth?"

Dr. Kleiman told Ali to touch the floor and his hips and put his hands in the air twenty times as Frazier had done. "*You* do it twenty times," Ali suggested. After the physical, Ali asked reporters if they wanted him to train in New York or return, as he originally planned, to Miami until Saturday or Sunday. "Stay here, stay here," they yelled. Of course, they wanted him to stay in New York. *The fight*, as it was now called by many, was only five days away. They needed to come up with a fresh angle every day, and with Ali around, that would not be difficult. He told them he would, as long as only the media were permitted to attend the workouts and a rollaway bed was placed in his dressing room for him to take a nap after training. Condon met both conditions.

Everyone was satisfied—everyone except Angelo Dundee, who worried that his fighter would deal with too many distractions in New York, hindering the training and the rest required to prepare for Frazier. The events over the previous couple of hours perfectly illustrated his point. When Ali arrived for the physical, extra police were needed to hold back the approximately two hundred fans waiting for him. In his dressing room, he was surrounded by people asking for autographs. "See what I mean?" Dundee said. "He'll get mobbed if we stay in New York. We've got to get back to the airport." A dark blue limousine descended to a loading zone in the basement of the Garden for Ali's getaway. Only this mob, like the teenyboppers chasing the Beatles in the movie *A Hard Day's Night*, was not easily outmaneuvered. As Ali stepped into the limo, the fans attempted to muscle their way past security. They got very close. The limo was able to take off in time, but as it sat in traffic on Thirty-third Street, people banged on the windows and the roof. Finally, the car was in the clear—well, almost in the clear.

"Nobody was left but this one kid, maybe in his late teens or early twenties," said Budd Schulberg, who went along for the ride. "We'd get to the next stop light and he would still be plugging along. The guys in the car were cynical about him, laughing, saying what a clown he was. But after about the tenth light, Ali said, 'Let's stop the car. Any kid that keeps running that far and tries that hard, I think we ought to stop the car.' He rolled down the window, shook his hand and talked to him, saying something like 'Boy, you must be training, you run pretty good.' The kid was so elated, finding it hard to believe he was actually talking to Ali."

Approaching JFK airport, Ali was still not totally convinced that flying back to Miami was necessary. He floated the idea of driving to his home in New Jersey. Dundee was in a tough spot. "Angelo knew that he could not tell Ali what to do," Schulberg said. "All he could do was set up possibilities and make Ali feel that it was Ali who was deciding it. He was very clever at doing that." In this case, they got to Ali through his stomach. He was told that a couple of steaks were waiting for him on the plane. Soon he was on board. "You had to trick him," Pacheco explained. "It was easy. You just had to know what he wanted."

And off went the whole gang, back to Miami, leaving behind a pack of writers forced to search for other pre-fight material. "I was no hero," Dundee said. "I just made him come back to train, which was important. He would have stayed there, and he was the kind of kid who would try to accommodate everyone." Perhaps the most disappointed was Condon, who had arranged for Ali to appear that evening on *The Tonight Show* with Johnny Carson, which was based in New York in those days. "I don't care what he was upset about," Dundee said. "We did enough to sell that fight." Carson was not too pleased, either. He said Ali would not be invited back. "I really kind of hate to do that," Carson said, "but damnit, it makes me angry. This is the second time it has happened, and I think two is enough." Carson gave him another chance; Ali was a guest on the show a few months later. During the telecast, according to Ali associate Gene Kilroy, "Ali said, 'You were mad at me,' and Carson said, 'I guess I had too many fights,' playing like he was punch drunk."

Everyone started to weigh in with predictions. In Las Vegas two days before the fight, the line was 7–5 in favor of Frazier; with London bookmakers, 11–8, Ali. Joe Louis picked Frazier, and so did Jose Torres and Jerry Quarry. Jimmy Ellis went with Ali. Just about the only prominent person in the fight game who did not offer a prediction was, ironically enough, Ali himself. He said that he would read it in front of a camera in the dressing room. The people watching on closed circuit, whom he considered *his* people, would hear it first. "They can't afford the fancy prices at Madison Square Garden," Ali said, " . . . so I'm going to give them the scoop." The prediction was supposedly kept by John Condon for days in a sealed envelope. According to Condon, *Sports Illustrated* even offered him $1,000 for it. The prediction was, in fact, handed over by Condon to his assistant, Patti Dreifuss, who left it in her unlocked desk until the day of the fight.

The search for last-minute tickets was frantic. "I was offered bribes like crazy," Dreifuss said. One call came from the manager of singer Johnny Mathis. "I can't remember exactly what he offered me, but I do know my answer was, 'You could pay my rent for a whole year and I still couldn't get you a ticket.'" Joe Hand heard from the owner of a Cadillac dealership who wanted two ringside seats. "You give me the seats and $1,000," the dealer said, "and you can come down and take any Cadillac you want out of here." Hand declined.

On the final afternoon, the scene got so crazy that Harry Markson left his office. "He just couldn't handle it," Kenville said. "The phone rang every thirty seconds and he didn't have any seats. I didn't know where he was. I did not want to know." At one point, Condon entered Kenville's office and shut the door. "I know that you have two tickets," Condon told him. "I don't want to see where they are. I will turn around and face the door and you will put the two tickets in my hand. Don't protest. I know you've got them hidden." Kenville retrieved the two tickets from his drawer and did not utter a word. Condon left. "I was holding them for last-minute emergencies," Kenville admitted.

Around the same time, Chartwell's Don Loze was wrapping up a few details with a banker in Manhattan, his excitement growing by the second. After nearly two months of criss-crossing the country to help secure territories, Loze could finally relax and watch the fight in person. Just then, the banker asked for a ticket. Loze immediately knew what he had to do. He gave him his ticket. "He was the guy in charge of coordinating the flow of the money from the local promoters into the bank account," Loze said. "I wanted the deal to work." It seemed that the only ones with extra tickets were the scalpers. "We could have sold out ten Madison Square Gardens," said Alvin Cooperman, the Garden's executive vice president.

Ali seemed as confident as ever in the final days. "He was calm and serene," Pacheco said. "He thought he was going to beat him. He never lost! He beat Sonny Liston and Sonny Liston was way meaner and more dangerous than Joe Frazier. Frazier was little. People don't really remember. Ali said, 'This guy is little. I'm going to lean all over him.' Little is not good in heavyweight championship boxing." Despite all the clowning and the willingness to let his sparring partners pound away at his body, Ali was in better shape than he had been for Jerry Quarry or Oscar Bonavena. He had taken Bonavena lightly and certainly was not about to make the same mistake with Frazier. He ran three miles a day, compared to Frazier's five or six, but, as Dundee pointed out, "None of my fighters ran more than three miles. They're not marathon runners. They get their legs in shape. You work hard in running. You work hard in the gym, what do you have left for the fight?"

An obvious drawback Ali faced was that he could not spar, as Dundee put it, against a "clone of Joe Frazier. Joe Frazier was Joe Frazier." In Ali's final workout in Miami Beach, he skipped rope and hit the light bag and the heavy bag. Afterward, he talked about the red-tasseled white shoes, imported from Germany, that he planned to wear on Monday night. One who was not particularly thrilled about the shoes was Ferdie Pacheco. "What the fuck are you doing with those tassels?" he later asked Ali. "So that the judges can be impressed when I'm dancing—makes me look like I'm going faster," Ali said. "What if they knock you on your ass and the tassels are dangling in the air where your legs are?" Pacheco said. Ali told him, "That's never going to happen." Howard Cosell, who came to the Fifth Street Gym to tape a fight preview for ABC, was not fooled by Ali's bravado. "I watched Ali intently in his last workout," he wrote in his autobiography. "I didn't like what I saw. He didn't seem in any sense to be the old Ali. He seemed tired."

On Saturday, March 6, Ali and Frazier returned to New York. Ali, who had logged 3,276 miles on three flights since Wednesday morning, set up headquarters at the Hotel New Yorker, a block from the Garden. Frazier checked into the City Squire Motor Inn at Seventh Avenue and Fifty-second Street, although he switched over to the Hotel Pierre after the City Squire received a bomb threat. Four city detectives were added to the four who came with Frazier from Philadelphia. A week earlier, an anonymous letter followed up by a phone call had warned Frazier to "lose or else." Also providing protection was Tom Payne, a former Philly cop. Payne met Yank Durham in 1964.

"One day, he said to me that Joe was going to become champion, and I said if he's going to be the next champ, he's going to need a bodyguard," Payne said. "I was totally B.S.ing. I just threw it out to have something to say." Payne spoke to Durham infrequently over the next three years. In 1967, the phone rang. "You ready?" Durham asked. "Ready for *what*?" Payne said. It was time, Durham told him, for the bodyguard. Payne was put on the payroll. During training camp, wherever Joe Frazier went, so did Payne. He watched the cooks prepare Frazier's food. He slept in the same room, a gun under his pillow. "That was a habit with me," Payne said. The death threats and sudden switch in hotels did not faze Frazier. "I never saw him unnerved," Payne indicated, "other than the fact that he doesn't like earthworms." On the night of the fight, about two hundred special uniformed guards and plainclothesmen, along with close to three hundred of New York's finest, patrolled the grounds.

On Sunday afternoon, Ali invited a small group of writers to his suite, including Budd Schulberg and *Los Angeles Times* columnist Jim Murray, for what essentially became a three-hour monologue. "Frazier's no real champion," Ali said. "Nobody wants to talk to him. Oh maybe Nixon. Nixon will call him if he wins. I don't think he'll call me. But 98 percent of my people are for me. They identify with my struggle. Same one they're fightin' every day—in the streets and against the police. If I win, they win. I lose, they lose. Anybody black who thinks Frazier can whup me is an Uncle Tom."

Later that evening, Frazier was watching television in his room when, he claimed in his autobiography, he received a call from Ali.

"Joe Frazier, you ready?" Ali asked.

"I'm ready, brother," Frazier said.

"I'm ready too, Joe Frazier," Ali told him. "And you can't beat me. 'Cause I am the greatest."

"You know what," Frazier said, "you preach that you're one of God's men. Well, we'll see whose corner the Lord will be in."

The repartee was reminiscent of a conversation the two had held about six months earlier in Frazier's car on the way from Philadelphia to New York. Ali, still without a license, asked Frazier if he could interview him for his book. Each bragged about what he would do to the other if the opportunity ever arose. Now, finally, it was only hours away.

"We were laughin' and havin' fun," Frazier said, referring to the 1970 trip. "We were friends, we were great friends. He was a brother. He called me Joe: 'Hey, Smokin' Joe!'"

Those days seemed a lifetime ago. These days, Ali was calling him a Tom, not Joe. Frazier could not wait to make him pay for his attacks. "He kept saying, 'Just watch this guy. Make sure he gets into the ring,'" said George Kalinsky, who spoke with Frazier on several occasions between the photo shoot in January and the fight. 'Make sure nothing happens to him.' He was saying that tongue-in-cheek."

Frazier was ready, all right. He had sparred for about 200 rounds in camp. "We had to rein him in because he was peaking too soon," Les Pelemon said. "We laid off training for a little while and then threw him back to get his adrenaline going." The champion was so confident that he planned a "victory party" at the Statler Hilton Hotel featuring Duke Ellington's orchestra. If he was feeling good enough, Frazier would also perform with the Knockouts. Ali could not resist the opening. "The Joe Frazier victory party," Ali joked, "is going to be like a wedding where the groom don't show up."

On the eve of the fight, those who opposed Ali remained vehement. William Loeb, the owner of the ultra-conservative *Manchester Union-Leader* in New Hampshire and a few other New England newspapers, did not accept any advertisements related to the event, and in the final week rejected any related news stories as well. "Any able bodied American who will not fight for his own country," Loeb wrote in a front-page editorial, "doesn't deserve to be allowed to fight in the prize ring." Earlier, the city council in Oklahoma City had voted 5 to 3 to prohibit the Civic Center Music Hall from being used for a closed-circuit telecast. Ali was under no illusions. He knew there were millions around the United States hoping to see him receive a beating they felt he richly deserved. He knew there were also millions hoping to see him administer the beating, to prevail over the Establishment, which could put him down but not out.

No fight in boxing history, not even the famous Louis-Schmeling rematch, had ever received this kind of hype. During these last few weeks, Muhammad Ali and Joe Frazier were everywhere: On the cover of *Life* and *Time*. On a television commercial for Vitalis hair products. On the minds of those who knew everything about the sport, and those who knew nothing. For the first time ever, two undefeated heavyweight champions, in a classic duel of the boxer versus the slugger, were going to meet in the ring. (John L. Sullivan and James J. Corbett were also unbeaten when they met in 1892, but each had a draw on his record.) "I don't know how you could have been in America and not have cared about that fight," Larry Merchant said.

8

March 8

Wearing a white T-shirt and yellow sweatpants, Joe Frazier woke up. It was 8:30 a.m., Monday, March 8, 1971.

Fourteen hours to go.

"Countdown!" he shouted.

"This is the day, champ," Pelemon told him.

The day began as many did for Frazier, music blasting from the record player. He walked to the mirror and, assuming a slight crouch, unleashed a flurry of left hooks and right crosses against an imaginary opponent. "I'm gonna kill this scamboogah tonight," he vowed, according to Pelemon. After his brief workout, Frazier chatted with the detectives, mostly about music.

The day began differently for Muhammad Ali. For a change, the shepherd did not tend to his flock. He did not go shopping as he had hours before the Bonavena fight. He did not field calls from friends asking for tickets as he had hours before the Quarry fight. By spending the extra three days in Miami Beach, Ali wisely avoided the distractions of the big city, and he wouldn't deal with them at this late juncture. He needed to concentrate on the enormous task ahead. He was not fighting Jerry Quarry or Oscar Bonavena. He was fighting the toughest man around. In twenty-six fights, Joe Frazier had knocked out twenty-three opponents, a .885

percentage. No top heavyweight had ever recorded a higher knock-out rate, not even Marciano. Of the twenty-three victims, eighteen were stopped in the first five rounds. As hundreds of his followers hung out in the lobby, Ali remained in his room.

Twelve hours to go.

Around 11 a.m., Frazier and his party left for the weigh-in at the Felt Forum. Once again, the athletic commission's Edwin Dooley decided to keep the fighters apart, scheduling Frazier for 11:30, Ali an hour later. The weigh-in ritual had been a non-event in professional boxing until that unforgettable day in February 1964 when Ali, then Cassius Clay, went berserk before his first fight against Sonny Liston in Miami Beach. "Somebody's gonna die at ringside tonight!" Clay screamed. "You're scared chump! You ain't no giant! I'm gonna eat you alive!" With Clay's blood pressure twice its normal level, Dr. Alexander Robbins determined that he was "emotionally unbalanced, scared to death, and liable to crack up before he enters the ring."

Clay's outburst, as was often the case, was an act—an hour later, his pulse was back to its usual rate—and many fell for it, including Sonny Liston. Liston believed that Clay was truly crazy, which worked to Clay's advantage. A crazy person, Liston figured, would not be scared of him like the rest of the human race was. Because of Dooley's decision, any chance for an encore with Frazier was removed. On his way to the weigh-in, Frazier spoke about his wife, his kids, and finding a new home for his mother in South Carolina. "It seems he wanted to talk about anything but the fight," Pelemon said. "If you ask me, he's calmer for this fight than any fight I've ever been with him." Frazier tipped the scales at 205½, slightly heavier than he hoped he would be, but nothing to worry about. His beard was gone, shaved off in the morning, and soon he was gone, too. Back in his hotel room, he enjoyed a steak, a baked potato, and a salad.

Nine hours to go.

Ali was next. The Hotel New Yorker was only a block away, but the journey turned into another chaotic one for the rock star that Muhammad Ali had become. The first mission was escaping the hotel before the fans blocked his path. The mission was accomplished, barely. The second was reaching the designated drop-off area. This mission was not accomplished. The driver of the black Cadillac limo made a wrong turn, got stuck in one-way traffic, and then circled the building three times before finally docking at a truck delivery entrance. By taking this unplanned route, the Ali entourage was left with only one of New York's finest—and oldest—to usher everyone safely inside.

"The car ground to a halt before a ramp door that slowly opened and then closed, castle-drawbridge fashion," Pacheco wrote, "sealing off the humanoids who discovered our presence, rushed after us with a collective roar, and swallowed the old policeman." One can assume that Joe Frazier never went through a similar experience. "We were constantly surrounded by humanity," Dundee said. "Frazier could have walked around the block and nobody would have bothered him. That is where the difference was. I had to be very careful that he [Ali] didn't have a mass of humanity ruining him."

More chaos greeted them in the dressing room. A camera crew shot Ali conversing with Burt Lancaster. It was around this time, according to Neal Marshall, that Ali opened the envelope and read his prediction, to be shown live during the closed-circuit telecast: "FLASH. I Predict, First of all, that all the Frazier fans, and Boxing experts, will be shocked at how easy I will beat Joe Frazier, who will look like an Amateur Boxer compared to Muhammad Ali, and they will admit I was the Real Champion all the time. FRAZIER FALLS IN 6." Finally, about one-thirty, an hour behind schedule, Ali, donning a white terrycloth robe over red trunks, was ready for his close-up. John Condon again introduced him as the "former" world heavyweight champion, and Ali again pretended to take offense. "I am the champion," he yelled. "I am the king. . . . I am going to straighten this thing out tonight for all of you experts who have been picking Frazier. I am going to whip Frazier, Jack Dempsey, Joe Louis and all you experts." Ali weighed in at 215, three pounds more than he had for Bonavena, and the heaviest of his career.

Ali did not return to the hotel after the weigh-in. The Garden had decided several days earlier that sending him back into the streets in the middle of the day would likely create another mob scene, and after what had taken place already, nobody, including Ali, raised an objection. "It was the only way to go," Pacheco said, "and it was the first time we had ever been in anything quite like that, where you cannot walk across the street back to your own hotel. The only way to keep him out of it was to keep him hidden." Ali was stashed in the press lounge on the first promenade (the room was available because it was not big enough to accommodate the hundreds of reporters with credentials), which was supposed to cater to his every whim—color TV, phone, bed. Except that when the group got there, according to Pacheco, there was no TV and no phone, and the bed was a cot. Pacheco quickly secured a folding bed from Harry Markson that was not exactly ideal for a man six-foot-three, but it was better than a cot. Everyone settled in to kill the remaining hours.

"They stayed there all day," Tom Kenville said. "There must have been a total of fifteen people and I believe they ran up a bill of about four thousand dollars in food and beverages." Ali, as usual, could not keep still. With the Garden virtually empty, "he started running around the promenade, moving through the circular aisles that go around the place," Kenville added. "I was numbering the press seats and talking with Burt Lancaster when he started hollering, 'What are you doing down there? Get it right.' Then he went back in his room."

Kenville was not the only one Ali heckled. Neal Marshall and Art Fisher were staging a rehearsal with boxers from Gil Clancy's gym on Twenty-eighth Street standing in for Frazier and Ali. They did not care about their fistic or acting credentials. All that mattered was that each fighter came as close as possible to resembling the skin tone of the combatant he portrayed. The goal was to determine how the image of the fighters on the canvas would translate to the screen. Marshall and Fisher were aiming to avoid a repeat of the embarrassing five-second blackout that occurred when Frazier

knocked Jimmy Ellis out in 1970. When the Ali double fell to the
floor, the real one shouted from the balcony: "Ain't no way that
Ali is getting knocked down. That is never going to happen!" He
issued instructions to the fighter playing him. "Speed up! Float like
a butterfly," he said. At 2:30, Ali ate his last prefight meal, which,
like his rival's, consisted of a steak, a potato, and a salad.

Eight hours to go.

For most of the day, Arthur Mercante was in his office at 485
Madison Avenue. Mercante worked in sales for the Schaefer Brew-
ing Company. Only, on this special day, Mercante was not thinking too much about how to market beer, and who could blame the
guy? He was hoping for a call from the New York State Athletic
Commission telling him to show up at the Garden a few hours later.
Once inside, as was custom, he and two others would soon find out
who had been selected by the commission as the referee for the
night's main event, Ali versus Frazier; the two who did not get it
would end up with other responsibilities. "Of course I was dying to
get the assignment," Mercante wrote in his autobiography. "Everyone was. The minutes, then the hours, ticked away interminably."
Also reportedly in contention for the job were Barney Felix, Zack
Clayton, Al Berl, Johnny Lobianco, Mark Conn, and Tony Perez.

Conn's chances were perhaps lessened by his inability in the
Ali-Bonavena bout to make certain that Ali went to a neutral corner after knocking his opponent down in the fifteenth round. A
referee can stop the count if the fighter fails to abide by the rule,
and start over once he reaches the neutral corner. The most
famous example came in the Dempsey-Tunney rematch in 1927,
known as the long-count fight. Because Dempsey did not proceed
to the corner after knocking Tunney down in the seventh round,
the count did not start for several seconds, allowing Tunney extra
time to recover; Tunney prevailed by unanimous decision. Durham
demanded that the commission select a referee who would guarantee that Ali obeyed the rules. He complained that Ali also failed to

retreat to a neutral corner in the second Liston fight, and when he defeated Cleveland Williams.

"He walked away when he wanted to," Durham said. "The referees let him get away with it." The Frazier and Ali camps were allowed to voice their objections about specific referees, but the commission was not obligated to disqualify anyone.

Perez was perhaps the strongest candidate. He had worked Frazier-Ellis and Ali-Quarry, the two most significant heavyweight fights of 1970. At the same time, the Mercante résumé was very impressive. He began as a referee in the United States Navy during the war, and became a regular at the New York Golden Gloves tournament until he officiated his first professional match in 1957, Garnel Hart versus Charley Cotton, at St. Nicholas Arena in New York. His prior championship bouts included Floyd Patterson versus Ingemar Johansson II, Emile Griffth versus Dick Tiger, Benny "Kid" Paret versus Luis Federico Thompson, and Frazier versus Quarry. Mercante also did Frazier's fights with Mathis and Ramos. "My style of refereeing a fight has always been the same, to be in the scene, but be unseen," Mercante said. "A lot of referees are not in very good condition. They can't use that style because they get in a little too late if they have to break." Mercante was highly regarded within the industry. "Arthur was one of the best referees around, there was no question about that," said Tony Castellano, a boxing official since the early 1950s.

At 4 p.m., the phone rang. The call was the one Arthur Mercante was hoping for. He was to show up at the Garden, which officially meant he was still in the running, although, as he told Thomas Hauser in 1989, "that's when I knew I had it." He went first to the New York Athletic Club. He normally took a steam and a shower before a big fight, and they certainly did not come any bigger than this. "It totally relaxed me," Mercante said. Afterward, he ate a steak and hopped on the subway. At the Garden, he was given the official word. The fight was his. The work was not going to make Mercante rich—he took home only $500 and was back at the office by eight the next morning—but being the referee for the fight of the century was never about the money. "It was a great feeling," Mercante recalled, "but you know the heat's on and you better be prepared."

Everyone showed up early—the scalpers, the spectators, the people who wanted to be seen, and the people who wanted to see them. The traffic heading toward the Garden moved so slowly that some taxis and limos dropped their passengers off eight blocks away. There was certainly no shortage of cops. "We're using everything tonight," one sergeant said. Yet even with the heightened police presence, the scene at Eighth Avenue and Thirty-third Street was far from secure. "I saw one guy grab a ticket out of a lady's hand," said Edwin Pope, who covered the fight for the *Miami Herald*. "She yelled, and the doorman saw it, but there was nothing he could do about it. I have never seen people hired to keep order at a fight get so scattered like they were that night, just completely overwhelmed."

One victim was comedian David Brenner. Brenner was escorting his date, a redheaded model, when a kid, probably no older than nineteen or twenty, took the two tickets from his hand and sprinted down the steps. Brenner was wearing a tux, but that did not prevent him from reacting in the same manner he would have if the crime had taken place during his teenage days on the streets of Philadelphia. He jumped off a landing right on top of the thief, who was with four or five others, punched him several times, and retrieved his tickets. The crowd applauded. After brushing himself off, Brenner approached a policeman who witnessed the whole thing.

"I said to the cop, 'Why didn't you do something?'" Brenner said. "He said, 'Come on, Dave, I saw you had it under control.' I swear to God. I had to laugh."

Others were robbed, as well, by scalpers. Ringside seats with a face value of $150 were generally going for anywhere from $400 to $600, while $100 tickets were sold for three times as much. One scalper estimated that as much as 60 percent of the crowd spent above the listed price. "There's lawyers, doctors, accountants scalping tickets," the scalper said. "These are straight people, right? These are people who abide by the law, right? Well, when you can turn over a quick buck, you try it." For some buyers, money was definitely no object. "I had six or eight of the best seats in the Garden," Bob Arum said, "and I was offered something like $2,500 a ticket, which was unbelievable. I thought people were crazy to pay that money." In all, 20,455 showed up, producing a record indoor gate of $1,352,961.

Instead of just before the main event, Harry Markson, according to Tom Kenville, decided to have the national anthem performed hours earlier. "Harry thought that if it played before the introductions of Ali and Frazier," Kenville explained, "there would be too much noise in the house with all the celebrities, and all the excitement. It wouldn't get the proper respect that it deserved." The anthem was performed by the Garden organist, Eddie Layton. At 8:45 p.m., with the building about half-filled, the preliminary matches got under way.

Two hours to go.

In the opening bout, light heavyweight Tom Kocan put away Joey Vasquez in only seventy-two seconds. In the following two fights, the winners were heavyweights Paul Simonetti and John Griffin. Next up was Rahaman, Ali's younger brother. He did not fight very often (seven times in seven years) or very well, but he never lost—until now. With a right to the chin, England's Don McAlinden almost knocked Rahaman out in the fourth round, taking the six-round decision. After watching his brother from a back corridor, Ali went back to his dressing room. The defeat, according to Pacheco, did not bother Ali. "That's the thing that people don't understand about Ali," Pacheco said. "He is in his own little chamber. Believe me, you're not getting in there. It's boxing. People lose, people win."

*   *   *

Neal Marshall and Art Fisher were in the middle of final preparations when Jack Kent Cooke entered the production truck.

"Boys," Cooke said, "we have a problem. Our deal with distributors all over the world is that we must deliver an interview with Joe Frazier before the fight. I need you to go to his dressing room and convince him to do an interview." Marshall and Fisher left immediately. When they arrived at the champ's dressing room, they were greeted by Yank Durham, who turned down their request.

"Yank was determined to keep Frazier out of what he called 'the verbal path of combat.' He was going to talk to nobody," Marshall said. Somehow they managed to convince Durham to allow them to run the idea by his fighter. "Joe Frazier was getting ready, shadowboxing," Marshall said, "his focus in the ring. Art and I go into this babble, two fast-talking Jews trying to find some way to get him to talk." They were clearly not going to get anywhere on their own. Fortunately, when they told Frazier that Archie Moore, a fighter he greatly admired, would ask the questions, the champ relented. After the cameras stopped rolling, even with everything going on, Frazier's focus shifted for a moment from the ring to Fisher's unique Afro-like hairdo.

"How do you get your hair to do that?" Frazier asked. "Whenever I let my hair grow out, I can't get my hair to look like your hair."

"I have the magic comb," said Fisher, who pulled it out.

Frazier laughed.

About 10 p.m., many of the top names in show business took their seats. They included Gene Kelly, Woody Allen, Ed Sullivan, Joey Bishop, Peter Falk, Robert Goulet, Carol Lawrence, Dick Cavett, Lorne Greene, Diana Ross, Michael Caine, Bill Cosby, James Taylor, David Frost, Diahann Carroll, Buddy Rich, and Andy Williams. Taylor, in fact, had been booked to perform in the Garden on the same night. In exchange for releasing the Garden from its

contract, according to Alvin Cooperman, the singer was given fif-
teen pairs of free tickets and a new date. "They weren't great seats,"
Taylor admitted. "They were on the balcony somewhere but it was
an amazing event." Among the other celebrities were former vice
president Hubert Humphrey, Senator Edward Kennedy, Ethel
Kennedy, Senator John Tunney (son of heavyweight champion
Gene), Joe Namath, Sargent Shriver, New York City mayor John
Lindsay, and Apollo 14 astronauts Alan Shepard, Stuart Roosa, and
Edgar Mitchell, who had returned from the moon in February.

The evening's fashions rivaled the display in Atlanta. LeRoy
Neiman wore a red velvet suit with a bright yellow necktie. Diana
Ross showed up in black velvet hot pants. Barbi Benton, escorted
by Hugh Hefner, wore black silk hot pants, a see-through chiffon
blouse, and a monkey-fur coat. Hefner, according to Neal Marshall, initially asked whether he could view the fight at the Playboy Mansion in Chicago. Yes, Hef was told, but it would cost him
$30,000. Among the other costumes: a black coat trimmed with an
oversized white fox collar and cuffs, a camel-colored wolf coat and
matching hat with animal tails, and a floor-length fringed suede
vest worn over beige suede hot pants. By comparison, Colonel
Harland Sanders, of Kentucky Fried Chicken, was almost drab in
his traditional white suit.

Thirty minutes to go.

Meanwhile, crowds had begun to gather at closed-circuit locations
across the country. In New York, at Radio City Music Hall, sold
out for days, approximately 6,000 fans arrived to watch the fight in
color on a screen 40 feet wide and 30 feet high. According to John
Condon, this was the first time Radio City stopped their movies or
stage performances to show a sporting event. In Pittsburgh, about
5,500 brave souls went to Three Rivers Stadium, the only venue in
the Steel City to provide the telecast, despite 18-degree temperatures, occasional snowflakes, and winds gusting at 30 miles per
hour. The fight was displayed on a 40-foot drive-in-type screen
between first and third bases. Some made the trip from as far as

Buffalo, 200 miles away, where the fight was a sellout. In Chicago, only one of seventeen outlets did not sell out. Of the roughly 350 closed-circuit venues in the United States, 250 showed the fight in black and white. There was not sufficient equipment in those days for more screenings in color.

Around the world, the interest was just as great. In Buenos Aires, the streets were deserted. In London, many stayed up all night, the match getting under way at about 4:40 a.m. local time. In northern Italy, millions watched on TV in hotels, bars, and nightclubs, including French, Swiss, Germans, and Austrians who crossed the border. In Manila, children were requested to bring their televisions into school, with classes suspended for the duration of the fight. In rice paddies and barracks across Southeast Asia, thanks to the late negotiating session between the promoters and the Pentagon, U.S. servicemen listened to a blow-by-blow account on their transistor radios. Ultimately, an estimated 300 million people watched the fight.

Precisely what Muhammad Ali was thinking in the dressing room during these final moments is impossible to know. Outwardly, he seemed the same Ali. Butch Lewis, a member of the Frazier circle who accompanied Eddie Futch to Ali's dressing room to make sure his hands were properly taped, told Thomas Hauser that Ali got off the rubdown table and started to dance and throw jabs. "You take this back to Joe. I'm gonna knock him out." Ali said.

Inwardly, however, did Ali believe he was going to knock Frazier out? Was he honest with the most important person—himself? In the four years since defending his title for the last time, against Zora Folley, Ali had been between the ropes for only 18 rounds, less than an hour, and many of them were among the least impressive of his career. The Quarry fight proved he needed more work. The Bonavena fight proved he couldn't dance all night. What would the Frazier fight prove?

In the other dressing room, Joe Frazier was aiming to prove a lot. He had captured a piece of the heavyweight championship for the first time against Buster Mathis and prevailed against Jimmy Ellis, but many fans would not consider him the real champ until he beat Ali—and he knew it. He was furious about the cruel things Ali said about him. He tried to defend himself with words, but his words could never match his opponent's, and that he knew as well. He would answer Ali the only way he knew how, in the ring, where there would be no press, no escapes, just man against man, will against will. "He was not going to lose that fight," Joe Hand remembered, "unless he got killed." Frazier said a prayer before he left the dressing room. "I asked the Lord," Frazier later told his son Marvis, "Lord, help me to kill this man because he's not righteous."

At 10:30, ring announcer Johnny Addie began introducing greats from the past: James J. Braddock ("Cinderella Man"), Rocky Graziano, Willie Pep, Jack Dempsey, Archie Moore, Jack Sharkey, Sugar Ray Robinson, Billy Conn, Joe Louis. Louis received a huge ovation as he climbed into the ring. Life was often difficult for the Brown Bomber after boxing—he worked as a greeter at a Las Vegas casino—but then there were moments like this, the fans honoring him for the years he gave them, a hero to his race and his nation. Soon the crowd's focus shifted to the present heroes. They were coming, at last, down the aisles, Ali first, followed a short time after by Frazier.

They entered the ring, Frazier in the the green robe he chose with as much attention to detail as a Hollywood starlet picking a gown for the Oscars. On the back, in gold, was his name, and embroidered between the "Joe" and the "Frazier" were the names of his five children. Ali wore a white satin robe, and those white shoes with the red tassels he told Pacheco were sure to impress the judges. Ali started to glide around the ring, throwing jabs. When reaching Frazier's corner, he brushed lightly against him. His rival was not intimidated. "I just glared at him, and watched him dance away," Frazier wrote in his book. "Was nothing he could do that could unsettle me now. My time was here. This was real. Me and damn Clay in the four squares." Later, according to Larry Merchant, it was revealed that "Ali had been skipping and almost singing to Frazier, as well as to himself, 'two and a half million dollars. Can you believe, two and a half million dollars?'"

Addie seized the microphone. "Introducing from Louisville, Kentucky, he's wearing red trunks, he weighs 215, undefeated in 31 bouts, scoring 25 knockouts, here is Muhammad Ali." Ali's fans cheered. "His opponent," Addie said, "from Philadelphia, Pennsylvania, he's wearing green trunks, he's weighing 205½ pounds, undefeated in 26 bouts, scoring 23 knockouts, the heavyweight champion of the world, Joe Frazier." Frazier's fans cheered. The fighters met in the center of the ring for Arthur Mercante's instructions. Ali started talking. Frazier wrote years later that he let "the anger inside me fester," and then, as Ali "babbled on, I looked at him and told him: 'I'm gonna kill you.'" They headed back to their corners, Ali pausing for a final prayer.

Larry Merchant has been to hundreds of fights and other major sporting events during five decades as a writer and broadcaster. No sound compares to the one he heard in Madison Square Garden at roughly 10:40 p.m on March 8, 1971.

"There was this guttural roar," Merchant recalled. "I can still summon it in my mind's ear. It came straight up from the stomach, from a place that went beyond the heart, that the heart could not control, much less the mind. People could hardly believe the fight was going to happen."

And then it did. At last.

9

The Fight

Ali, a left to the head, followed by a right. Ali, moving well, landed the majority of punches in the opening round, which was to become the pattern for the rest of the fight. With a nearly seven-inch reach advantage, he scored with his superb jab, the key to his chances. He needed to keep Frazier as far away as possible. Ali launched another left, and a right to the head. If he was going to send Frazier to the canvas, round one might well be his best opportunity. Yet Frazier kept coming. Joe Frazier always kept coming, every round, every fight. He knew no other way. In scoring points, Frazier was typically a slow starter—he dropped the first round to Buster Mathis and Jerry Quarry and Jimmy Ellis, and was not particularly sharp against Bob Foster—but against Ali he got in some hard shots to the body. *If you kill the body, the head will die.* He did not ignore the head either, scoring with a left to the jaw. As usual, Frazier bobbed and weaved, making him appear even shorter in comparison to the six-foot-three Ali. No heavyweight moved his head and upper body as much as Frazier.

Always the showman, Ali shook his head several times to indicate to the crowd that none of these punches inflicted any real damage. Maybe they didn't, but at the very least they reached their destination, and that was enough for now. Before Ali was stripped of his crown, that did not happen too often. Frazier connected with a

181

solid left to the body as Ali tied him up. Ali fought back with a couple of left jabs, but Frazier scored with a left to the jaw. Mercante, who warned Ali for grabbing Frazier around the head, a manuever he often employed, and judge Artie Aidala awarded the round for Ali. Judge Bill Recht gave it to Frazier.

"Who won the round?" Ali asked Dundee when he approached the corner. The answer was obvious.

Early in the second round, Frazier landed a left hook to the head, though he paid for it with a left-right combination and two lefts to the head. Yet Frazier kept going forward, scoring again with a shot to Ali's jaw, another to the body. Frazier knew precisely what he was doing. "He would be forced to fight my fight," he explained in his autobiography, "and that smug expression of his would fade like grease before a spot remover. . . . I wasn't worried that he was hitting me with the jab because I was forcing him to jab so that he would be vulnerable to my left hook."

For the time being, however, Ali was fighting *his* fight. If not dancing as he did in the first round, Ali, utilizing his tremendous hand speed, connected with two lefts and two rights. He took another round, this time in the view of all three judges. Both fighters were told by Mercante to stop talking. Don Dunphy could not believe it. "They have time for that?" Dunphy said on the closed-circuit telecast.

When the round was over, Ali waved his glove derisively, letting the fans know that he did not think too much of what he had witnessed up to that point from the *official* world heavyweight champion. He even refused to sit on his stool between rounds. A hook to the chin had appeared to sting Ali late in the round, but he winked to observers at ringside after Dundee splashed water in his face. Frazier, however, knew better. "I gave all those Clay fans a sneak preview of what was to come," he wrote. "[Clay] threw his arms around me as if I was a treasured possession."

In the third, Ali started off with a hard left to the head, but was promptly tagged by a Frazier left to the body. Ali put together two left-right combinations, but they did not keep Frazier from pressing ahead. Frazier connected with a right to the head and a left to the ribs. Ali again attempted to curtail Frazier's pursuit with a left and a right to the head, but nothing could stop him. Not on this night. "It's amazing that Frazier can stand up under that battering," Dunphy said. Ali found himself against the ropes, the absolute worst place to be against Frazier, who scored with a left to the jaw, followed by another left and right. Ali, covering up when the bell sounded, seemed a bit shaken, although after consulting with his corner, he assured his supporters he was in control. He was not. The round, Frazier's first, was awarded to him by all three judges. He was gaining inside position, which was not an encouraging sign for Ali. That was how Frazier always caused the most harm.

Ali was back on the ropes in the fourth, although he was able to score with left jabs. Yet Frazier, too, was scoring, with a left hook to Ali's jaw and a short right. Soon came a left hook to the head, a right to the ribs, and another left to the jaw. Ali wasn't moving much, although, Pacheco said, the strategy was by design. "When he saw that Frazier was determined and stuck to him," Pacheco maintained, "he thought he better come down and do some fighting because he could not stand on his toes and fight for fifteen rounds. He would be exhausted and he knew it." The plan, according to Pacheco, was "to get Joe tired of punching while, at the same time, he would get punched pretty good." The plan made a lot of sense against the average Joe (and, known as the *rope-a-dope*, would be especially successful three years later, in Zaire, against George Foreman), but not this Joe. Frazier did not seem to mind if Ali landed two or three punches to his one. He knew that his one, the left hook especially, would be the punch that mattered the most. All three judges again gave the round to Frazier. The fight was even.

Even so, Ali did not stop fooling around.

"Noooooooooo contest," he often said when Frazier got in a good lick. Except it was very much a contest, and he was in jeopardy of losing it.

"The joke was on him," Frazier wrote. "I was fighting in earnest, and he was just trying to disguise the fact that he was stalling." At one point in the early rounds, according to Frazier, Ali said, "Don't you know I'm God," to which the champion replied: "God, you in the wrong place tonight. I'm kicking ass and taking names."

In any case, Ali must have realized he was in for the fight of his life. In the fourth round, he later wrote, Ali felt the "first of the hard hooks explode against my jaw . . . bells ring in my head . . . I stab back but he drives in again, bobs, weaves and comes under."

In the fifth, Frazier connected with a left to the body and a hard left to the head. Ali landed a left and right, but the momentum clearly belonged to the defending champion. Frazier was so confident that he began to do his own taunting. He lowered his hands, inviting Ali to take his best shot, and when he did, a left, and then a right, Frazier laughed. He wanted Ali to know that "I could take anything he could dish out," Frazier said. Durham, however, was not very amused. "He [Frazier] was just indulging himself and I guess you can't blame him. Yank admonished him between rounds not to do stupid things," Eddie Futch said. "There was so much emotion involved, so many things to prove." Frazier forced Ali into a corner, landing another left hook to the head. Ali responded with a left-right combination to the head, but these punches, like the others, were not very effective.

One thing was becoming clear. All those days in training camp, when Ali allowed himself to be belted in the midsection over and over by his sparring partners to toughen his body for Frazier, were obviously not paying off. Nothing could toughen his body for this kind of punishment. Frazier was pounding Ali in places where Ali had never been pounded before. When he later examined Ali, Pacheco was amazed at the extent of the damage that Frazier caused. "Joe was small and he was smaller because he was ducking down," Pacheco said, "so he was at the level of Ali's hips. He wasn't hitting his ribs or his shoulders. He was hitting his hips. The hips don't have any protection. I never saw anybody hit somebody in the hips two hundred times!" At the same time, Frazier was not exactly escaping unscathed; Ali was connecting against Frazier, and often. Ali was not known as a slugger who routinely put away his rivals with a single devastating strike; they fell, normally, as the result of a steady accumulation of blows.

"Those jabs were not ordinary jabs. They were much harder than most jabs because Frazier was moving so hard into them,"

Merchant pointed out. Nonetheless, Aidala and Mercante gave the fifth round to Frazier, his third in a row.

The bell sounded for round six. Round six was pivotal for Muhammad Ali. He had told the world, "Frazier falls in 6," and he always worked extremely hard to make good on his predictions. Against Bonavena, he might have tried too hard. Bonavena unloaded with a left hook and a right hand in round nine that hurt Ali. Ali later joked that he was almost predicting against himself. How Ali fared over these next three minutes might very well say a lot about his prospects the rest of the way. Frazier was ready. "I was looking across the ring at him," Frazier wrote, "knowing this was the round he'd called, and eager to make a liar out of him. When the bell rang, I sprang off my stool like a sprinter to meet him in center ring. 'Come on, sucker,' I shouted. 'This is the round. Let's go.'"

Frazier struck early. After taking several punches, he hit Ali with a left to the ribs. He pinned him against the ropes, again. Ali felt the punches, and the pressure. "Something has gone out of me," he wrote. "I feel tired and the fight is not half over. I know from experience that if I hold on, I will grow stronger. But the air in my lungs is hot, my arms are heavy. I look out at the crowd. I think how the world is watching. I've got to do what I said I would do." Ali landed a few left jabs, but Frazier, laughing, was not deterred. He was not falling in six, that much was obvious. He pummeled Ali with a right to the body, a left to the jaw. "Ali almost a sitting duck here," Dunphy declared. Yet it also became obvious that Frazier was not the only one to possess the grit of a champion.

"What's holding him up?" Frazier asked Durham after the round.

Aidala and Recht awarded the round to Frazier, Mercante siding with the challenger. Ali may have been trying to preserve energy, as Pacheco contended, but Frazier surely had a lot to do with why he was spending so much time on the ropes. "If Frazier is coming after you, you are not going to get away," writer Dave Kindred explained. "Ali had no choice. He had to fight the way he did."

Pacheco was concerned. "I had the feeling we were standing under a building which was crumbling," he said, "and that any minute, the whole building was going to fall on us." While others in the Ali corner believed the former champ would, as usual, find a way to pull out the victory, Pacheco thought to himself, "Not this fight. Unless he does something big, he ain't getting out of here."

Before the seventh got under way, Ali's handlers urged their fighter on, but there would be no rally, not this round. Instead, Frazier moved in again, scoring with powerful left hooks to the body, and a left and right to the head near the ropes. Ali threw a right and a short left to the head, but almost every exchange seemed to favor Frazier. He drove Ali to the ropes, getting off a sharp right to the body at the bell. Frazier was going after the head perhaps more than the experts had anticipated, but was very effective. Ali shook his head once more to reassure his fans. They weren't buying it. He lost another round, and the fight was almost half over. He was in trouble and they knew it. "Ah-lee, Ah-lee, Ah-lee," they chanted before the bell rang for round eight. He raised his right arm to acknowledge them, then pointed to Frazier's corner, to the crowd, and, finally, to himself, to make sure his opponent knew that he, Ali, was the one the people were cheering for, not him. His corner was unable to get him back on track. Could the fans?

At the Chicago Coliseum, fans were not chanting. They were rioting, and it was not because of what they saw on the screen. It was because of what they did *not* see. The projector broke down before the fight started. The approximately 7,000 spectators who forked over $10 per ticket were instructed to leave and check the newspapers for information on how to get their money back. That was not what they were hoping to hear. "We want it now, we want it now," they kept saying. Fans threw ticket counters, folding chairs, and bottles. The box office was smashed. Ironically, the person responsible for repairing the projector could not get past the police cordon.

Three other closed-circuit locations in the United States experienced equipment breakdowns. In Portland, Maine, the projector also didn't work. In Duluth, Minnesota, the audio worked but the picture did not. Fans huddled around the speakers as they did in the days of Dempsey and Louis. At Hunter College in New York, the screen was blurry for the first seven rounds and went dark in the eighth. Yet the vast majority of the roughly 1.5 million people in the United States and Canada who watched the fight on closed circuit got their money's worth. Those living near the Mexican border of Texas, meanwhile, fared even better, catching it on television by picking up the feed from a station in Monterey that aired the telecast from Independencia Mexicana Network in Mexico City. The bout was carried in Spanish, but at least one overjoyed Texan did not mind. "I don't care a hang about the commentary," he said. I just want to see the fight."

Back at the Garden, photographer Neil Leifer was having a pretty good night, except that he was making the same error he made during the 1969 Super Bowl in Miami when he took too many pictures of the heavily favored Baltimore Colts from the established NFL, and not enough of the AFL's New York Jets and their star quarterback Joe Namath. Like everyone else, Leifer figured the Jets did not have a chance.

"Everytime Ali would throw a punch, I would shoot a sequence," he recalled, "and when Frazier was throwing punches, unless it was something really good, I held up a bit. I thought those pictures were going to be wasted. The story of this fight was going to be Ali beating Frazier." Around the eighth or ninth round, Leifer started to reconsider his approach.

"I woke up to reality," he said. "I thought, 'Holy shit, Frazier might be winning the fight!'"

Ali started well in round 8 with a series of solid combinations. Moments later, though, he was again on the ropes, Frazier pounding away with two rights to the head. When Ali responded with playful taps on Frazier, fans began to boo. There was a limit to the amount of clowning they would tolerate, even from Muhammad

Ali. Merchant, sitting at ringside, started to wonder if Ali was making a crucial mistake. "I remember thinking," he said, "were Ali's
antics going to hurt him with the judges?"

After Mercante broke up the fighters, Ali urged Frazier to come
straight at him, which he did, and, not surprisingly, with more success. After Ali connected with two weak lefts, Frazier landed a strong
hook to the jaw. They were soon back at the ropes. "My weariness
is greater now," Ali wrote. "I wonder if Joe Louis is right about
those three and a half years. . . . The bell rings. I go back to my
corner. I've got to turn the fight around." The judges awarded
another round to Frazier, Dundee appearing quite annoyed. "Stop
playing," he admonished Ali. "Do you want to blow this fight? Do
you want to blow everything?" At the same time, perhaps there was
another explanation for Ali's decision to confront Frazier in the
trenches.

"I think this was a chance to prove he could really take it, so
instead of finessing and dancing, which he may not have been able
to do successfully, in any case, he was going to fight on Frazier's
terms," suggested the *New York Times*'s Robert Lipsyte. If that was,
indeed, Ali's rationale, to demonstrate his manhood, he was making the point but losing the fight. When the round was over, fans
started to chant, "Joe, Joe, Joe." While perhaps more spectators
in the Garden rooted for Ali, there was a substantial number of
Frazier admirers, who, *New York Post* columnist Pete Hamill wrote,
were cheering for a man who, in contrast to his adversary, "believed
in the ritual of this mean craft, who thought the form itself had a
certain value, and that there were some things you did not do."

Then, remarkably, Ali came to life. Late in the ninth round, he
landed a series of consecutive shots—lefts, rights, jabs, uppercuts—
to Frazier's head. As the bell sounded, Ali connected with another
sharp left hook to the jaw. The boos turned into cheers. "The
troops of Ali's second corps of energy had arrived," Norman Mailer
wrote in his *Life* piece, entitled *Ego*, "the energy for which he had
been waiting long agonizing, heart-sore vomit-mean rounds." Frazier had a lump over his left eye and was bleeding from the nose,

but kept his ground. "I refused to acknowledge their effect," Frazier wrote, "and just kept wacking at him, as if he hadn't showed me shit." Frazier, meanwhile, showed Ali a great deal. "Now I know he'll die before he quits," the former champion later wrote. Still, all three judges gave the ninth to Ali, the first time since the second round. The rapid pace of the fight was perhaps finally getting to Frazier. "Joe punched himself out in the prior round," Merchant said.

Nonetheless, after a rest, Frazier, as usual, was ready for further combat. Ali may have slowed him a bit in the ninth, but Frazier aimed to return the favor, connecting with a left to the jaw and a right to the ribs. It was during this round that Mercante made an error that could have been monumental. Prior to then, he was on the scene, although, as he liked to phrase it, "unseen." Mercante, boxing historian Bert Sugar noted, "did one thing that I was always impressed with. When he had to break, he would stand in the middle and make sure nobody got any type of advantage. He knew what to do." Maybe, but in breaking up a clinch in the tenth round, the experienced referee accidentally poked Frazier in the eye. An angry Frazier waved to Mercante. "Wait a minute," Frazier said. "Damn it, Yank," he went on. "I've got two fuckin' guys banging on me now." Mercante felt awful. "Right then a terrifying thought flashed through my mind," Mercante relayed in his autobiography. "What if Frazier decided on the spot that he wasn't going to fight anymore, with both Ali and Mercante taking pokes at him? The 'Fight of the Century' would, thanks to me, become the controversy of the century." He tried between rounds to apologize, but Durham was not in a very forgiving mood. Fortunately, for Mercante, and the sport, there was to be no controversy, then or ever. Frazier was not injured, scoring late in the round with solid lefts to the head and body, and another left to Ali's jaw as the bell rang. Although losing the round, Frazier remained ahead on two (Aidala, 6–4; Recht, 7–3) of the three cards; Mercante had Ali winning, 6–4. At one point in the tenth, Ali shouted to those at ringside, "He's out," referring to Frazier. Frazier was tired, to be sure, but he was far from *out*. "The real story was that Clay was so tired that all he could do was just stand there, taking my punches," Frazier wrote. There was certainly no panic in the Frazier corner. "He got hit a couple of good shots," Eddie Futch said afterwards, "but he was going with the punches. Clay wasn't setting himself that much, or the damage would have been greater."

The damage *was* greater in round 11—to Ali, not Frazier. The first part of the round was fairly uneventful, with nobody seizing a distinct advantage. Ali fell to the floor in the early moments, but Mercante immediately ruled that it was a slip. Perhaps the furious pace Frazier and Ali set would finally subside for an entire round, both conserving their stamina for the last two or three in a duel that could easily go the distance. Perhaps not. About two minutes into the round, Ali was backed up to the corner again when it came, the left hook, naturally, to his head, "the hardest hook I've ever taken in my life," he admitted. Ali's knees buckled. Frazier followed with a right and another left. Ali wobbled near the ropes, his eyes glassy. "He was on Queer Street," Brown said. "I prayed for him." Ali bent "forward like a sapling struck with an ax," Pete Hamill wrote. Ali was on his feet, barely. Nobody had ever seen him quite like this. The two times he was sent to the canvas, by Sonny Banks in 1962 and Henry Cooper in 1963, he recovered to win by technical knockout. Even against Liston, his fiercest combatant until Frazier, Ali was never seriously hurt.

This time was different. One more powerful shot and Ali would surely go down, and might not recover. The shot never came. As Ali flopped around, his movements became so exaggerated that it appeared to some, perhaps to Frazier, that he was faking how severely he was injured to lure him into a trap. "I was trained, you always got to remember a man is dangerous when he's hurt," Frazier explained decades later. Finally, mercifully, for Ali, the bell rang. "I don't know how the kid survived the eleventh round," Dundee recalled. Dundee, Chickie Ferrara, and the other handlers worked on getting him ready for the next round. Brown was in tears. Dr. A. Harry Kleiman from the New York State Athletic Commission stopped by to make sure Ali was alert enough to continue. Mercante also checked him out. Both saw no reason to call the fight. Pacheco was concerned, but did not give up hope. "Anybody else, you would have said, 'We're fucked,' but not Ali," he said. "If you had been with Ali through all the fights, you were used to his wacky luck. When you had that kind of faith in your fighter, you abandoned common sense."

An eager Frazier rose from his stool. He might have squandered his opportunity to finish off Ali in the eleventh, but he was not about to hold back at this point. "I was crazy to get at him," Frazier wrote, "knowing he was running on empty, knowing the hurt I put on him. . . . I was enjoying it and having a ball getting the job done." Early in round 12, Frazier landed more lefts to the jaw, Ali holding on. Then came another left to the head and a left to the ribs. Ali was on the ropes, Frazier firing away with both hands to the body. Ali tried to battle back with a left-right-left combination, but Frazier was in total control, grunting, laughing, steering the action toward the ropes again. The round ended, another for the champion. Nonetheless, "for someone who was virtually out on his feet the round before," Burt Lancaster said between rounds (only Dunphy, as he had insisted, spoke during the actual fighting), "I would say that Ali made a great comeback but he's a tired boy."

In round 13, however, Ali summoned the energy to get back on his toes, landing two lefts to Frazier's head, followed later by a solid left and right. Yet there was little power in these punches, Frazier continuing to press forward with solid rights to the body. Ali was back on the ropes. The bell sounded. Mercante and Recht gave the round to Frazier, Aidala to Ali. Only six more minutes and the decision would go to Frazier—unless he were to knock Ali out sooner.

Then, amazingly, in round 14, Ali came to life once more. Perhaps Ferdie Pacheco was right. Perhaps, with Muhammad Ali, you did abandon common sense. "Frazier's right eye looks as though it might be closing," Dunphy said. Yet Frazier kept coming. He kept bobbing and weaving as he had since the opening round. He landed a solid hook to the head and a left to the body. Although

Ali finished strong, with several punches to the head and took the round, his first since the tenth, with only one to go, he would need a knockout to pull out the victory. He had found a way against Bonavena, who had never been knocked out before. Of course, Oscar Bonavena was no Joe Frazier.

When the bell rang, the Garden's Tom Kenville rounded up members of the press to escort them to the interview room. Otherwise, they would probably not make it through the crowded aisles once the fight ended. They could catch the last three minutes on the TV monitors.

The bell rang. Muhammad Ali and Joe Frazier came out for the fifteenth and final round. It was hard to believe that after nearly three years of sparring in the press and forty-two minutes in the ring, the most anticipated duel in boxing—in all of sports—was almost history. If there had never been a Vietnam War, and if Ali had not been stripped of his crown, he would most likely have taken on Frazier in 1968 or 1969. They would not have received $2.5 million apiece. They would not have done a commercial for Vitalis hair products. They would not have appeared on the covers of *Time* and *Life*. Ali versus Frazier would not have been the fight of the century or even the fight of the decade. But there was a war, which tore two countries apart, and although, in early 1971, no end was in sight, at least this particular conflict, between two mortals, could last no longer than three more minutes. If it was hard to believe, and in a bizarre way, sad, it was also comforting.

They went at it again. Whatever they had, and granted it was not much, they were going to give if it killed them, and it looked as if it just might. Ali scored with two lefts and a right to the head. "I want to circle, jab and come through with a straight right," he later wrote. "I see an opening." The opening was there, all right—for Frazier. Less than thirty seconds into the round, it came again, the left hook to the jaw, and this time Ali did not wobble.

Ali fell.

"He toppled backwards toward me like a tree," the *Times*'s Dave Anderson said. "There was this tremendous thunder clap of a crash. The rings are metal underneath and they're noisy, especially when somebody gets knocked down." The Frazier fans cheered. The Ali fans cringed. Their hero was down, slain by Joe Frazier, the enemy, the hero of the white man. The writers who had been on their way to the interview room immediately went back to their seats. "There was absolute pandemonium when Frazier knocked him on his ass," Kenville remembered.

However, Ali was back on his feet in a hurry. Even Pacheco could not believe that he got up so fast.

"He went down hard and he was dog tired," Pacheco said. "If he had gone down like that in the fifth, no problem. Tenth round, no problem. But, in the last round, it's easy to stay down but he didn't."

After Ali took the mandatory eight count, Frazier landed a left hook and a right to the jaw, and a combination to the body. Soon came another left to the jaw, two more shots to the body, and a hard left to the face. The seconds could not go by quickly enough for Muhammad Ali. His eyes were glazed, his face swollen, his invincibility gone, for good. He was fortunate that Frazier was as exhausted as he was or the end could have been much worse.

"Hard as I tried," Frazier wrote, "I just couldn't get across the finisher."

The bell rang. Frazier raised his arms. In his autobiography, Frazier claims he told Ali: "I kicked your ass." Ali staggered to his corner. Soon the ring was packed.

Johnny Addie made the announcement: *"Ladies and gentlemen . . . Referee Arthur Mercante scores it eight, six, one even, for Frazier. Artie Aidala nine to six for Frazier."* The score from Bill Recht (Frazier, 11–4) was not relevant. Still undefeated, and still the heavyweight champion of the world, was Smokin' Joe Frazier. He leaped into Durham's arms as he had after knocking out Jimmy Ellis. Except this time, Frazier was truly *free at last*. Angelo Dundee once said Frazier would never lick Ali in a "million years," but Frazier licked him, licked him good. At the same time, Ali performed admirably. After only two tune-ups since the end of his exile, he took on the most ferocious fighter in the heavyweight division and lasted the whole way. Considering the obstacles, it was one of Ali's greatest nights in the ring. Even in defeat, he, too, was a winner.

The decision was not questioned. While Ali had landed more punches, Frazier was more aggressive, capturing the two most dominating rounds, 11 and 15, and was never close to going down. The margin surely would have been more substantial if the bout were scored on a points system, with Frazier winning round 15, 10–8, and perhaps round 11 as well. Still, the knockdown provided an important touch of finality that guaranteed there would be no controversy over the scoring.

"Frazier won the drama of the fight with that punch," Merchant said. "That was the final act of a great drama, with the curtain about to come down. It all comes together now at this moment, everything the playwright and the actors are trying to tell us."

The experts told us that if the fight went the distance, Ali, the superior boxer, would prevail. The experts were wrong. Not everyone, however, thought a decision would go to Ali. The *Daily News* polled one hundred celebrities for their views. Forty-six picked Frazier but only one nailed it. "Frazier by a decision," the celebrity said. "Clay laid off too long." The prophet was—it figured—baseball's Yogi Berra. "I laughed at him when he told me," said the *Daily News*'s Phil Pepe. In the *Life* issue that previewed the bout, sports editor Bill Bruns predicted that Frazier would knock out Ali in two minutes and twenty-one seconds of the eleventh round, extremely close to the moment when the Frazier left hook stunned Ali, and, essentially, paved the way for his triumph. After Addie announced the decision, the knockdown was replayed on the closed-circuit telecast sixteen times.

"You can't play it enough," Art Fisher told Neal Marshall. "You can't play it enough."

The celebrating went on.

"You done it, Joe, you done it," Durham said. Afterward, Frazier spoke to the press, some of whom had doubted him for years but could doubt him no longer.

"What are you guys going to say now?" Frazier asked. "You've been writing about the great Ali and what he was going to do to me. I can read, you know." Frazier said he wanted Ali to apologize for the names he had called him, but, he claimed, Ali "just mumbled something and turned to his corner." To his credit, Frazier was also gracious. He praised his opponent's ability to take a punch.

After the session, back in the dressing room, Frazier looked in the mirror. "You flat-footed, you dumb, you ugly," he said, mimicking Ali. "Hah, we saw about that." Later he soaked his face in a sink full of ice. He "kept it there so long, I thought he was going to drown," said Dave Wolf, a member of the Frazier camp. Frazier, according to Lester Pelemon, said he wanted Ali to crawl to him, as he had promised during the gathering at Toots Shor's in December, "but Yank said, 'Leave that man alone, that man hurt bad.'"

10

After the Fight

Yank Durham was right. *That man* was hurt bad. So bad, in fact, he needed to go to the hospital for X-rays on his jaw. "The goddamn thing looked like a grapefruit," Pacheco said. "It had to be a big fracture." Even so, Ali did not lose his sense of humor. In the dressing room, with Ali still in his trunks, a sobbing Diana Ross wrapped her arms around his calf. When Ali noticed Jerry Perenchio, he told the pop diva: "Diana, say hello to the man who gave me two and a half million dollars to get my ass whupped." Another deeply affected by the defeat was *Life* photographer Gordon Parks. Parks was the only one with a camera allowed into the dressing room after the fight. He was also a friend.

"Hi, champ," Parks said while Ali lay prone. "We had bad luck tonight." Ali answered, "Yup, I got whupped—just got whupped." Brown began to dress Ali. He put on his socks and lifted Ali's legs into his trousers before realizing they were on backward. Parks watched the whole scene, ready to take the one historic picture photographers dream about, an image destined to live a lot longer than them. The image does not exist. Parks placed his friendship above his profession. "I couldn't bring myself to release the shutter," he said. Many Ali supporters were devastated. "I cried my eyes out," said Bryant Gumbel. "I'm sure most people did. You were so certain that you were right to support Ali, that you were right to oppose the war, that the cause of Civil Rights was just, and when he lost, it was almost like, 'I can't be on the wrong side of those things. I just can't be.'" At a closed-circuit screening in Harlem, one black fan summed up how numerous African Americans felt. "Whitey won again," the Ali fan said.

Brown was suspended indefinitely two days later by the New York State Athletic Commission for "acts detrimental to boxing." He was cited for soaking a sponge in a water bucket and spraying water in Ali's direction after he was knocked down in the fifteenth round. "Trying to revive my soldier," Brown later explained. "My, you'd think I'd climbed into the ring to get Frazier with a baseball bat." Brown also violated the rule against coaching during a round.

By the time Tom Kenville made it to the dressing room, Ali was gone. "They were standing around," Kenville recalled, "like it was a wake, especially Herbert Muhammad. Jimmy Ellis was there, and Bundini, and some of the Black Muslims." Kenville got right to the point. "I understand the champ has gone to the hospital," he said, "but I've got to have somebody for the postfight interview. Frazier is over there now. I've got to have somebody in there or it's going to be all Frazier. There will not be anybody from your side." Kenville's plea worked. "I'll go," Brown chimed in. The reporters were not thrilled. They wanted to hear from Ali, not Bundini Brown. Ali was always eager to talk when he won or when there was a fight or a cause to promote. Now, a loser in the ring for the first time, Ali was silent for the first time. "Look," Brown told them, "he'd be here if he could. The man's hurt. He just can't make it." Brown assured the press his boss would live to fight another day. "I asked him if we're through," Brown said. "He said, 'Just get the gun ready. Set the traps. We'll be back.'"

The ride to Flower and Fifth Avenue Hospitals, at Fifth Avenue and One-hundred-sixth Street, about seventy blocks uptown from the Garden, took forever. "Must've been a helluva fight 'cause I'm sure tired," said Ali from the back seat. Inside the hospital, Ali closed his eyes while lying on the table for X-rays and had to be nudged each time the technician needed to take a different shot. The jaw, it turned out, was not broken. The X-rays revealed hematoma, a collection of blood between the skin and the bone. There remains, however, no record of the X-rays, which were apparently stolen from the hospital. Nonetheless, despite the encouraging results, Pacheco and the doctors on the scene felt that Ali should spend the night in the hospital.

"When you take a big beating like that," Pacheco pointed out, "you don't know exactly what kind of brain damage you have. It would have been safer to keep him sedated in a quiet room instead of a place where the press is going to come, and your friends and everybody will come. He should have stayed about a week, at least."

He didn't stay for a week. He stayed for less than an hour. Ali did not want it said that Joe Frazier put him in the hospital. Just after 1 o'clock, his arms draped over the shoulders of Dundee and Pacheco, Ali made his way toward the limo. "I got to get to bed," he said. "I got to get to bed." The limo headed down Fifth Avenue. By around 1:30, he was back at the New Yorker. The fans cheered when he walked through the lobby.

"You still the greatest," they said.

"I know, I know," Ali responded. "Gotta get to bed."

At the St. Regis, Jerry and Jacquelyn Perenchio hosted a small gathering of friends in their suite. The final numbers from the closed-circuit telecast would not become official for weeks, but from early indications, Perenchio and Cooke had fared extremely well. The party began to break up around 2 a.m., except, as Jacquelyn recalled, the actor Patrick O'Neal, a friend of Burt Lancaster's, was not quite ready to leave. A frustrated Perenchio phoned Lancaster, who was also staying at the hotel. "I'll be right there," he said. Lancaster, according to Don Loze, entered the suite in a terrycloth wraparound, "grabbed [O'Neal] by the collar and threw him in the hall. 'You're bothering my friends,' he said. When he got to the bottom of the hotel, he put him in the spinning around thing, spun the door and the guy went out onto the street. He put him in a cab. 'I never want to see you again,' Burt said. Burt Lancaster became my hero forever. He was the real Burt Lancaster." After everyone left, Perenchio and his wife reflected on the remarkable night.

"He said something to me I have never forgotten," Jacquelyn said. "He said, 'Do you ever think I'll do anything as big again?' It was sad. I couldn't understand why he couldn't enjoy it rather than wonder what was going to happen to him."

By 10 a.m. Tuesday, Ralph Graves was in the *Life* offices on the Avenue of the Americas in New York City. Graves had a magazine to put out. One immediate priority was to choose which photo of the fight would make the cover. The photos, including the ones taken by Francis Albert Sinatra, had been processed hours earlier. The deadline was so tight that the prints went directly to Graves instead of the usual chain of editors. Neil Leifer said he knew which photo would be picked as soon as he saw the six possible covers laid out on the wall.

"They were all mine except one," Leifer said, "and all of mine were better pictures than the one Sinatra had. I remember thinking, 'that takes care of that.'" Sure enough, Graves selected a shot Sinatra had taken of Ali and Frazier near the ropes. Even Leifer agreed with the decision. "If I were editor of *Life* magazine," Leifer said. "I would have run it. There were three blurbs [in the ad in the *New York Times*]. The first one said, 'The fight,' the second, 'The writer, Norman Mailer,' the third, 'The photographer, Frank Sinatra.' That wouldn't have quite worked with Neil Leifer." Two other Sinatra pictures, including one he took by tilting his camera, also appeared in the issue.

Graves spent much of the next two days editing Mailer's article, which arrived by messenger, a few pages at a time. Mailer, who lived in Brooklyn, wrote by longhand on lined yellow paper. His assistant typed it and handed the pages to the messenger. Mailer possessed more control over his prose than the typical *Life* contributor. "I was free to make suggestions and he was free to take them or not take them," Graves said. "He had the right to say no." In this case, they were in agreement except for a minor fix that Graves made, with Mailer's approval, in reference to the scoring system. Mailer's name was put on the cover, as well as Sinatra's. The other *Life* photographers complained. Their names rarely went on the cover. "I thought Sinatra's name was a nice bit of good luck for us," Graves explained.

On the day after the fight, lying in his bed at the Hotel New Yorker, a sheet covering his legs, Ali finally spoke to a group of reporters. The performance was almost as impressive as any he delivered between the ropes. Hours after dropping one fight, Ali took the first round of the next, the fight to prove he was still the greatest. He downplayed the significance of his defeat—"The way I look at it," he said, "I've made a lot of people lose in my time, so now it's my turn"—while saying he did not believe that he lost in the first place. "I think I won at least nine rounds," he insisted. "Look at my face—forget the bruise. Then go look at him, and you'll see who really won." At one point, he put the sport in perspective by bringing up the horror of plane crashes and assassinations. In another, he said the judges were biased against him.

"Ali was the master spinner of all time," Dave Kindred said. "By the next morning, he convinced himself that he had won and he would soon convince the world."

Joe Frazier did not meet with a group of reporters the day after the fight, although he did grant an interview in his hotel room to the *New York Post*. Frazier did not have to convince the world of anything. He convinced the judges, and those were the only three people who mattered. Ali, though, was right about one thing: Frazier looked a lot worse than he did. With his jaw swollen and knots on his face, he refused to pose for photographers.

During the press conference in December, when Perenchio estimated the potential gross between $20 and $30 million from the live gate and ancillary income, Ali broke up the room when he turned to Frazier and said, "We've been taken." Looking back, neither the fighters nor any of their advisers should be faulted for going with the guaranteed money. No prizefighter had ever made anywhere close to $2.5 million for a single bout. They had to accept it. The risk would have been too enormous. What if a blizzard blanketed the Midwest or Northeast on March 8? What if there was a sharp economic downturn in January or February? What if people were unwilling to pay the high ticket prices at the closed-circuit venues? By settling for the sure thing, Ali and Frazier did not have to be concerned with the accuracy of the final accounting. They got their money and they were satisfied; of course, they would have been more satisfied if Uncle Sam had not seized such a sizable chunk of their paychecks. After taxes and expenses, Ali estimated he would be left with about $370,000. On the other hand, if they had gone with the offers from the Garden or Top Rank, Ali and Frazier would likely have pocketed a lot more.

"Perenchio made the deal of the century in only paying the fighters $2.5 million each," HBO President Ross Greenburg said. "Clearly the big winner that night was Jerry Perenchio, as well as Joe Frazier."

The other big winners were the fans. The fight surpassed expectations, and not because it was the greatest *fight* ever. It was not. There were better fights before March 8, 1971, and there have been better fights since. The fight, however, remains the greatest *event* in the history of boxing. What separates this fight, what makes it the fight of the century, was what Muhammad Ali and Joe Frazier fought for, and against, and how they fought heroically, under the kind of pressure, from each other and from society, that nobody else, except Joe Louis and Max Schmeling, ever encountered in the ring.

It was almost 1 a.m. The fight had been over for about an hour. Tom Kenville was still in the Garden, and he was far from alone.

"People were just standing around, just looking down at the ring," Kenville said. "I guess they thought they witnessed something that would be talked about forever. They didn't want to leave."

Muhammad Ali and Joe Frazier were to meet again, only five days later, in a New York television studio, to talk about the fight with Howard Cosell for ABC's *Wide World of Sports*. For Ali and Frazier, this was their first opportunity to promote the inevitable rematch, to be staged, most likely, in 1972 at Jack Kent Cooke's Fabulous Forum in Los Angeles.

The opportunity would have to wait. Frazier did not show up. The official reason relayed by Cosell to his viewers was that the champion was suffering from the flu. The official reason was apparently not the real reason. "Yank was very concerned that Ali would put Frazier down," a Frazier aide admitted. "He didn't want the show turned into a circus." There was another reason. Frazier was suffering, all right, except it was much worse than a flu. "I couldn't urinate," he wrote in his autobiography. "I couldn't stand up and walk. I couldn't eat or drink. My eyes were puffed and sensitive to light. We kept the shades drawn and the doors closed, and it also helped to stick my head in a sink filled with ice water." Frazier, the aide added, remained in his New York hotel room because he did not want his kids to see him "until his face gets better."

Frazier did not get better. On March 16, he was admitted to St. Luke's and Children's Hospital in Philadelphia for what his doctor termed "high blood pressure." The rumors spread in a hurry: Frazier has a detached retina. Frazier is retiring. Frazier is . . . dead!

Gene Kilroy, a member of the Ali circle, received a call from Budd Schulberg, who passed on the report of Frazier's demise. Kilroy informed Ali.

"If he did," a shaken Ali replied, "I'll never fight again."

Kilroy contacted Dr. James C. Giuffre, the hospital's medical director, who assured him that Frazier was going to be okay. Kilroy told Ali. "All praises due to Allah," Ali said.

Frazier's medical difficulties, Dr. Giuffre told the press, were not connected to the fight. To lower his blood pressure, Frazier was fed intravenously for twenty-four hours and his diet was restricted. Dr. Giuffre said Frazier had an inflammation of the eye. "It wasn't Clay's punches," Frazier wrote, "so much as the effort I'd put in with a body that was not one hundred percent to begin with. I was drained, ten to fifteen pounds lighter than when I walked into that ring."

Whatever the diagnosis, Frazier was in greater danger at first than the public was ever led to believe, according to Cloverlay's Joe Hand.

"I stayed there with him through the night," Hand said. "He couldn't talk. He was laying in the bed, nearly to death." Hand did a lot of crying that night, and a lot of thinking, and the more he thought, the angrier he became. "I thought of all these sons of bitches," Hand explained, "who made a good buck on him and were not there." Hand's disgust was not aimed, however, at Durham, who would have been at the hospital but was out of the country at the time.

Frazier was kept in a private room for a few weeks, he wrote in his autobiography, although he claimed that after a while he left the hospital every night. Either way, the extended stay forever provided Ali with the ammunition for his argument that he was the true winner of their struggle.

"What a weasel," Frazier wrote. "All it proved was that I needed a rest after The Fight, while Clay had rested during it."

Frazier recovered—physically, that is. Emotionally he did not, then and perhaps ever. A few weeks after Frazier returned to Philadelphia, *Newark Star-Ledger* columnist Jerry Izenberg paid a visit to his gym on Broad Street. "I walked in," Izenberg remembered, "and there was a full-sized wall picture already of Ali on his ass." Frazier and Izenberg took off to grab a bite. "We drove over to this deli and three little schoolboys were running down the street, screaming, 'Joe Frazier, Joe Frazier.' So he goes to the car and gets some pictures for the kids. He talks to them for a while and says, 'Stay in school, don't hurt nobody, and it will be okay.' One of the kids says, 'My daddy said that you drugged Ali,' and I thought he was going to hit an eight-year-old kid. I could see the rage in his eyes. Then he said to the kid, 'Yeah, I drugged him. I drugged him with a left hook. Go to school.'"

*   *   *

"We've got to get him right back in the saddle," Herbert Muham-mad told Bob Arum, Ali's attorney, soon after the loss to Frazier. Arum agreed.

Ali should never have taken on Frazier before at least two or three additional tune-ups, but the money was there and so was the possibility of him going to prison. To wait was too risky. Now, how-ever, there was a chance for Ali to get in the work he needed before meeting Frazier again. On June 25, 1971, in Dayton, Ohio, he fought in an exhibition against Rufus Brassell, Eddie Brooks, and J. D. McCauley. This time Jerry Perenchio, who reportedly along with Jack Kent Cooke grossed about $20 million from the Ali-Frazier fight, did not stop it. Ali was no longer his prized invest-ment. Next, on June 30, in Charleston, South Carolina, Ali was set to appear in an exhibition against Brooks and Alex Mack. This time, the County Council did not stop it.

Before Charleston, Ali won another fight. This one was more important even than the fight of the century. This one was the fight for his freedom. On June 28, the Supreme Court ruled 8–0 (Justice Thurgood Marshall abstained, as he was the solicitor general when Ali was convicted) to clear him of the 1967 draft evasion charges. The court determined that the Justice Department misled Selective Service authorities by advising them that Ali's claim as a conscien-tious objector was neither sincere nor based on religious tenets. The sincerity of his beliefs, and their foundation in religious train-ing, the court declared, were not in question. Ali received the news in Chicago. "I'm not going to celebrate," he said. "I've already said a long prayer to Allah, that's my celebration."

On July 26, Ali faced his friend and sparring partner Jimmy Ellis in the Astrodome, scoring a technical knockout in the twelfth round. Missing from Ali's corner was Angelo Dundee, who, with the ex-champion's approval, worked with Ellis to collect a larger share of the purse. Over the next nineteen months, Ali seemed intent on making up for his three and a half years of inactivity. He fought nine times, a total of 91 rounds, beating, in succession, Buster Mathis, Jurgen Blin, Mac Foster, George Chuvalo, Jerry

Quarry, Alvin Lewis, Floyd Patterson, Bob Foster, and Joe Bugner. Ali was far from the dancer who was so dominant against Cleveland Williams and Zora Folley. Each match went past the sixth round, four (Mathis, Mac Foster, Chuvalo, Bugner) going the distance. In Ali's first 32 bouts, only 14 made it into the seventh, just 7 going the distance.

On March 31, 1973, Ali faced Frazier's former sparring partner Ken Norton in San Diego. Ali trained only a few weeks, since he did not view Norton as a difficult test, and neither did the boxing establishment. For the first time since 1966, a fight featuring Ali was shown on network television, not closed circuit. Ali and the boxing establishment underestimated Norton. Trained by Eddie Futch, who realized perhaps better than anyone how to exploit Ali's fundamental weaknesses, Norton broke his opponent's jaw during the second round and won a 12-round split decision. Ali's future was suddenly uncertain. He did not fight for six months, but after outdueling Norton in another split decision and Rudi Lubbers a month later, he prepared to avenge his only other setback.

After his triumph over Ali, Frazier did not defend his crown for ten months, until recording a fifth-round TKO over Terry Daniels in New Orleans. Four months later, in Omaha, Nebraska, Frazier put away Ron Stander in the fifth. Terry Daniels and Ron Stander were not exactly among the premier heavyweights of the early 1970s, but on January 22, 1973, in Kingston, Jamaica, Frazier took on a young fighter who clearly was, the 1968 Olympic champion, George Foreman. Foreman, 37–0 as a professional, posed such a threat that, according to Jane Durham, her husband was opposed to the match.

"That was the one time that Joe did not listen to him," she said. "Yank was telling him, 'Look, I took you this far, and I am telling you that you are not ready for George Foreman,' and Joe said, 'I'm out of kindergarten now.'" Yank Durham was right, again. Frazier was not ready for George Foreman. Foreman knocked Frazier to the canvas three times in the opening round, three more in the second, prompting the unforgettable Cosell call: "Down goes Frazier. Down goes Frazier." Out went Frazier, late in the second. The title, which he had owned at least a share of since beating Buster Mathis in March 1968, was gone, and he would never get it back. Six months later, Frazier outdueled Joe Bugner in England. Then came another loss, this one out of the ring. In August, Durham died suddenly of an aneurysm. He was only fifty-two.

"Joe took it very hard," Yank's widow recalled. "He stayed at the hospital the whole time." Eddie Futch took over as his trainer and did an excellent job with Frazier, but nobody could replace Durham.

In the fall of 1973, the rematch with Ali was signed at last. With Bob Arum as the promoter, the scheduled 12-rounder was to be held again at Madison Square Garden, in January. Ali and Frazier were each guaranteed $850,000, or 32½ percent of the live gate and ancillary income, whichever was higher.

"So there we were, me and damn Clay again," Frazier wrote.

They met first, five days before the fight, to speak with Cosell about their 1971 duel for *Wide World of Sports*. The last time they were to appear together in this forum, Frazier had stayed away, partly, an aide said, due to the concern that Ali would turn it into a circus. Well, it definitely became a circus this time. Around 2:30 p.m., as Ali and Frazier watched the tenth round, the conversation centered on the subject of Ali's swollen jaw, which required X-rays after the fight.

"That's what he went to the hospital for," Frazier said.

"I went to the hospital for ten minutes," Ali responded. "You went for a month."

"Be quiet," Frazier said. "I was resting. I was in and out."

"That shows how dumb you are," Ali said. "People don't go to a hospital to rest. See how ignorant you are."

"Why you think I'm ignorant?" Frazier said. "I'm tired of you calling me ignorant all the time. I'm not ignorant."

Frazier threw his earphone to the ground, got up, and clenched his fists. "Why you think I'm ignorant?" he asked. "Stand up, man."

Rahaman Ali rushed to join his brother.

"You in this too?" Frazier asked. And then it began.

Ali grabbed Frazier's shoulders and pinned his arms. They wrestled to the ground, falling off a platform about a foot high, as others attempted to separate them. There were no punches. Ali was smiling. Frazier was not. Frazier was furious. Holding the broken band of his watch, he stormed from the studio with Futch.

"See you Monday night," Ali shouted.

"Be on time," Frazier said.

Once Frazier was gone, Ali joked on the air that the entire incident was staged. "It was just the way we rehearsed it," Ali said. "The code word was ignorant."

The incident, however, was not staged, at least not Frazier's part. "I was ready to rock and roll," Frazier wrote. "It wasn't a gimmick fight, like a lot of people thought who watched it. I wanted a piece of him."

Ali and Frazier were each fined $5,000 by the New York State Athletic Commission for conduct that "demeaned the sport of boxing." They were threatened with more fines, Frazier indicated in his book, if they were to misbehave during the weigh-in, but, as was the case in 1971, the commission wisely chose to have the fighters appear separately. Ali tipped the scales at 212, three pounds lighter than he was at their first fight, Frazier, at 209, almost four pounds heavier.

On January 28, 1974, thirty-four months after their first battle, Muhammad Ali and Joe Frazier finally met again, in the ring.

So much was different from before. The Vietnam War, if not officially over (the last U.S. troops would leave the roof of the American Embassy in Saigon on April 30, 1975), was no longer at the forefront; the press was fixated on the Watergate scandal, one revelation of wrongdoing after another crippling the Nixon presidency.

The racial component also did not come into play as it had leading up to their first confrontation. Finally, Ali and Frazier were
not vying for the crown, though whoever prevailed would surely
receive a chance to dethrone Foreman. The public was simply not
as enthralled as it had been in 1971, but how could it be? The fight
of the century comes along once a century. Nonetheless, this was
still Ali versus Frazier, and, boosted no doubt by the theatrics at the
studio, interest in their clash remained high. Once again, the Garden
sold out, while closed-circuit venues across the United States were
packed. In fact, by accepting a percentage instead of a flat fee, the
fighters, Ali claimed in his autobiography, earned slightly more than
they did in 1971.

Ali started strong again. In the second round, a straight right
nailed Frazier in the jaw. Wobbling toward the ropes, he was in
serious trouble. However, Tony Perez, the referee, believing that
the round was over, soon stepped between the fighters. Once Perez
was notified of the mistake, the round continued, but the extra seconds of rest might have saved Frazier from going down, and perhaps out. During the middle rounds, Frazier returned to his familiar role, the relentless stalker, but was never able to land the one
devastating punch, as he did in round 11 of the first fight, to assert
command. In the eighth, after Frazier connected with a right to the
jaw, Ali smartly backed off to avoid any further damage.

Another difference was that Ali did not clown around. His
antics may have cost him a couple of rounds with the judges in the
first meeting, and he could not afford to throw away a single round
this time. Although Ali might have been hindered by an injury to
his right hand he suffered in the Norton rematch, he again landed
the majority of punches, and was rewarded. Perez scored the fight,
6–5–1 for Ali; judge Tony Castellano, 7–4–1 for Ali, and judge Jack
Gordon, 8–4 for Ali.

Frazier complained that Ali intentionally tied him up in clinches,
133, according to Futch's count. "Clay didn't want to rumble," Frazier suggested in his autobiography. "His strategy was to limit the
action. He would do his damnedest to make the fight a nonfight,
to make the night a punch-and-grab show as if we were fighting

under the rules of the World Wrestling Federation rather than of the Marquis of Queensberry." Frazier also argued that Perez should not have allowed Ali to continually place his forearms around his neck. Perez, however, claimed that a violation occurs only when a boxer holds and hits at the same time, which, he contended, Ali did not do. Either way, Ali remained on track for another shot at the title, while Frazier would be forced to wait. On October 30, 1974, Ali pulled off his stunning eighth-round upset of Foreman in Zaire, "The Rumble in the Jungle." After defending his crown against Chuck Wepner, Ron Lyle, and Joe Bugner, Ali agreed to a third duel with Frazier, set for October 1, 1975, in Manila. Frazier, in the interim, recorded technical knockouts over two previous victims: Jerry Quarry in the fifth, Jimmy Ellis in the ninth.

They were old men—Ali, thirty-three, Frazier, thirty-one—and big men, Ali, 224½, Frazier, 215½. They were not close to who they were in 1971, and never would be again. Yet here they were, together again, one final time, and it made perfect sense. After all, they could never finish their rivalry tied for eternity at one victory apiece. Whatever Ali and Frazier represented in their profession and their times, by design or due to circumstances beyond their control, their duel, like all classic duels in history, required a winner and a loser. During the prefight buildup, Ali was again crueler than he needed to be, referring to his opponent as a gorilla. "It will be a killer and a chiller and a thrilla when I get the gorilla in Manila," Ali said. Frazier wrote years later that his kids were teased in school and returned home in tears.

In the final days, Ali found himself in another feud, this one with his wife, Belinda. In the Philippines, he spent a lot of time in public with a model, Veronica Porche. When the story was widely reported, Belinda left the United States for Manila and confronted her husband in his hotel room. "I could hear both voices," the late journalist Dick Schaap said, "and there's no doubt that Belinda's was the louder." Publicly, Ali attempted to downplay the situation, but she did not play along. "I don't like an imposter coming in,"

Belinda said before leaving the country, "and taking over my family after eight years and destroying my life." The dispute was quite embarrassing for Ali, though apparently it did not adversely affect his preparation for Frazier. "This type of thing actually helped Ali get ready," suggested Dave Wolf, who spent a lot of time with Frazier in those days. "It allowed him not to get tied up in knots worrying about the fight itself."

At 10:45 a.m. local time to suit closed-circuit viewers back home, the fight, in front of an estimated 25,000 people, including President Ferdinand Marcos and his wife, Imelda, began.

For the third time in a row, Ali seized control, scoring early and often with the right hand, yet again Frazier held his ground. From rounds 5 through 11, he went after Ali's head and body. Ali was often against the ropes, covering up, as he did during their first fight and his battle with Foreman. Nonetheless, just as in their 1974 sequel, Frazier could not deliver the one punch to make a difference, and, in the twelfth round, Ali regained command. In the thirteenth, he knocked Frazier's mouthpiece out. By this juncture, Frazier was fighting with one eye, his left shut. In his autobiography, he claimed that an exam days later revealed he was legally blind in the left eye, which, he said, was already in poor shape due to a cataract. A subsequent exam, he indicated, showed 20/70 vision. "Sit down, son," Eddie Futch told his fighter after the fourteenth round. "It's all over. No one will ever forget what you did here today." The fight went down officially as a TKO in round 14. Frazier was beaten up like never before, and so was Ali, who said it was the closest he ever came to dying in the ring.

"I think that was the beginning of Ali being over," Robert Lipsyte suggested.

Months turned into years, years into decades. Yet for Frazier, the animosity he felt toward Ali did not go away.

Burt Watson, Frazier's ex-business manager, rode with him from Philadelphia to Florida during the late 1980s. They were in the middle of a harmless conversation about former heavyweight champions Larry Holmes, George Foreman, and Floyd Patterson when Watson made the unfortunate mistake of complimenting Ali. "I don't know how the hell he was able to take those punches," Watson said. Frazier did not say a word. Shortly afterward, they stopped for gas in the Carolinas. Watson went inside to buy candy. When he came out, Frazier was gone. Watson waited for a half hour, and started to worry. Finally, Frazier pulled up.

"Where the hell did you go?" Watson asked.

"If you ever think something like that again, you keep it to yourself," Frazier said.

In 1988, Frazier and Ali, along with Holmes, Foreman, and Ken Norton, met in Las Vegas for the taping of the boxing documentary *Champions Forever*. Thomas Hauser, who was working on his Ali bio, watched Frazier shadow his longtime rival. "Joe had some alcohol at the luncheon," Hauser recalled, "and Joe does not hold his liquor particularly well. Ali was sort of floating around like Mr. Magoo. Joe was in a ugly mood and would sort of brush up against him. You could see trouble coming. So wherever Joe walked, Larry Holmes would walk with him and interpose himself between Joe and Ali. It was fascinating. Everyone in the room could see it, except Muhammad. He was oblivious to it all. Larry did this for about ten minutes and then George walked over to Larry, and said, 'I'll take over.' "

In March 1996, Frazier's autobiography, *Smokin' Joe*, written with Phil Berger, was released. His wounds were exposed more than ever. "I'd like to rumble with that sucker again—beat him up piece by piece and mail him back to Jesus," Frazier wrote. "I ain't forgiven him for what he said and did. I stood up for him when few others did. . . . I'll open up the graveyard and bury his ass when the Lord chooses to take him. You see what the Lord did to him. He shut him down, the ungrateful scamboogah."

Frazier's timing could not have been worse. In July, the world watching, his body trembling from Parkinson's disease, Ali lit the torch during the opening ceremonies of the 1996 Summer Olympic Games, the second comeback he launched in Atlanta. The first, in 1970, made him into a contender again; the second, an icon.

Somehow Frazier did not appear to grasp that a fight with Ali in print was one he could never possibly win, but, like the Frazier of old, he did not back off. "It would have been a good thing," Frazier said, incredibly, "if he would have lit the torch and fallen in. If I had the chance, I would have pushed him in." According to Ferdie Pacheco, however, Frazier has also shown compassion toward Ali since their fighting days ended. When Ali was in the early stages of the Parkinson's, Pacheco said, "Joe asked me, 'Doc, is it true that he's in such bad shape?' I said, 'Yes, it is,' and he said, 'Man, I'm sorry. Think I did that?' I said, 'No, I think everybody did it, but you were a big part of it.'"

Ali has apologized for the things he said about Frazier. "I'm sorry I hurt him," he told Hauser in the late 1980s. "Joe Frazier is a good man. I couldn't have done what I did without him, and he couldn't have done what he did without me. And if God ever calls me to a holy war, I want Joe Frazier fighting beside me."

Where Are They Now?

The ages given below are current as of the time of this writing. Oscar Bonavena was shot to death on May 22, 1976, outside a high-wire fence surrounding the Mustang Ranch Brothel near Reno, Nevada. Willard Ross Brymer, a security guard at the ranch, was charged with the murder, but after a mistrial he pleaded guilty to voluntary manslaughter and served only fifteen months in prison. Bonavena was thirty-three.

Drew "Bundini" Brown remained in Ali's corner until his final fight in the Bahamas against Trevor Berbick in December 1981. Brown also appeared in several films, including *The Color Purple*. In 1987, Brown, fifty-seven, died after suffering a stroke.

George Chuvalo, seventy, was never knocked out in ninety-three fights from 1956 to 1978. Chuvalo, who lost two sons to drug overdoses and another to suicide, gives speeches about drug abuse. He was inducted into the Canadian Sports Hall of Fame in 1990.

Jack Kent Cooke sold the Los Angeles Lakers in 1979 to Dr. Jerry Buss for a record $67.5 million. In the same year, he and his wife, Jeannie, were divorced; the $49 million settlement was the largest ever at the time, according to the *Guinness Book of World Records*. Cooke died of cardiac arrest in 1997. His net worth was estimated at $825 million.

Howard Cosell announced fights for ABC until the 1982 heavyweight title mismatch between champion Larry Holmes and Randall "Tex" Cobb. "I am tired of the hypocrisy and sleaziness of the boxing scene," Cosell said. Cosell, seventy-seven, died of a heart embolism in 1995.

Angelo Dundee went on to work with another charismatic boxing champion, Sugar Ray Leonard. Dundee, eighty-six, was inducted into the International Boxing Hall of Fame in 1994.

Don Dunphy called more than 2,000 fights, including 200 with a title at stake. He also did the closed-circuit telecast in 1974 for the Ali-Foreman fight in Zaire. He passed away on July 22, 1998, at the age of ninety.

Jimmy Ellis, after falling to Ali, and to Frazier for a second time, appeared in the ring only once more, knocking out Carl Baker in May 1975. Ellis, sixty-seven, who still lives in Louisville, suffers from dementia pugilistica, or punch-drunk syndrome.

Bob Foster appeared in nineteen fights after his second-round loss to Frazier, losing only three times. After his career was over, Foster went into law enforcement, and became a deputy sheriff in Albuquerque, New Mexico. Foster, sixty-nine, has retired.

Fred Hofheinz was elected mayor of Houston in 1973, serving two two-year terms. Hofheinz, sixty-nine, works in the oil, gas, and real estate business in Houston, and practices law.

J.D. Hudson, eighty, took a leave of absence from the Atlanta Police Department in 1972. Hudson was appointed as the director of the city's Department of Corrections, where he remained until his retirement in 1990.

Leroy Johnson served in the Georgia State Senate until 1974. After leaving the legislature, he was part of a group that bought the Atlanta International Hotel, the largest owned by African Americans at the time. Johnson, seventy-nine, practices law in Atlanta.

Robert Kassel never promoted another fight after the Ali-Quarry bout in Atlanta. In 1985, he went into the investment banking business, retiring in 2003. Kassel, sixty-seven, lives in Lake Tahoe, Nevada.

Burt Lancaster received an Academy Award nomination in 1981 for his portrayal of a small-time gangster in *Atlantic City*. His final significant screen appearance came in 1989's *Field of Dreams*. Lancaster died of a heart attack in 1994.

Neal Marshall, sixty-five, works as a writer and producer in Hollywood. Marshall co-wrote the screenplay for *The Flamingo Kid*. In 1981, he produced the first pay-per-view concert, in which the Rolling Stones appeared. His former business partner, Art Fisher, died in a helicopter crash in the 1980s.

Sam Massell was dethroned in 1973 by the city's vice mayor, Maynard Jackson, who became Atlanta's first African American mayor. Massell, eighty, manages the Buckhead Coalition, a nonprofit group comprised of CEOs in an affluent section of Atlanta.

Buster Mathis appeared in 10 fights after he was knocked out by Frazier, losing to Ali, Quarry, and Ron Lyle. The fight with Lyle, on September 29, 1972, was his last. His weight reached over 500 pounds after he left boxing. Mathis died of a heart attack in 1995. He was fifty-two.

Arthur Mercante worked as a referee into his eighties. He officiated at about 200 fights. Mercante, eighty-seven, was inducted into the International Boxing Hall of Fame in 1995.

Larry Merchant has been HBO's boxing analyst since 1978. At seventy-six, he is a member of the World Boxing Hall of Fame and lives in Los Angeles.

Ferdie Pacheco went into television after leaving the Ali circle in 1977. For twenty-five years, he served as a boxing commentator for NBC and Showtime, winning two Emmys. Pacheco, seventy-nine, continues to paint and write. He lives in Miami Beach.

Jerry Perenchio promoted another historic duel in 1973, Billie Jean King versus Bobby Riggs, at the Astrodome. He later ran Univision, the largest Spanish cable network. In 2006, *Forbes* magazine ranked Perenchio, seventy-six, as the eighty-fifth richest person in the United States, with a net worth of approximately $3 billion.

Tony Perez officiated at the Ali versus Chuck Wepner fight in 1975, and numerous title bouts in the 1980s and 1990s. Perez, sixty-eight, still works as a boxing judge in New Jersey.

Jerry Quarry continued to fight until 1977. He tried two come-backs, including in 1992 at the age of forty-seven, dropping a decision to Ron Crammer. Jerry finished with fifty-three wins, nine losses, and four draws. In the 1990s, he was diagnosed with dementia pugilistica. Jerry passed away in 1999.

Kathleen Quarry was divorced from Jerry in 1973. In 1987, she remarried. She has two children from her first marriage. Kathleen, sixty-one, lives in Moreno Valley, California.

Muhammad Ali appeared in ten fights after his 1975 triumph over Joe Frazier in the Philippines. He held on to his title until 1978, when he was upset by Leon Spinks. Seven months later, Ali beat Spinks by a decision and won the crown back for a third time. Ali, sixty-five, remains afflicted by Parkinson's disease.

Joe Frazier, after losing to Ali in Manila, fought only two more times. He lost again to George Foreman in 1976 and officially ended his career five years later with a draw against Floyd Cummings in Chicago. Frazier, sixty-three, and his son Marvis run a gym in Philadelphia.

Acknowledgments

For about a year, living with me was a challenge, to put it gently. My body may have been in the present, but my mind was trapped in the early 1970s. I tried to keep up with current events—Iraq, the 2008 presidential race, and whether Jennifer and Vince were still together (are they?)—but I was consumed with Muhammad and Joe and Jerry and Oscar and Jimmy, and the only war that occupied my thoughts ended more than thirty years ago, in Southeast Asia. I cared about the Paris Peace Talks, not Paris Hilton. Fortunately, my wife, Pauletta, understood my frequent lapses into the past. For her patience and advice, I thank her. She believed in this project as much I did. I can't possibly overstate how much that has meant to me.

I also want to thank my mother, Celia Wiseman, who encouraged me to pursue my dreams. After my father died, she displayed remarkable courage. Another supporter has been my daughter, Jade, who asked questions that helped me probe even deeper. I'm very grateful for her love.

I owe a tremendous amount to two wonderful and dedicated public servants at the Library of Congress. I cannot imagine how I could have conducted my research without their assistance. Whenever I needed something, they came through. I spent countless hours sifting through the microfilm, reading stories from the *New York Times*, *Ring* magazine, the *Washington Post*, the *Atlanta Constitution*, the *Atlanta Journal*, the *Louisville Courier-Journal*, the *Chicago*

Tribune, the *Los Angeles Times*, the *Philadelphia Inquirer*, the *Philadelphia Daily News*, and the *Philadelphia Evening Bulletin*. I used these sources and relied on the wire services for the punch-by-punch accounts of the fight, as well as Ali-Quarry, Ali-Bonavena, Frazier-Ellis, and numerous other duels. Also, for detailed fight records of the combatants in this book, I referred to www.boxrec.com.

Unable to speak to either Ali or Frazier, I depended on interviews with third parties and quotes attributed to each fighter in various publications, as well as their autobiographies. I realize that the words and tone in celebrity autobiographies aften come from the collaborator and not the protagonist. Furthermore, portions of *The Greatest*, Ali's book, have been discredited over the years. Nonetheless, I believe the interpretation of events detailed in these books contributes to the narrative of my book.

Another who was invaluable each time I bugged him, which was quite often, was Jeff Brophy at the International Boxing Hall of Fame in Canastota, New York. Jeff supplied dozens of *Ring* magazines from the 1960s and 1970s. At the Amateur Athletic Foundation of Los Angeles, which contains an impressive collection of sports books, Michael Salmon was also extremely helpful.

I will never claim to be a boxing expert, which is why I am very grateful to those in the profession who educated me on a number of occasions, such as HBO's exceptional analyst, Larry Merchant. Besides granting several interviews, Larry hosted a gathering at his home in California, which included veteran Los Angeles sportswriters Doug Krikorian and Steve Springer and boxing publicist Bill Caplan. We ate Chinese food and watched a tape of the fight, without any announcers. They were not necessary. The commentary Merchant and the others provided was enlightening and entertaining. It was an experience I will always cherish. Thomas Hauser, who wrote the definitive Ali biography, graciously read the manuscript and made a number of excellent points.

The highlight of my research was, without question, the two days I spent in Miami Beach with Ferdie Pacheco and his wife, Luisita. They were remarkably warm and open from the moment we met. Ferdie and I spoke dozens of times. I looked forward to each talk with much anticipation and was never disappointed. I am extremely grateful for his insight and suggestions. The same goes for the former *New York Times* columnist Robert Lipsyte. He spoke with an eloquence and a perspective that constantly inspired me during those times when the challenge felt overwhelming. Also inspirational was the extraordinary Budd Schulberg, who, in his early nineties, reminisced about his days hanging around Ali and the boxing scene.

There were many others who came through over and over with their sharp recollections, such as Dave Anderson, Marvin Arrington, Bob Arum, Reggie Barrett, Marc Berman, George Berry, Furman Bisher, Julian Bond, David Brenner, Bill Bruns, Zev Buffman, Paul Cardoza, Ed Casey, Tony Castellano, Dean Chance, George Chuvalo, Gil Clancy, Bud Collins, John Kent Cooke, Miguel Diaz, Patti Dreifuss, Angelo Dundee, Jimmy Dundee, Jane Durham, Nancy Durham-Parson, Mary Ellis, Bouie Fisher, Johnny Flores Jr., Bob Foster, Eddie Foy III, Don Fraser, Frank Fried, Tony Fulwood, Bud Furillo, Vince Furlong, Eva Futch, Bill Gallo, Howard Gosser, Ralph Graves, Dick Greco, Ross Greenburg, Phil Guarnieri, John Hall, George Hill, Jesse Hill, Stan Hochman, Fred Hofheinz, Larry Holmes, J.D. Hudson, Jerry Izenberg, Cleopatra Johnson, George Kalinsky, Hank Kaplan, Jeffe Keating, Neil Kelleher, Bonnie Kellogg, Tom Kenville, Gene Kilroy, Dave Kindred, Tom Knight, Jim Lacher, Neil Leifer, Al Lewis, Don Loze, Jim Mahoney, Don Majeski, Sam Massell, Arthur Mercante, Joey Orbillo, Johnny Ortiz, Tom Payne, Lester Pelemon, J Russell Peltz, Phil Pepe, Jacquelyn Perenchio, Tony Perez, Scott Pett, Edwin Pope, Arwanda Quarry, Dianna Quarry, Janet Quarry, Kathleen Quarry, Freddie Roach, Alan Rothenberg, Stan Sanders, William Saunders, Hank Schwartz, Bob Short, Philip Sigler, Leon Silverman, Ron Scott Stevens, Bert Sugar, Claude Sutherland, Harold Taber, Robin Thaxton, Ronnie Thompson, Jose Torres, Marilyn Tracy, Bruce Trampler, Jim Turner, Pete Waldmeir, Burt Watson, Henry Winston, and David Woroner. I thank all of them.

Of the more than a hundred people I interviewed, nobody was more accommodating than former Georgia state senator Leroy Johnson. We spent many hours talking about his work on securing the license for Muhammad Ali to resume his boxing career. Without Johnson's political skills, it is unclear when Ali would have fought again. Robert Kassel, whose father-in-law, Harry Pett, made the initial contact with Johnson during the summer of 1970, was also extremely helpful in laying out the sequence of events that led to the Ali-Quarry bout. Others who must be singled out are Joe Hand, Neal Marshall, and Shelly Saltman. Hand offered plenty of insights into the career of Joe Frazier, while Marshall brought to life the story of how the closed-circuit telecast was put together. Saltman, the former president of Fox Sports, provided a lot of information in our lively conversations.

Numerous friends and others made contributions. Las Vegas boxing writer Kevin Iole shared his contacts and his wisdom. Ed Schulyer, the Associated Press boxing writer who covered the sport for many years, went out of his way a few days before Christmas to make a copy of the fight and mail it to me. I received assistance as well from Lorenzo Benet, John Beyrooty, Ron Cherney, David Davis, Bernard Fernandez, Steve Fraidstern, Christopher Fraser, Mark Greenslit, Stephanie Harris, Erin Hinkebein, Mike Kern, Stuart Kirschenbaum, Pat Patierno, Simcha Pearl, Melissa Scroggins, Ron Sirak, Tyrone Spriggs, Liz Stillwell, Robert Stilwell, Kim Taylor, Mike Towle, Sue Warner, and Robert Zizzo.

I would like to thank my agent, Jay Mandel, and his assistant, Charlotte Wasserstein. As always, they were there for me throughout the process. I can't conceive of an author benefitting from a stronger support team. After the first draft, senior production editor Lisa Burstiner at John Wiley & Sons guided me wonderfully to the finish line. Camille Acker was also very helpful.

Finally, this book would not have come together without the efforts of my outstanding editor, Stephen Power. From the beginning, with passion and patience, Stephen made one superb suggestion after another. He knew precisely what the book was about and made certain I stayed on track. I will never forget the afternoon he and I met at his office in the summer of 2005. I threw out a few ideas, but nothing clicked. The hour was getting late. Finally, I brought up the Ali-Frazier fight. He loved it. I could not wait to get started.

Notes

1. Beating the System

3   *"Cassius Marcellus Clay!"*   Thomas Hauser, *Muhammad Ali: His Life and Times* (New York: Simon & Schuster, 1991), p. 169.

3   *The officer called him by his . . . accept service*   David Remnick, *King of the World: Muhammad Ali and the Rise of an American Hero* (New York: Random House, 1998), p. 290; Hauser, *Muhammad Ali: His Life and Times*, p. 169.

3   *"I refuse to be inducted into the armed forces"*   Hauser, *Muhammad Ali: His Life and Times*, p. 169; Federal Bureau of Investigation files.

3   *"Man, I ain't got no quarrel with them Vietcong"*   Ibid., p. 145.

4   *"Regarded by the commission to be detrimental"*   Thomas Rogers, "New York Lifts Crown in Swift Move," *New York Times*, April 29, 1967.

8   *"Desecrate the land"*   Peter Wood, "Return of Muhammad Ali, a/k/a Cassius Marcellus Clay Jr.," *New York Times*, November 30, 1969.

9   *"I think Mr. Frazier can easily beat Mr. Clay"*   Tom McEwen, "Clay vs. Frazier in Tampa? Maybe." *Tampa Tribune*, December 10, 1969.

9   *"We Object Conscientiously"*   *Tampa Tribune*, editorial, December 11, 1969.

9   *"While I would like to see Frazier put his fists right on Mohammed Blah"*   Jim Selman, "Kirk Now Opposes Clay Fight in Florida," *Tampa Tribune*, December 13, 1969.

11   *"I could announce tomorrow"*   Phil Pepe, *Come Out Smokin': Joe Frazier—the Champ Nobody Knew* (Coward, McCann, & Geoghegan, 1981), p. 128.

11–12   *Under one plan . . . closed-circuit outlets*   Martin Kane, "Welcome Back, Ali," *Sports Illustrated*, September 14, 1970, p. 23.

13 *"For days, I refused even to answer the phone"* Muhammad Ali, with Richard Durham, *The Greatest: My Own Story* (New York: Random House, 1975), p. 269.

14 *"The old South rested everything on slavery and agriculture"* "Henry Grady Sells the 'New South,'" www.historymatters.gmu.edu/d/5745, accessed April 25, 2007.

17 *"An enemy of the country"* "Martin Luther King," www.ourgeorgiahistory.com/chronpop/1360, accessed April 25, 2007.

18 *"I think Clay deserves another chance"* Kent Mitchell, "Maddox Gives Okay to Clay," *Atlanta Journal*, August 14, 1970.

18 *"A man of great compassion"* Kent Mitchell, "Clay Fight Still On— Despite Maddox Opposition," *Atlanta Journal*, August 16, 1970.

19 *"They can come up tomorrow"* Muhammad Ali, "I'm Sorry but I'm Through Fighting Now," *Esquire*, May 1970, p. 120.

20 "I'd be pickin' and pokin'" Ibid., p. 121. Emphasis in original.

21 *"This don't bother me none"* Robert Lipsyte, "The Mystery Guest," *New York Times*, August 9, 1969.

21 *Butch Lewis, a friend, said Frazier,* William Nack, "The Fight's Over, Joe," *Sports Illustrated*, September 30, 1996, p. 59.

22 *"Mr. Muhammad plainly acted"* Quoted in Hauser, *Muhammad Ali: His Life and Times*, p. 194.

22 *"He was right and I was wrong"* Jack Fried, "Cassius Clay Says He'll Tell All," *Philadelphia Evening Bulletin*, September 25, 1969.

22 *"I don't want to fight Frazier"* Ibid.

24–25 *"I knew that unless my exile ended soon"* Ali, *The Greatest*, p. 270.

25 *After schmoozing with Sam Massell* Ibid., p. 273.

27 *"Prominent speakers"* and *"cross lighting"* *Atlanta Journal*, September 2, 1970.

27 *"I have a lot to see in eight rounds"* United Press International, "Clay Set Tonight for 2 Exhibitions," *New York Times*, September 2, 1970.

27 *"What he—and everyone else—saw in three separate bouts"* Kane, "Welcome Back, Ali," p. 23.

27 *"I kept talking to him in the corner"* Kent Mitchell, "Hang Frazier's Scalp in City Hall," *Atlanta Journal*, September 3, 1970.

27 *If Ali did not feel* Hauser, *Muhammad Ali: His Life and Times*, p. 136.

28 *Responding to Brown's pep talk . . . necessary to reclaim the crown* Kane, "Welcome Back, Ali," p. 23.

28   *"Way down in our hearts, we didn't know if the bell"*   Mitchell, "Hang Frazier's Scalp in City Hall."

28   *"At the time, among Morehouse students"*   David Davis, "Knockout: Muhammad Ali and the Fight Nobody Wanted," *Atlanta*, October 2005, p. 121.

30   *"I've always wanted to fight him"*   Dave Anderson, "Ali Finds Crown Fits and Wears It," *New York Times*, September 11, 1970.

2. "Back in My Old Life Again"

32   *"Which disqualifies a person from participating in"*   Darrell Simmons, "Legal TKO Ends Maddox Fight Ban," *Atlanta Journal*, September 30, 1970.

35   *"He gave me a long list of championships"*   Thomas Hauser, *Muhammad Ali: His Life and Times* (New York: Simon & Schuster, 1991), p. 35.

36   *The punch thrown by . . . he was really hurt.*   Muhammad Ali with Richard Durham, *The Greatest: My Own Story* (New York: Random House, 1975), pp. 290–291.

36   *"Like a terrible toothache shooting through bones"*   Ibid., p. 290.

37   *"Trying to overcome"*   Ibid., p. 300.

37   *"Shoot, I been out there running"*   Darrell Simmons, "Bonavena Not for Ali, Quarry," *Atlanta Journal*, October 23, 1970.

39   *"Draw more nuts and Maddox will say"*   Ali, *The Greatest*, p. 317.

41   *"Owned by organizations that normally display"*   "No Closed-Circuit Fight Showing Here," *Scranton Times*, October 24, 1970.

42   *"For the purpose of prostitution"*   "Knockout: Failing to Defeat Him in the Ring, His Enemies Take Him to the Courts," www.pbs.org/ unforgivableblackness/knockout/mann.html, accessed July 1, 2007.

42   *"It's about me"*   Leticia Kent, "I See No Prestige in Show Business," *New York Times*, 1969.

42   *"Boxing needs a white champion"*   Dave Anderson, "Quarry Gains Title Final, Stopping Spencer in 12th," *New York Times*, February 3, 1968.

43   *"I should reach my peak at about 30"*   Darrell Simmons, "Ali's Partner Feels a Sting," *Atlanta Journal*, October 22, 1970.

44   *"He hasn't gotten wet since Folley"*   Milton Gross, "A Vote for Ali," *New York Post*, October, 26, 1970.

46   *"I was put on this earth to do something"*   Paul Zimmerman, "Quarry Has Seen Rougher Days," *Los Angeles Times*, December 14, 1966.

46 *"Are boxing fans finally getting the idea"* John Hall, "Not Such a Happy," *Los Angeles Times,* July 16, 1966.

48 *X-rays taken afterward* David Davis, "The 13th Round," *Los Angeles Weekly,* March 17–23, 1995, p. 24.

49 *"Finally the time has come"* Mark Kram, "The Brawler at the Threshold," *Sports Illustrated,* June 16, 1969, p. 28.

50 *"I've had too many complaints in the past"* Sandy Padwe, "Steam Engine Smokes Upstairs," *Philadelphia Inquirer,* June 24, 1969.

50 *"I would hope that Clay gets beat"* Dave Anderson, "Politicians Spar over the Ali-Quarry Bout," *New York Times,* October 23, 1970.

50 *"Oh, yeah, there'll be a lot of my folks here"* Robert Lipsyte, "Freshest Mouth in Town," *New York Times,* October 24, 1970.

51 *"Everybody would go to him like he was a magnet"* David Davis, "Knockout: Muhammad Ali, Atlanta, and the Fight Nobody Wanted," *Atlanta,* October 2005, p. 150.

52 *More pressing issues surfaced* Budd Schulberg, *Loser and Still Champion: Muhammad Ali* (Garden City, NY: Doubleday, 1972), p. 81.

53 *"Would suggest that the forces of blind patriotism"* George Plimpton, "Watching the Man in the Mirror," *Sports Illustrated,* November 23, 1970, p. 87.

54 *He taped his shoelaces* Ibid., p. 102.

54 *"It's been so long"* Mark Kram, "He Moves Like Silk, Hits Like a Ton," *Sports Illustrated,* October 26, 1970, p. 16.

56 *During a talk in Ali's bedroom* Leonard Lewin, "Ali Can't Hit a Lick—Quarry," *New York Post,* October 27, 1970.

56 *"If I can knock him out in the first"* Arthur Daley, "Muhammed Ali Is Back on Top," *New York Times,* October 28, 1970.

56 *"With the first punch"* Ibid.

57 *"All that went through my mind"* United Press International, "Quarry Forgives Trainer for Call," *New York Times,* October 27, 1970.

57 *"There'd been a big controversy"* Hauser, *Muhammad Ali: His Life and Times,* p. 212.

57 *Only two doctors were used for the prefight examination* Milton Gross, "Quarry: Fighting Mad," *New York Post,* October 23, 1970.

57 *"They want equal rights and that crap"* Ibid.

57 *In the end, four doctors were assigned* Leonard Lewin, "Family Decision," *New York Post,* October 27, 1970.

57 *Why none of them examined the cut remains* Ibid.

57 *"In my 50 years in boxing"* Associated Press, "Garden Yell: Champ," *New York Post,* October 27, 1970.

58   *"My jab was off target"*   Ali, *The Greatest*, p. 324.

59   *"As soon as we get rid of Foster"*   "Bout with Ali Looms in Frazier's Dreams," *New York Times*, October 27, 1970.

59   *"For me . . . it meant that Clay was back"*   Joe Frazier with Phil Berger, *Smokin' Joe: The Autobiography of a Heavyweight Champion of the World* (New York: Macmillian USA, 1996), p. 90.

59   *"A giant surrounded by dwarfs"*   Associated Press, "The World Cheers Ali," *New York Post*, October 29, 1970.

59   *"the wonder boxer"*   Ibid.

59   *"This win is actually a blow to racists"*   Ibid.

59   A *"living example of soul power"*   Robert Lipsyte, "Ali Says Frazier Will Be Easier," *New York Times*, October 27, 1970.

59   *"A champion of justice"*   Ibid.

59   *The only incident occurred*   Davis, *Atlanta*, October 2005, p. 152.

60   *The investigation . . . centered on*   Ibid.

3. Joe

62   *He received a guarantee of $333 a month*   Thomas Hauser, *Muhammad Ali: His Life and Times* (New York: Simon and Schuster, 1991), p. 30.

62   *Running out of savings, Frazier and his three children*   Peter Wood, "In This Corner . . . the Official Heavyweight Champ," *New York Times*, November 15, 1970.

62   *A ton of donations poured in*   Joe Frazier with Phil Berger, *Smokin' Joe: The Autobiography of a Heavyweight Champion of the World* (New York: Macmillian USA, 1996), p. 37.

62   *Goss was supposed to fight Johnny Deutch*   Jack Fried, "Kitten Gets Everything—Victory, Boos," *Philadelphia Evening Bulletin*, August 17, 1965.

62   *One opponent soon followed another*   Jack Fried, "Frazier's 4th Victim Out in 2:38," *Philadelphia Evening Bulletin*, November 13, 1965.

63   *Critics complained that Durham was bringing*   Stan Hochman, "Durham: He Led Joe to Fame, Fortune," *Philadelphia Daily News*, February 24, 1971.

64   *Every morning, Frazier jogged*   Frazier, *Smokin' Joe*, p. 24.

64   *He became such a regular*   Ibid.

64   *"I felt disgusted about how sloppy"*   Ibid., pp. 23–24.

64   *Beginning in the early 1950s*   Hochman, "Durham: He Led Joe to Fame, Fortune."

64   *"I was a cook and we were getting the food"*   Charles Maher, "Trainmen to Trainer," *Los Angeles Times*, February 19, 1971.

64   *After spending two years in hospitals*   Phil Pepe, *Come Out Smokin': Joe Frazier—the Champ Nobody Knew* (New York: McCann & Geoghegan, 1981), p. 75.

65   *"The trainers pit their prestige against"*   Stan Hochman, "Can Joe Avoid Jinx of Philly Fighters?" *Philadelphia Daily News*, March 3, 1971.

65   *"The champ" and "beat them all"*   Joe Falls, "Exactly Who Is This Joe Frazier," *Detroit Free Press*, November 17, 1970.

66   *"He used to think I was a damn fool"*   Tom Cushman, "Durham Shoved Joe Straight Ahead," *Philadelphia Daily News*, March 5, 1971.

67   *"Undersized aggressors"*   Frazier, *Smokin' Joe*, pp. 28–29.

68   *"In his debut against Elwood Goss"*   Ibid., p. 39.

70   *"I told him he better get rested"*   Cushman, "Durham Shoved Joe Straight Ahead."

70   *Durham told him to bring*   Phil Pepe, "Night the Light Almost Went Out for Joe," *New York Daily News*, March 16, 1971.

71   *"I was in a hurry to get to the top"*   Frazier, *Smokin' Joe*, p. 52.

71   *"That was the turning point of Joe's career"*   Hochman, "Durham: He Led Joe to Fame, Fortune."

71   *"I'll never forget Machen afterwards"*   Cushman, "Durham Shoved Joe Straight Ahead."

72   *"He's like a leech"*   Mark Kram, "A Sad Farewell, a Glad Hello," *Sports Illustrated*, March 6, 1967, p. 44.

72   *"I don't need Clay right now"*   Ibid., p. 46.

73   *"He punches like a woman who's washing clothes"*   Thomas Hauser, *Observer Sport Monthly*, November 2, 2003.

74   *"But he has never"*   Red Smith, "Could Clay Beat Joe Frazier?" *Philadelphia Inquirer*, July 21, 1967.

74   *"All that fat boy had done"*   Frazier, *Smokin' Joe*, p. 30.

74   *"When they offered to X-ray it,"*   Ibid., p. 34.

75   *When, in March 1965, he introduced*   Hauser, *Muhammad Ali: His Life and Times*, p. 102.

76   *"To us, and to millions of other blacks"*   C. Gerald Fraser, "Fight at Garden Will Be Picketed," *New York Times*, March 1, 1968.

76   *"Those black radicals could say this and that"*   Frazier, *Smokin' Joe*, pp. 59–60.

77   *"After Mathis, I was willing to fight"*   Cushman, "Durham Shoved Joe Straight Ahead."

78   *"Man, are you kidding?"*   Jack Fried, "Joe Wants Ellis Next after Brawl with Oscar," *Philadelphia Evening Bulletin*, December 11, 1968.

79   *"He had a style that for me"*   Frazier, *Smokin' Joe*, p. 68.

79   *It was "not a true championship fight"*   Ray Kelly, "Cassius Unimpressed, Barred from Frazier," *Philadelphia Evening Bulletin*, December 11, 1968.

79   *"That's all right"*   Ibid.

79   *"I'd like to button his big mouth"*   Associated Press, "Joe Frazier Calls Clay 'Big-Mouth Phony and a Disgrace'," *Philadelphia Inquirer*, June 5, 1969.

80   *"Here I am"*   Tom Cushman, *Philadelphia Daily News*, September 24, 1969.

80   *"By not joining Ali in the Park"*   Mark Kram, *Ghosts of Manila: The Fateful Blood Feud between Muhammad Ali and Joe Frazier* (New York: Harper Collins, 2001), p. 28.

80   *"Six weeks, that's all I would need"*   Sandy Padwe, "Ali and Frazier Stage Old Vaudeville Act," *Philadelphia Inquirer*, September 26, 1969.

80   *"Every time you'd breathe"*   Ibid.

80   *After the show, they tussled*   Jack Fried, *Philadelphia Evening Bulletin*, September 24, 1969; Kram, *Ghosts of Manila*, p. 28.

80   *"You crazy mothafucka"*   Kram, *Ghosts of Manila*, p. 28.

80   *"If the showdown ever comes"*   Padwe, "Ali and Frazier Stage Old Vaudeville Act."

82   *"I am thinking of quitting boxing"*   John Hall, "One More Cinderella," *Los Angeles Times*, April 29, 1968.

83   *"Boys from 18 to 23 years old"*   Dave Anderson, "Zyglewicz's Manager Hints Frazier Might Need Shelter: 'Ziggy Throws Bombs'," *New York Times*, April 20, 1969.

84   *While in New York for the final week*   Dean Eagle, "Frazier Came Up Hard Way: Ellis Says He'll Go Down Easier," *Louisvile Courier-Journal*, February 13, 1970.

85   *"How can you give away something"*   Dean Eagle, "As Underdog to Underdog: Jim Braddock Picks Ellis," *Louisville Courier-Journal*, February 11, 1970.

85   *"When Frazier and Ellis climb in that ring"*   Sandy Padwe, "'I'll Be the Winner, Even in Jail,' Ali Claims," *Philadelphia Inquirer*, February 15, 1970.

85   *"The Philadelphia columnist Stan Hochman"*   Stan Hochman, "The Mongoose vs. the Hippo," *Philadelphia Daily News*, February 16, 1970.

86   *"The first round, I'm a little tight"*   "I Got a Surprise for Clay," Joe Frazier interview with Martin Sharnik, *Sports Illustrated*, February 22, 1971, p. 30.

87   *"Sure I smiled through that mouthpiece"*   Frazier, *Smokin' Joe*, p. 79.

87   *"Sissy, you can't hit"*   Frank Dolson, "The Next Fight Is Markson's," *Philadelphia Inquirer*, February 17, 1970.

88   *"He could never lick Clay"*   Tom Cushman, "Ellis Groggy Addition to Frazier Crypt of Losers," *Philadelphia Daily News*, February 17, 1970.

88   *"I want Frazier"*   Donald Janson, "Clay in Vocal Form, Is Looking to Rock Frazier," *New York Times*, February 17, 1970.

88   *"Absolutely nuts"*   Frazier, *Smokin' Joe*, p. 73.

88   *"The more people tell him not to"*   Martin Kane, "The World Champion Nobody Knows," *Sports Illustrated*, November 16, 1970, p. 37.

4. The Tune-ups

92   *It was only the second time since Tiger*   Chris Cozzone, "I was Cocky . . . but Damn, I Was Good," www.newmexicoboxing.com/history .newmexicoboxing/bobfoster.html, accessed June 6, 2007.

92   *"I'm sorry but I don't know"*   Joe Falls, "Exactly Who Is Joe Frazier?" *Detroit Free Press*, November 17, 1970.

94   *"There's a man out there trying to take"*   Peter Wood, "In His Corner . . . the Official Heavyweight Champ," *New York Times*, November 15, 1970.

95   *While Frazier demonstrated*   Phil Pepe, *Come Out Smokin': Joe Frazier—the Champ Nobody Knew* (New York: McGann & Geoghegan, 1981), p. 127.

95   *The fight's press agent, Murray Goodman*   Shirley Povich, "This morning . . .," *Washington Post*, November 18, 1970.

95   *"I want Joe Frazier"*   United Press International, "Ali Says Frazier Can't Move Fast," *New York Times*, November 19, 1970.

95   *"I want to know within myself"*   Dave Anderson, "Ali Calls Bonavena 'Perfect Test of Whether He Has Champion's Touch'," *New York Times*, December 6, 1970.

95   *"Fix, fix, fix"*   Lincoln A. Werden, "Clay Loses Stature Despite Victory over Jones," *New York Times*, March 15, 1963.

96   *"The commission was well"*   Robert Lipsyte, "Our Best Shot," *New York Times*, May 4, 1970.

96   *"An intentional, arbitrary and unreasonable discrimination"*   Craig R. Whitney, "3-Year Ban Declared Unfair," *New York Times*, September 15, 1970.

96   *"A disgrace to the people of New York State"*   Associated Press, "Bout Called Disgrace," *New York Times*, December 4, 1970.

96   *"An affront to the memories of American soliders"*   Ibid.

97   *"Utter chaos"*   Phil Pepe, "Ali Pops and Pops Off for 12 Rounds," *New York Daily News*, December 5, 1970.

97   *Teddy Brenner claimed he took a few*   Teddy Brenner and Barney Nagler, *Only the Ring Was Square* (New York: Prentice Hall, 1981), p. 103.

97   *"I didn't sleep nights"*   Ibid., p. 104.

98   *"He's the greatest natural heavyweight"*   United Press International, December 1964.

99   *"I never had one bit of trouble"*   Thomas Hauser, *Muhammad Ali: His Life and Times*, p. 215.

99   *"My idea is an appeal to Clay's pride"*   Gene Ward, "Word to the Wise," *New York Daily News*, December 3, 1970, p. 27.

100   *"Why you no go"* Robert Lipsyte, "Are You Crazy?" *New York Times*, December 5, 1970.

101   *"Where is that boxing?"*   ABC's *Wide World of Sports*, December 12, 1970.

101   *"I was givin' him hell cause he was letting"*   *ESPN Classics*, January 21, 2006.

101   *"I told Muhammad to get serious"*   Gene Ward, "Word to the Wise," *New York Daily News*, December 10, 1970, p. 133.

101   *"Dance and box"*   Dick Young, "Young Ideas," *New York Daily News*, December 8, 1970.

102   *"Can you continue?"*   Gene Ward, "Oscar Had Heart, Crowd Said," *New York Daily News*, December 8, 1970.

102   *"The night before the fight with Bonavena"*   David Condon, *Chicago Tribune*, March 3, 1971.

103   *"Every day in the gym, he'd talk Frazier"*   Dick Young, *New York Daily News*, February 26, 1971.

103   *"I only cared that he'd won"*   Joe Frazier with Phil Berger, *Smokin' Joe: The Autobiography of a Heavyweight Champion of the World* (New York: MacMillian USA, 1996), p. 92.

104   *"Joe Frazier's here"*   Vic Ziegel, "Frazier, Durham Rap Ali," *New York Post*, December 8, 1970.

104   *"If Joe Frazier dreamed he was here"*   Ibid., 1970.

5. Jack, Jerry, and the Deal

106   *Those hoping to promote the fight*   Dave Anderson, "Garden Wins Out as Site of Ali-Frazier Heavyweight Title Bout March 8," *New York Times*, December 28, 1970.

106   *Soon after the Ali-Bonavena fight*   Teddy Brenner and Barney Nagler, *Only The Ring Was Square* (Englewood Cliffs, NJ: Prentice-Hall, 1981), p. 106.

107   *"He hadn't planned to charge $100"*   Dave Anderson, "Ticket Shortage Has Markson Ducking," *New York Times*, February 14, 1971.

108   *"He (Sullivan) pounded Mr. Wilson"*   "Mr. Sullivan's Failure," *New York Times*, July 18, 1882.

108   *"Just short of murder"*   Zander Hollander, *Madison Square Garden: A Century of Sport and Spectacle on the World's Most Versatile Stage* (New York: Hawthorn Books, 1973), p. 94.

108   *"Cruel and inhuman"*   Ibid.

108   *Sullivan did not*   Ibid., p. 95.

108   *The Garden resurfaced . . . Mike Jacobs took over*   Ibid., p. 96.

109   *Markson . . . closed-circuit venue*   Thomas Hauser, *Muhammad Ali: His Life and Times* (New York: Simon and Schuster, 1991), p. 218.

109   *"Yank, Joe, Harry Markson, and I"*   Ibid., p. 218.

110   *When he was thirteen, he overheard*   Adrianne Kinnane, *Jack Kent Cooke* (Jack Kent Cooke Foundation, 2004), p. 6.

110   *"Wait until I'm your age"*   Ibid.

110   *In 1934, . . . did not fare much better*   Ibid., pp. 9–10; Adrian Havill, *The Last Mogul: The Unauthorized Biography of Jack Kent Cooke* (New York: St. Martin's Press, 1992), pp. 40–41.

111   *"I saw the local grain elevator operator"*   Dave Kindred, *Washington Post Magazine*, August 19, 1982, p. 12.

111   *As evening approached . . . he hit bottom*   Havill, *The Last Mogul*, p. 41.

111   *In 1936, he started working for . . . weddings*   Kinnane, *Jack Kent Cooke*, pp. 7–8, 11.

112   *Gradually, under Jack's guidance . . . every cent*   Ibid., pp. 12, 16.

112   *In 1951, Jack bought . . . turned down,*   Ibid., p. 29.

112   *"That was a dopey idea, retiring"*   Dave Kindred, "Jack Kent Cooke," *Washington Post*, October 26, 1979.

112 *Jack became involved in the cable . . . another $16 million* Kinnane, *Jack Kent Cooke*, pp. 37–38.

113 *"There were intercoms in the offices"* Dave Kindred, "Jack Kent Cooke," *Washington Post Magazine*, August 22, 1982, p. 10.

114 *Starting at age twelve, Jerry received* Lewis MacAdams, "Silent Running," *Los Angeles Times*, July 2001, p. 64.

114 *"Biggest showman and promoter"* Meg James, "A Hollywood Player Who Owns the Game," *Los Angeles Times*, June 20, 2006, p. 1.

114 *His father, reportedly, squandered most* "The Many-Moneyed World of Jerry Perenchio," *Broadcasting*, August 6, 1979, p. 129.

114 *"I'm busted, I'm broke—no more allowances"* Ibid.

114 *Jerry started over . . . grossing $500,000 per year* MacAdams, "Silent Running."

114 *In less than two years, he became* Jerry Kirshenbaum, "Sport's $5 Million Payday," *Sports Illustrated*, January 25, 1971, p. 22.

115 *By 1971, his share* Kirshenbaum, "Sport's $5 Million Payday"; MacAdams, "Silent Running."

115 *"I knew right away I wanted it"* Kirshenbaum, "Sport's $5 Million Payday."

116 *Jerry ran the idea* Ibid.

116 *Jack later informed reporters* Jack Kiser, "Cooke Gets His Championship at Last," *Philadelphia Daily News*, March 1, 1971, p. 46.

118 *Also dropping out of the talks* Anderson, "Garden Wins Out as Site of Ali-Frazier Heavyweight Title Bout March 8," *New York Times*, December 28, 1970.

117–118 *"When Jerry offered a $250,000 deposit* Kirshenbaum, "Sport's $5 Million Payday," p. 25.

118 *In addition, because Chartwell was not* Phil Pepe, "Garden's $5M Wins Ali-Frazier Fight March 8," *New York Daily News*, December 28, 1970, p. 75.

118 *For a guaranteee of $500,000* Kiser, "Cooke Gets His Championship at Last," March 1, 1971.

118 *Bring the Garden into the equation* Kirshenbaum, "Sport's $5 Million Payday," p. 23.

118 *Once the money was right* Brenner and Nagler, *Only the Ring Was Square*, p. 108.

118 *Jerry phoned Jack* Kirshenbaum, "Sport's $5 Million Payday," p. 23.

118 *"I'm disappointed it won't be in the Forum"* Ibid.

119 *Jack was offended* Ibid.

119   *At this point, Jack reportedly hesitated*   Kinnane, *Jack Kent Cooke*, p. 40.

119   *The next morning, Jack agreed to give*   Ibid.

119   *"He had gone to his ranch near Bakersfield"*   Red Smith, "Okay, Guam! Take It Away," *Philadelphia Evening Bulletin*, March 3, 1971.

119   *"I wanted them to squirm a little"*   Kiser, "Cooke Gets His Championship at Last."

119   *About 10 a.m on December 30*   Kirshenbaum, "Sport's $5 Million Payday," p. 23.

119   *"I'm the real champ"*   Phil Pepe, "Ali-Joe Ink for March 8 Garden Go," *New York Daily News*, December 31, 1970.

119   *"They got us cheap"*   Dave Anderson, "Ali and Frazier Make It Official: They Sign for Title Fight Here March 8," *New York Times*, December 31, 1970.

119–120 *"Not because of Joe Frazier"*   Pepe, "Ali-Joe Ink for March 8 Garden Go." *New York Daily News*, December 31, 1970.

120   *"Let him do the talking"*   Ibid.

120   *Ali, with his usual clowning*   Milton Gross, "Frazier's Warning," *New York Post*, January 21, 1971.

120   *"Sit down and shut up"*   Jim O'Brien, "Ali-Frazier Mar. 8 in Garden," *New York Post*, December 30, 1970.

120   *"I was sitting right next to Joe Frazier"* *Ali-Frazier I: One Nation Divisible*, HBO Productions, 2000.

6. The Show

122   *Maybe, but in Perenchio's opinion*   Art Fisher and Neal Marshall, *Garden of Innocents* (New York: E.P. Dutton, 1972), p. 82.

122   *"The people there were shouting"*   Dave Anderson, "Lancaster Turns Down Sparring Role," *New York Times*, February 23, 1971.

123   *"I'll say this for Burt"*   Howard Cosell, *Cosell* (Chicago: Playboy Press, 1973), p. 213.

123   *"I'm in my fifties now"*   Ibid., p. 214.

123   *"No group ever acted so defiantly"*   Bill Braucher, "First Frazier . . . Then Cosell, Says Clay," *Miami Herald*, March 7, 1971.

123   *ABC claimed the price to carry it*   Les Gapay, "Going for Broke, Promoting a Big Fight May Not Be Bonanza That It First Seemed," *Wall Street Journal*, March 3, 1971.

123–124 *Perenchio contended an offer was never made*   Ibid.

124   *"I felt I was compelled"*   Joe Falls, "What's a Title Bout without Don Dunphy?" *Detroit Free Press*, November 19, 1970.

124 *"The rhythm between us just wasn't there"* Don Dunphy, *Don Dunphy at Ringside* (New York: Holt, 1988), p. 191.

126 *He scanned hours of film* Fisher and Marshall, *Garden of Innocents*, p. 134.

127 *At the press conference in December* Phil Pepe, "Ali-Joe Ink for March 8 Garden Go," *New York Daily News*, December 31, 1970.

127 *After paying $5 million to Ali and Frazier* Ibid.

128 *"You've got to throw away the book"* Jerry Kirshenbaum, "Sport's $5 Million Payday," *Sports Illustrated*, January 25, 1971, p. 20.

128 *Perenchio suggested closed-circuit* Dave Anderson, "Ali and Frazier Make It Official: They Sign for Title Fight Here March 8," *New York Times*, December 31, 1970.

128 *For starters, unlike the standard 50-50 split* "Jerry Perenchio . . . The Real King of the Ring?" *New York Daily News*, March 7, 1971.

128 *"What we have here is the Mona Lisa"* Thomas Thompson, "The Battle of the Undefeated Giants," *Life*, March 5, 1971, p. 41.

128 *In hopes of . . . would stay dark* Gapay, "Going for Broke, Promoting a Big Fight May Not Be Bonanza That It First Seemed."

128 *"He won't get the split he's asking"* Ibid.

128 *The Michigan territory was sold to an exhibitor* Ibid.

128 *Exhibitors were required to guarantee half* William N. Wallace, "Most Will Watch on Home Screens," *New York Times*, March 7, 1971.

128 *Fight of Champions kept the guarantee* Gapay, "Going for Broke, Promoting a Big Fight May Not Be Bonanza That It First Seemed."

128–129 *"I know how to book Andy Williams"* Kirshenbaum, "Sport's $5 Million Payday," p. 22.

130 *Days before the fight* William N. Wallace, "Most Will Watch on Home Screens," *New York Times*, March 7, 1971.

130 *"Is there a projector there"* Jim O'Brien, "The Title Fight on the Phones," *New York Post*, February 21, 1971.

130 *"I bleed when it just doesn't come"* Ibid.

130 *"If the A.T.&T. building blows up"* Wallace, "Most Will Watch on Home Screens."

130 *"He is the ebullient theatrical booking agent"* Gapay, "Going for Broke, Promoting a Big Fight May Not Be Bonanza That It First Seemed."

131 *Perenchio counted on interest* Ibid.

131 *"It was a false assumption on their part"* Ibid.

131 *He was also facing over $50 million* Thompson, "The Battle of the Undefeated Giants."

131   *Perenchio cited the $7 milllion in guarantees*   Milton Gross, "The Promoter," *New York Post*, March 5, 1971.

131   *"There's no risk here"*   Jim Murray, "Inside Darkest America," *Los Angeles Times*, March 5, 1971; Wallace, "Most Will Watch on Home Screens."

131   *Cooke was to receive 60 percent*   Fisher and Marshall, *Garden of Innocents*, p. 41.

132   *"We're business people"*   "$5 Million Decision Is Made in 10 Minutes by Promoter," *New York Times*, December 31, 1970.

132   *His plans included a feature-length*   Gapay "Going for Broke, Promoting a Big Fight May Not Be Bonanza That It First Seemed."

132   *"If a movie studio can auction"*   Kirshenbaum, "Sport's $5 Million Payday," p. 21.

132   *Ali was lying on the rubbing table*   Ferdie Pacheco, *Fight Doctor* (New York: Simon and Schuster, 1976) pp. 102–103.

132   *"This ain't no plantation deal"*   Bud Schulberg, *Loser and Still Champion: Muhammad Ali* (Garden City, NY: Doubleday, 1972), p. 117.

132   *Perenchio, who reportedly invested*   "Jerry Parenchio . . . the Real King of the Ring?"

132   *"We got a contract for this"*   Schulberg, *Loser and Still Champion*, p. 117.

132   *In another example, when the Mutual Broadcasting System*   Gould, "Broadcast of Fight Barred to Many GI's."

133   *They also wanted a guarantee that*   Fisher and Marshall, *Garden of Innocents*, p. 86; Gould, "Broadcast of Fight Barred to Many GI's."

133   *During negotiations with Pentagon officials*   Gould, "Broadcast of Fight Barred to Many GI's."

133   *In one memorable meeting, Cooke asked Marshall*   Fisher and Marshall, *Garden of Innocents*, p. 120.

133   *"Where's Chick Hearn?"*   Ibid., p. 121.

134   *"Who gets the other seat?"*   Ibid., p. 122.

134   *"If I want a photographer"*   Ibid., p. 123.

136   *"We're like a guy in an orchard"*   Thompson, "Battle of the Undefeated Giants."

7. The Countdown

145   *Deeply held*   Fred Graham, "High Court Backs Draft Exemption for Ethical View," *New York Times*, June 16, 1970.

145   *"It was a little pressure waiting"*   United Press International, "Only Thing on Ali's Mind Now Is Beating Frazier," *New York Times*, January 12, 1971, p. 40.

145   *"The only thing I care about"*   Ibid.

146   *Perenchio later said he paid $10,000*   Jim McCulley, "Ali Wants Ellis Tuneup Bout But Perenchio Yells No," *New York Daily News*, February 11, 1971.

146   *"I need a good competitive workout"*   Ibid.

146   *Perenchio even threatened to sue Ali*   Ibid.

146   *"The man is driving us nuts"*   Ibid.

146–147 *"I called the gym at the time"*   Tom Cushman, "Ali's Warmup for Frazier? Ellis!" *Philadelphia Daily News*, February 16, 1971.

147   *Harry Markson called it the biggest ticket rush*   Dave Anderson, "Garden Considers Halting Mail Orders on Ali Bout Tickets," *New York Times*, January 10, 1971.

147   *Markson was charging a record $150*   Thomas Hauser, *Muhammad Ali: His Life and Times* (New York: Simon & Schuster, 1991), p. 218.

148   *"They've immobolized me with no more seats"*   Shirley Povich, "This morning . . . ," *Washington Post*, February 8, 1971.

148   *"Moshe," she said, "who's going to win the fight?"*   Ibid.

149   *When a photographer for the* Village Voice   Charles Maher, "Pain in the Head," *Los Angeles Times*, March 6, 1971.

149   *Condon worked sixteen hours*   Hauser, *Muhammad Ali: His Life and Times*, p. 221.

149   *"I have been called prejudiced toward whites"*   Tom Cushman, "Super Tickets? Super Headache!" *Philadelphia Daily News*, March 3, 1971.

149   *Those he turned down included*   Jim O'Brien, "And in This Literary Corner . . . ," *New York Post*, February 26, 1971, p. 65.

150   *"Ain't my* lungs"   Tex Maule and Morton Sharnik, "He's Gonna Be the Champ and the Tramp," *Sports Illustrated*, February 1, 1971, p. 15.

151   *"No, I'm not putting Joe Frazier down"*   Ibid., p. 17.

151   *"Frazier will catch hell"*   Si Burick, "A Mere Handful See Ali Training for Mar. 8 Bout," *Dayton Daily News*, January 15, 1971.

151   *During training, Ali stayed at Octagon Towers*   Budd Schulberg, *Loser and Still Champion: Muhammad Ali* (Garden City, NY: Doubleday, 1972), p. 110.

151   *When his stay ended, the residents*   Ibid., p. 111.

151–152 *The basic strategy mapped out by Dundee*   Dick Young, "Young Ideas," *New York Daily News*, February 26, 1971.

152   *"I can't wait to see how Frazier will react"*   Ibid.

152   *"I know what's going to happen"*   Shirley Povich, "A Super Show from Ali," *New York Post*, January 15, 1971.

152   *Ali delivered the line with a laugh*   Ibid.

153   *When he was fourteen, a white boy called him*   Joe Frazier with Phil Berger, *Smokin' Joe: The Autobiography of a Heavyweight Champion of the World* (New York: MacMillian USA, 1996), pp. 17–18.

153   *"Cynical attempt by Clay to make me feel isolated"*   Ibid., p. 96.

153   *"Only those who were bigots"*   *Ali-Frazier I: One Nation Divisible*, HBO Productions, 2000.

156   *"He catches up with me every day"*   United Press International, "Ray Anderson's Willing to Bet $10,000 on Frazier," *New York Daily News*, February 13, 1971.

157   *"That's what wears them down"*   Jack Fried, "He Throws Me, I Drop Him over Ropes," *Philadelphia Evening Bulletin*, February 13, 1971.

157   *"I had to devise ways and means"*   Gerald Eskenazi, "Eddie Futch, Who Trained Fighters His Way, Dies at 90," *New York Times*, October 12, 2001.

158   *Durham was just as stern . . . concerns with Jack Kent Cooke*   Stan Hochman, "'Super Fight' Pickets Make It Lousy Day for Frazier," *Philadelphia Daily News*, February 19, 1971.

158   *"I still feel the same way I did before"*   Ibid.

158   *"I've been suspicious of Don Warner"*   Stan Hochman, "Who's Ali's Spy? Warner Suspect," *Philadelphia Daily News*, February 25, 1971, p. 48.

159   *Warner claimed he received crank phone calls*   Frank Dolson, "A Little Man Takes a Beating," *Philadelphia Inquirer*, February 28, 1971.

159   *"Maybe it wasn't the ideal setup"*   Frazier, *Smokin' Joe*, p. 102.

160   *Once his workouts ended*   Ibid., p. 102.

160   *"I don't think the fight will go more than ten rounds"*   Jim McCulley, "Joe—I'll Stop Ali within 10 Rounds," *New York Daily News*, March 4, 1971.

160   *"I think it's going to be bad"*   Robert Lipsyte, "Please Open Your Mouth and Say . . ." *New York Times*, March 4, 1971.

160   *"Former heavyweight champion of the world!"*   Phil Pepe, "Doc Okays Joe & Ali and away They Go," *New York Daily News*, March 4, 1971.

160   *"Was he smoking?"*   Lipsyte, "Please Open Your Mouth and Say . . ."

160   *"Is there any . . ."*   Ibid.

160   *"You do it twenty times"*   Pepe, "Doc Okays Joe & Ali and away They Go."

161   *"Stay here, stay here"*   Dave Anderson, "Ali Flits Like a Butterfly, Flees like a Bee," *New York Times*, March 4, 1971.

161   *When Ali arrived for the physical*   Ibid.

161   *"See what I mean?"*   Schulberg, *Loser and Still Champion*, p. 123.

162   *"I really kind of hate"*   Bob Williams, "Carson KOs Ali over Tonight Show Snub," *New York Post*, March 4, 1971.

162–163   *"They can't afford the fancy prices"*   Dick Young, *New York Daily News*, February 19, 1971.

164   *"We could have sold out ten Madison Square Gardens"*   *Ali-Frazier I: One Nation Divisible*, HBO Productions, 2000.

165   *"I watched Ali intently"*   Howard Cosell, *Cosell* (Chicago, Playboy Press, 1973), p. 216.

165   *"Frazier's no real champion"*   Schulberg, *Loser and Still Champion*, p. 134.

165   *Later that evening, Frazier was watching television*   Frazier, *Smokin' Joe*, p. 106.

166   *"Joe Frazier, you ready?"*   Ibid.

166   *"We were laughin' and havin' fun"*   William Nock, *Sports Illustrated*, September 30, 1996.

166   *"The Joe Frazier victory party"*   David Condon, "In the Wake of the News," *Chicago Tribune*, March 5, 1971.

166–167   *"Any able bodied American"*   "Joe Frazier Switches Hotels after Threat on His Life," *Philadelphia Daily News*, March 8, 1971, p. 58.

8. March 8

168   *Wearing a white T-shirt*   Leonard Katz, "Frazier's Day: Music Maker," *New York Post*, March 9, 1971.

168   *"Countdown"*   Ibid.

168   *"This is the day, Champ"*   Ibid.

168   *"The day began like many did"*   Ibid.

168   *After his brief workout, Frazier chatted*   Ibid.

169   *As hundreds of his followers hung out in the lobby*   Robert Vale, "Ali's Day: No Crowds," *New York Post*, March 9, 1971.

169   *Around 11 a.m., Frazier and his party left*   Katz, "Frazier's Day: Music Maker."

169   *"Somebody's gonna to die at ringside tonight!"*   Thomas Hauser, *Muhammad Ali, His Life and Times* (New York: Simon & Schuster, 1991), p. 70.

169   *"Emotionally unbalanced, scared to death"*   Ibid., p. 71.

169   *On his way to the weigh-in, Frazier spoke*   Katz, "Frazier's Day: Music Maker."

169   *"It seems he wanted to talk about anything"*   Ibid.

169   *Back in his hotel room, he enjoyed a steak*   Ibid.

170   *"The car ground to a halt"*   Ferdie Pocheco, *Fight Doctor* (New York: Simon & Schuster, 1976), p. 111.

170   *"I am the champion"*   Jack Fried, "Ali Has Weight Edge over Joe, 215–205$^1/_2$," *Philadelphia Evening Bulletin*, March 8, 1971.

172   *"Speed up!"*   Art Fisher and Neal Marshall, *Garden of Innocents* (New York: E. P. Dutton, 1972), p. 166.

172   *At 2:30, Ali ate his last prefight meal*   Vale, "Ali's Day: No Crowds."

172   *"Of course I was dying to get the assignment"*   Arthur Mercante with Phil Guarnieri, *Inside the Ropes* (Ithaca, NY: McBooks Press, 2006), p. 5.

172   *Also reportedly in contention for the job*   Jim Barniak, "A $500 Ref in Spotlight" *Philadelphia Evening Bulletin*, March 8, 1971.

172   *Conn's chances were perhaps lessened*   Dave Anderson, "Durham Demand-ed a Referee Who Can Control Ali," *New York Times*, March 1, 1971.

173   *"He walked away when he wanted to"*   Ibid.

173   *"That's when I knew I had it"*   Hauser, *Muhammad Ali: His Life and Times*, p. 228.

174   *"We're using everything tonight"*   Steve Cady, "Decision Satisfies Most Buffs," *New York Times*, March 9, 1971.

175   *"There's lawyers, doctors, accountants"*   Gerald Eskenazi, "A $1,000-a-Seat Bid Is Rejected," *New York Times*, March 9, 1971.

175   *After watching his brother . . . to his dessing room*   Phil Pepe, "Bad Start," *New York Daily News*, March 9, 1971.

176–177 *In exchange for releasing the Garden*   *Ali-Frazier I: One Nation Divisible*, HBO Sports, 2000.

177   *"They weren't great seats"*   Ibid.

177   *According to John Condon . . . to show a sporting event*   Charles Maher, "Pain in the Head," *Los Angeles Times*, March 6, 1971.

178   *"You take this back to Joe"*   Hauser, *Muhammad Ali: His Life and Times*, p. 226.

179   *"I asked the Lord"*   *Ali-Frazier I: One Nation Divisible*, HBO Sports, 2000.

179   *"I just glared at him"*   Joe Frazier with Phil Berger, *Smokin' Joe: The Autobiography of a Heavyweight Champion of the World* (New York: MacMillian USA, 1996), p. 107.

180   *"The anger inside"*   Ibid., p. 107.

9. The Fight

182   *"Who won the round?"*   Phil Pepe, *Come Out Smokin': Joe Frazier—the Champ Nobody Knew* (New York: Coward McCann & Geoghegan, 1972), p. 180.

182   *"He would be forced to fight my fight"*   Joe Frazier with Phil Berger, *Smokin' Joe: The Autobiography of a Heavyweight Champion of the World* (New York: MacMillian USA, 1996), p. 108.

182   *"They have time for that?"*   Don Dunphy, closed-circuit telecast of the fight.

182   *"I gave all those Clay fans a sneak preview"*   Frazier, *Smokin' Joe*, p. 108.

183   *"It's amazing that Frazier can stand up"*   Dunphy, closed-circuit telecast of the fight.

183   *"The joke was on him"*   Frazier, *Smokin' Joe*, p. 109.

183–184 *At one point, according to Frazier*   Ibid.

184   *"First of the hard hooks"*   Muhammad Ali with Richard Durham, *The Greatest: My Own Story* (New York: Random House, 1975), p. 350.

184   *"I could take anything"*   Larry Fox, "Does Ali Want a Rematch?" *New York Daily News*, March 9, 1971.

184   *"There was so much emotion involved"*   Stan Hochman, "Frazier Wins Medals after 'War of Attrition'," *Philadelphia Daily News*, March 9, 1971.

185   *"I was looking across the ring at him"*   Frazier, *Smokin' Joe*, p. 110.

185   *"Something has gone out of me"*   Ali, *The Greatest*, p. 352.

185   *"Ali almost a sitting duck here"*   Dunphy, closed-circuit telecast of the fight.

185   *"What's holding him up?"*   Frazier, *Smokin' Joe*, p. 110.

186   *"We want it now, we want it now"*   David Wiessler, "Fight Packs Punch around the World," *Pittsburgh Press*, March 9, 1971.

187	*"I don't care a hang about the commentary"*　Ibid.

187　*"I don't care a hang about the commentary"*　Ibid.

188　*"My weariness is greater now"*　Ali, *The Greatest*, p. 352.

188　*"Stop playing"*　Pepe, *Come Out Smokin'*, p. 186.

188　*"Believed in the ritual'"*　Pete Hamill, "Champion," *New York Post*, March 9, 1971.

188　*"The troops of Ali's second corps"*　Norman Mailer, "Ego," *Life*, March 19, 1971.

189　*"I refused to acknowledge their effect"*　Frazier, *Smokin' Joe*, p. 110.

189　*"Now I know he'll die before he quits"*　Ali, *The Greatest*, p. 352.

189　*"Wait a minute"*　Milton Gross, "A Question of Courage," *New York Post*, March 11, 1971.

189　*"Damn it, Yank"*　Arthur Mercante with Phil Guarnieri, *Inside the Ropes* (Ithaca, NY: McBooks Press, 2006), p. 114.

189　*"Right then a terrifying thought flashed through my mind"*　Ibid.

189　*"He's out"*　Phil Pepe, "Frazier Topples Foe in 15th; Ali May Have Fractured Jaw," *New York Daily News*, March 9, 1971.

190　*"The real story was that Clay"*　Frazier, *Smokin' Joe*, p. 111.

190　*"He got hit a couple of good shots"*　Hochman, "Frazier Wears Medals after War of Attrition."

190　*"The hardest hook I've ever taken"*　Ali, *The Greatest*, p. 353.

190　*"He was on Queer Street"*　George Girsch, "Clay Legend Is Ended," *Ring*, June 1971, p. 12.

190　*"Ali bent forward like a sapling"*　Hamill, "Champion."

190　*"I was trained, you always got to remember"*　*Ali-Frazier I: One Nation Divisible*, HBO Sports, 2000.

191　*"I was crazy to get at him"*　Frazier, *Smokin' Joe*, p. 111.

191　*"For someone who was virtually out on his feet"*　Burt Lancaster, closed-circuit telecast of the fight.

191　*"Frazier's right eye"*　Dunphy, closed-circuit telecast of the fight.

192　*"I want to circle, jab"*　Ali, *The Greatest*, p. 354.

193　*"Hard as I tried"*　Frazier, *Smokin' Joe*, p. 112.

193　*"I kicked your ass"*　Ibid., p. 113.

194　*"Frazier by decision"*　Bill Gallo and Phil Pepe, "Yogi Knew," *New York Daily News*, March 10, 1971.

195　*"You done it, Joe, you done it"*　Frazier, *Smokin' Joe*, p. 113.

195　*"What are you guys going to say now?"*　Deane McGowen, "Frazier Says Blows to Body Won," *New York Times*, March 9, 1971.

195　*"Just mumbled something and turned to his corner"*　Ibid.

195　*"You flat-footed. You dumb"*　Pepe, *Come Out Smokin'*, p. 210.

195   *He "kept it there so long"*   Thomas Hauser, *Muhammad Ali: His Life and Times* (New York: Simon & Schuster, 1991), p. 232.

10. After the Fight

196   *In the dressing room*   *Ali-Frazier I: One Nation Divisible*, HBO Sports, 2000.

196   *"Diana, say hello to the man"*   Ibid.

196   *"Hi, champ"*   Ralph Graves, "Some Very Special Help for the Big Fight," *Life*, March 19, 1971.

196   *Brown began to dress Ali*   George Plimpton, "No Requiem for a Heavyweight," *Sports Illustrated*, April 5, 1971, p. 86.

196   *"I couldn't bring myself to release the shutter"*   Graves, "Some Very Special Help for the Big Fight."

196   *"I cried my eyes out"*   *Ali-Frazier I: One Nation Divisible*, HBO Sports, 2000.

197   *"Whitey won again"*   Arthur Daley, "The Mirror Told a Distressing Tale," *New York Times*, March 10, 1971.

197   *"Acts detrimental to boxing"*   Dave Anderson, "Brown, Ali Aide Is Suspended for Throwing Water over Ring," *New York Times*, March 11, 1971.

197   *"Trying to revive my soldier"*   Plimpton, "No Requiem for a Heavyweight," p. 85.

197   *"Look . . . he'd be here"*   Paul Zimmerman, "Ali Praise: 'A Real Champ'," *New York Post*, March 9, 1971.

197   *"I asked him if we're through"*   Ibid.

197   *"Must've been a hellava fight"*   Plimpton, "No Requiem for a Heavyweight," p. 89.

197–198   *Ali closed his eyes while lying on the table*   Ibid., p. 90.

198   *"I got to get to bed"*   Tom Fox, "All-Night Jab and Jabber Is Finished," *Philadelphia Daily News*, March 9, 1971.

198   *"You still the greatest"*   Roy McHugh, "Fall of a King," *Pittsburgh Press*, March 9, 1971.

200   *On the day after the fight*   Milton Gross, *New York Post*, March 10, 1971.

200   *"The way I look at it"*   Tom Cushman, "Ali Takes His Turn at Losing with Class," *Philadelphia Daily News*, March 10, 1971.

200   *"I think I won"*   George Artz, "Ali: 'I Think I Won'," *New York Post*, March 9, 1971.

200   *In another, he said*   Ibid.

200   *"Look at my face"* Cushman, "Ali Takes His Turn at Losing with
        Class."

200   *Frazier looked a lot worse than he did* Dave Anderson, "Manager
        Foresees No Fights for Frazier before Next Year," *New York Times*,
        March 10, 1971.

202   *"Yank was very concerned"* Gerald Eskenazi, "Frazier, Ill at Ease,
        Shuns TV Review," *New York Times*, March 14, 1971.

202   *"I couldn't urinate"* Joe Frazier with Phil Berger, *Smokin' Joe: The
        Autobiography of a Heavyweight Champion of the World* (New York:
        MacMillian USA, 1996), p. 114.

202   *"Until his face gets better"* Eskenazi, "Frazier, Ill at Ease, Shuns TV
        Review."

202   *The rumors spread in a hurry* Robert Reilly, "Frazier on the Ropes?
        Doctor KOs Rumor," *Philadelphia Inquirer*, March 18, 1971.

202   *"It wasn't Clay's punches"* Frazier, *Smokin' Joe*, p. 114.

203   *"What a weasel"* Ibid., p. 115.

204   *This time Jerry Perenchio* Gerald Eskenazi, "Ali Favored over
        Frazier in Battle of Ex-Champions," *New York Times*, January 27,
        1974.

204   *The court determined* David Rosenbaum, "Ali Wins in Draft Case
        Appeal," *New York Times*, June 29, 1971.

204   *"I'm not going to celebrate"* Dave Anderson, "A Day for Victory
        outside Ring," *New York Times*, June 29, 1971.

204   *Missing from Ali's corner* Thomas Hauser, *Muhammad Ali: His Life
        and Times* (New York: Simon & Schuster, 1991), p. 240.

205   *Ali's trained only* Ibid., p. 251.

206   *"So there we were"* Frazier, *Smokin' Joe*, p. 142.

206   *"That's what he went to the hospital"* Dave Anderson, "'I'm Not
        Ignorant, Stand Up, Man,'" *New York Times*, January 24, 1971.

207   *"I was ready to rock"* Frazier, *Smokin' Joe*, p. 145.

207   *"Demeaned the sport of boxing"* Red Smith, "Demeaning What?"
        New York Times, January 28, 1974.

208–209 *"Clay didn't want to rumble"* Frazier, *Smokin' Joe*, p. 146.

209   *"It will be a killer and a chiller"* Ibid., p. 154.

209   *"Frazier wrote years later that his kids were teased"* Ibid., p. 155.

209   *"I could hear both voices"* Hauser, *Muhammad Ali: His Life and Times*,
        p. 319.

209–210 *"I don't like an impostor coming in"* Dave Anderson, "Ali Weighs
        $224^1/_2$ to Frazier's $215^1/_2$," *New York Times*, September 28, 1975.

210   *"This type of thing actually helped Ali"*   *Muhammad Ali: His Life and Times*, p. 320.

210   *In his autobiography . . . 20/70 vision*   Frazier, *Smokin' Joe*, p. 164.

210   *"Sit down, son"*   Tom Callahan, "Fight One More Round," *Time*, December 14, 1981, p. 90.

211   *"I'd like to rumble with that sucker"*   Frazier, *Smokin' Joe*, p. 196.

212   *"It would have been a good thing"*   William Nack, "The Fight's Over, Joe," *Sports Illustrated*, September 30, 1996, p. 55.

212   *"I'm sorry I hurt him"*   Hauser, *Muhammad Ali: His Life and Times*, p. 326.

Where Are They Now?

214   *"I am tired of hypocrisy"*   Leonard Shapiro, "Howard Cosell Dies at 77," *Washington Post*, April 24, 1995.

Bibliography

Ali, Muhammad, with Richard Durham. *The Greatest: My Own Story*. New York: Random House, 1975.

Brenner, Teddy. *Only the Ring Was Square*, Englewood Cliffs, NJ: Prentice-Hall, 1981.

Cosell, Howard. *Cosell*. Chicago: Playboy Press, 1973.

Dunphy, Donald. *Don Dunphy at Ringside*. New York: Holt, 1988.

Early, Gerald. *The Muhammad Ali Reader*. Hopewell, NJ: Ecco Press, 1998.

Frazier, Joe, with Phil Berger. *Smokin' Joe: The Autobiography of a Heavyweight Champion of the World*. New York: Macmillian USA, 1996.

Hauser, Thomas, *Muhammad Ali: His Life and Times*. New York: Simon and Schuster, 1991.

Havill, Adrian. *The Last Mogul: The Unauthorized Biography of Jack Kent Cooke*. New York: St. Martin's Press, 1992.

Hollander, Zander. *Madison Square Garden: A Century of Sport and Spectacle on the World's Most Versatile Stage*. New York: Hawthorn Books, 1973.

Kaiser, Charles. *1968 in America: Music, Politics, Chaos, Counterculture, and the Shaping of a Generation*. New York: Weidenfeld & Nicolson, 1988.

Kindred, Dave. *Sound and Fury: Two Powerful Lives, One Fateful Friendship*. New York: Free Press, 2006.

Kinnane, Adrian. *Jack Kent Cooke*. Lansdowne, VA: Jack Kent Cooke Foundation, 2004.

Kram, Mark. *Ghosts of Manila: The Fateful Blood Feud between Muhammad Ali and Joe Frazier*. New York: Harper Collins, 2001.

Lipsyte, Robert. *Free to Be Muhammad Ali*. New York: Harper & Row, 1978.

Margolick, David. *Beyond Glory: Joe Louis vs. Max Schmeling, and a World on the Brink*. New York: Alfred A. Knopf, 2005.

Marshall, Neal, and Art Fisher, *Garden of Innocents*. New York: E.P. Dutton, 1972.

Mercante, Arthur. *Inside the Ropes*. Ithaca, NY: McBooks Press, 2006.

Pacheco, Ferdie. *Fight Doctor*. New York: Simon & Schuster, 1976.

—————. *A View from the Corner*. New York: Birch Lane Press, 1992.

Pepe, Phil. *Come Out Smokin': Joe Frazier—the Champ Nobody Knew*. New York: Coward, McCann & Geoghegan, 1981.

Remnick, David. *King of the World: Muhammad Ali and the Rise of an American Hero*. New York: Random House, 1998.

Schulberg, Budd. *Loser and Still Champion: Muhammad Ali*. New York: Doubleday, 1972.

Short, Bob. *Everything Is Pickrick: The Life of Lester Maddox*. Macon, GA: Mercer University Press, 1999.

Torres, Jose, and Bert Randolph Sugar. *Sting Like a Bee: The Muhammad Ali Story*. New York: Abelard-Schuman, 1971.

Index

Page numbers in *italics* refer to illustrations.